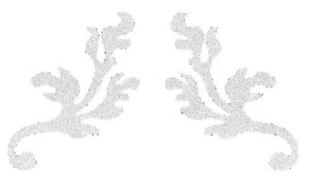

TREATY OF THE PAINT OF LIONARDO OF VINCI

Newly given back into light the life of the author only amongst themselves written by
RAFAELLE DU FRESNE and transcribed into English by Bryan Strong 2015

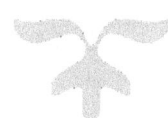

Date: 11/22/2015

ISBN-13: 978-1505430745

ISBN-10: 1505430747

Treaty

The Paint

By LIONARDO of VINCI.

Newly given into light

WITH THE LIFE OF THE SAME AUTHOR

Scribed

From RAFAELLE DU FRESNE.

One they are joined the three Books of the Painting, and to the Treaty
of the STATUE of Leon Battista Alberti
with the Life of the same.

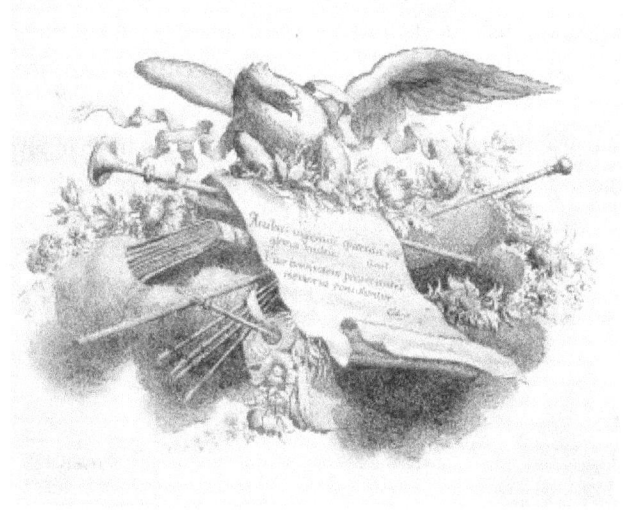

IN BOLOGNA

In the Institute of Sciences.)(1786)(With approval.

THE EDITOR
To courteous Bookbindery

The Treatise of the Painting, of the renowned Lionardo of Vinci fact firstly into Paris the year *1651. from Rafaello Trichet from Fresne* with the Figures designate from the hands talented of *Poussin,* and of the Errard (Wander), not due to the many editions afterwards that give, and the translation in order to also into various languages, being become rare, and from many therefore sought-after, me they are determined of reproduce, and in the same form of the Architecture, Painting, and Statue of Leon Battista Alberti, not many years they are, from me postpone to the light, proceed thus the launch reprinting of the Books more rare, and more advantage provided that negotiate of the three noble Arts Architecture, Painting, and Sculpture. Of the utility of this Work not occurs make advances at this point promise, being conceder sufficiently. Which that of it say the Bosse (Boffe) in his Treatise of Perspective, the Book is all scattered of admonishment, and of the teachings not in order to holy thursday fly, but necessary to the studies of the Art of the Paint, and of the Design. One experience, is true, the scholarly Author not contain into all perfection, be intended no things repeated, and other not declare sufficiently, same as of it advise despite the from Fresne same in the his Letter to the Bourdelot Doctor of the Queen Christina of Sweden, to the such as dedicated the Book, which here to see printed; however not pertain despite such any is the Book usefulness, and deserving delivery of one grand Master. Into these reprinting I have redirect into all the mentioned edition of Paris of the 1651. Just like it most perfect, and most accreditation, and hope not suspect to appear to a lesser extent agree to of the above-mentioned of Leon Battista Alberti. Enjoy the good spirit that I have of jovial, and anticipate even if next to of see proceed the commence my endeavor, since other Works I have ready of grave Author, which not you make to a lesser extent dear of these that I have already make public.

HIGHEST QUEEN.

Swede for long memory of the furthermore clearest histories lie status always tented into merit the art of the paint, And each one be able that Alexander, which for grandness of spirit and of facts departed the Savor of his century, he had into honor the grand Apollo. Nullity affirm of Fabio (Fabulist), which into that city whereas the King one throw honor of the title of citizen, for the mass of one noble art departed called the Paint, and of it leave the name to the his Family. Neither for induce the Majesty Yours to do valuation of this virtue creed that both necessary of making remember that Antoninus Emperor with those hands that entrust with the regulation to the mankind, with those remain one delighted of knead at times the brushes. To everyone is known the love that she threshold at Letters, and to all the fine Arts, and the admire the mankind same as protective and owning thus far of the most recondite science, and amaze to see without a lot of clothes virtuous joined one successfully the Imperious. Hoping therefore that this Work, whom from me come consecrated near his own merits, and threshold into front the august name of V.M. both for be from you gratitude, I have supplicate the Sir. Bourdelot, delicacies of the scholars of our nationality, and that has a particular taste of the thing of the Paint, of to want presentation to the Majesty Yours, accommodate for the gentleness of the donation the gift purchases most gratitude next to from you. The author, which wrote in the principle of the century past, late favored from Principles grands, And the King Francesco first, that same as it departed the Name tutelary of Virtuous, the direct, although laden of years, possess in the his Court, and one be able that he him died in arms. Adventurous Old man, being nowadays his fortune of revive in the hands of one Lady, that for the empire of tempt fair and bellicose nation one it can call the most potent, how for those of the virtue it more accomplished and illustrious Princess of the Universe, and which from those which speak the language of the God one duty to one voice call Queen of Parnassus. However for not penetrate most beyond in the broad field of the his praise, not being matter proportioned to the tenuous of my style, I come to beseech humbly the Majesty Yours of appreciate the my pains, having for the reputation of Leonardo of Vinci, and for the usefulness public, returned an Works much important, whom accompanied from the his bright name, defeat the darkness of the oblivion, has from pass through fine to the more distant posterity, And I to remain felicitous, one you one deem of receive with benign source, one just like I the gift and dedicate with deep affection of heart, being not less reverent of the his grandness, that admiration of the his glory.

OF YOUR MAJESTY

Humbled and devoted Servan
Rafaelle Trichet from Fresne.

To the Many Illustrious and Excellence Sir
THE SIR. PIETRO BOURDELOT,
First Medical of the Serene Queen of Sweden.
Many illustrious and excellence Sir, and free my revealing. ^me.

I have consider that the nobility of the art of the certain one elucidate the precepts into this work, and the merits of Leonardo from Vinci, that of it is the author, same as thus far the beauty and curiosity with whom one is printed the book, not one can embellish of a name more glorious of that of the his great Queen. I have believed thus far that if V. S. etc. ^ma me provide into these occasion the hands, more gratitude to wit the my oblation. And to me they are nimbly persuaded than invoke, same as I suit, you not to me deny this duty, so much for the long-lasting our friendship, how many for the love which you threshold to the painter: whom taste born into she and into me into a same time, namely when be in fashion with concern accuracy examining the beauty of the one and of the other Rome, crescendo with the continue application, is diviner, principality into she, always more fine and exquisite. To me they are value in the do printing this treaty of various manuscripts. More noble for a good number of figures, that there they are sketched from the erudite hand of the Sir. Poussin, is state those of the Sir of Ciantelou, whom the he had from the virtuous knight of the Pozzo (Well), in the time which he gone into Italy to the conquest of the beautiful things, whether for the glory of the kingdom not pass away the our great Cardinal, achieved result Rome without Paris. The other, which is affairs most correct, me is state announcement from the courtesy of the Sir. Tevenot, gentleman of each fate of beautiful letters and cognition adorned. However for the ignorance or negligence of who copies books, or for whichever to other occasion, few one they are chance upon the chapters, neither which not there both state some glitch, and principality into those whereas entered a little of geometry, that for the absurdity of the figure remained almost intelligible. I hope of have returned the all to her first purity. There remain however many things that seem desire the file: us they are many replicas unnecessary, a lot of reasoning truncated, the wording is into more places unregulated, and although there both some order neither chapters, nor is however such which one requires into a work perfect: whence one concludes easily that Lionardo from Vinci not the he gave mine the finish hand. Actually you is considerable, and of marvelous utility, and worth always more, how ago V. S. etc.^ma a rough cast of Michelangolo that four statues finished of whichever other sculptor poor. Possess therefore purged how much one can, for majorly illustrate one they are produce engrave them figure with those diligence that you to see. The Sir. Errard gifted painter, that for the profound science of the design not one he can compare if not with the more excellent men of the last centuries, and of the what he may be able to say some philosopher that for that true taste that he has of the things ancient, fusses surface treatment into he the soul of a few one of those first masters, is those to the which one be obliged the completion and the ornament of the work, possess added several figure, and between the other those that one to see direction the end of the book, whereas one reasons of the manner of draperies and of dress the figure: in the remainder one is served of those ideas and sketch of the Sir. Poussin, that one they are located in the manuscript of the Sir of Ciantelou. Similar is the history of this treaty. I have credited that V. S. etc.^me possess without care of expensive apprised. For the conformance of the material one they are adjoin the three books of the painting from Leon Battista Alberti, and the treaty of the statue of the same, whom not one come across more, not being my state printed sense one time sun. The Vasari scribed already the vice of the one and of the other author, however because he has omit many things worthy of be observed, me they are well-dressed to make of new, adjoin those that the reading of the books, and some cognition that I myself they are acquire of the things of Italy me they've suggested. I have written in language Italian, because pundit how much for be understood, me believe which that him request again the accompaniment of the work. If another time mean occasion of speak Latin or French, perhaps to me succeed best, and be able successfully elucidate the mine concepts. In the meantime supplicate V. S. etc. ^ma of to want be protector, and of extend to my writings that assistance which not it may be able to pear fortune from the creator their trust, manifesting the overabundance of his love in the multitude of mine defects. Is the kiss thousand times the hands.

Of V. S. most excellent.
Servant devoted and cordial   //   **Rafaelle Trichet from Fresne.**

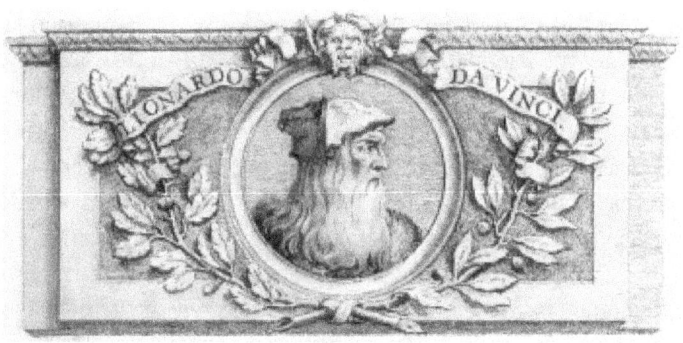

Life of LEONARDO from VINCI Described

By RAFAELLE of FRESNE

Whether the nobility of the blood, which is anything imaginary, ago one such distinction between the men, which the united raises above the other, who is he who that not esteem which that of attitude, which consist in virtue effective, and resides in the part that draw its origin from the heaven, not both for deliver him the men from the most lowest state ending to the confines of the divinity. Of this true and more resplendent nobility adorned Lionardo from Vinci, be able into glory and honors equate the more grand men of his century, and raise above the vile act of his birth, live, practice, and die away with the king and principles grand; and that who without few is concede, leave with immortality to the his name. Be born he in the castle of Vinci, position in the Valley of Arno of underside, not too much distance from Florence, and departed his father Piero from Vinci. This person notice of the genius of the children, which between the other his studies always expect to draw, one resolved of encourage that his natural inclination, is deliver to Florence deliberate of establish with Andrea Verrocchio painter into that time of certain reputation. This admiring the ingenuity of the young, of it whether that judgment which afterward the time demonstrated in truth, and accreditation for his disciple, as much more promised to serious Piero of apprentice, how much that proceed one handshake acquaintance between of them, and that Lionardo for the his beautiful manners, and costumes, him seem deserving of the his care. He in the school of Andrea, which not only one applied to the painting, but still departed sculptor, architect, engraver and goldsmith, learn not only the art of the paint, but of more all those other whereas the design intervened. And departed such the progress that he there make, which into little time one leave ago the progress master. Of the which one regulation that paint into one table, for the monks of Vallombrosa, which they are into St. Salvi beyond of Florence, the history of St. John when baptizes Christ, direct that Lionardo the assist, and he allocate to color an angel, which in the hands grasp no clothing. Preform he given at any rate mastery how much from Andrea him departed committed, that of great long overtaking the remaining of the work, and judged clearly each one that the other parts of the vignette they were many into beauty to the angel inferior. Upset the Verrocchio, is seeing passed from a lad his learner, indignant contrary his own paint brushes, never more direct employ colors, and indicate for always goodbye to the paint.

Exit from the school Lionardo, and being by now into age from be able govern whether same, produce into Florence those works that from the Vasari come imply, namely for the king of Portugal the carton of Adam and of Eve when commit a sin in the paradise Earth, in the which, beyond the two figures, there depiction of clear dark with incredible forbearance and diligence the trees and the herbs of the meadows. Make still to instance of Piero his father, for one his countryman from Vinci, above one wheel of righteous, one such composition by diverse and strange little animals, just like snakes, lizards, green lizard, crickets and locusts, which of all together soul formed one, a lot frightful and horrible, which to guise, of the head of Medusa render immobile from astonishment anyone the regards. However judging the father that this not era works from put into hands of peasant, sold to certain merchant departed then bought for 300. ducats from the duke of Milan. Produce into a painting one Madonna very rare, and between the other things there counterfeited one pitcher overflow of water with no flower inside, above whom with admirable artifice possess imitated it dew of the water: whom when he had then Pope Clement seventh. Ago still mention the Vasari of a design fact above a sheet for Antonio Segni his friend, in the what with rare invention, and with the its ordinary accuracy figure a Neptune into middle to the sea disturbed, with his chariot drawn from horses marine, accompanied of orcas, newts, and other things fantastic that the perfect to purpose for a such subject.

Into this place observe that although the Vinci be able to such signal into that object consisted those divine proportion that is mother of the beauty, which the his figures overflow of grace inspired love to the regarding, expression nevertheless a lot taste in the paint things bizarre and altered, that one he one chance upon into some lout that with face strange and somewhat beyond of the ordinary route a little bit in the ridiculous to take a fancy to from the bizarre of the objected the achieve continue daytime overall, pretense a lot of that possess one perfect idea return to home him sketch same as whether the contain repository present. And observe Paolo Lomazzo in the sixth of the painting caption. 32. that in his time Aurelio Lovino of it possess fifty into a book drawn of his hand. Into this genre is depiction that picture that one to see at this point to Paris between many other that one conserve into one room of the building real of the (Tuellerie) *Gallery* below it guard of the Sir the Maire painter, same as each an apprised, of not ordinary valor, in the what they are paintings two knights into action of remove for force to two other one flag: whom squall make segment of one work greater, namely of the cartoon that he made for the sitting room of the building of *Florence*, just like of beneath one enunciate, however for the her beauty departed from him painting in little foot (stalk) volume with taste and love incredible. At this point beyond the fury of the horses riders, and the oddness of the garments, one to see the witness of the combatants creases, to make red-hot and infuriate, with air so much extraordinary and extravagant, and for say thus load up, and of mascara, that in a same time destined and fear and laughter in the spirt of the scrutinize.

Return at first works of Lionardo from Vinci, says Giorgio Vasari that he commence into a picture to leaf one head of Medusa of extravagant invention, whom remained imperfect. Allocate still principle to one table of the adorations of the Magi, in which they were no beautiful witness; however not departed never ended, same as be in the habit of for the more intervene to all the things his. Because having he an infinity of beautiful cognition, and being of nature lively, and of fertile ingenuity, not one pragmatic contain commence one work, which him occur into thought of place into execution one other. And beyond the profession of the painting, which for that so much diligent manner from him encompass, be able occupy all, attentive to the sculpture, and modeled divinely well. Era intelligent of the geometry, and in the mechanical not ceased never of ponder to new ordnance, and departed inventor of diverse machine. Era delicious architect, and seem to the equal of none other the science of the mirrors, and the perspective. Studied still the property of the herb, and penetrating with the ingenuity fine in the sky one applied to the study of the astronomy, and made many observation regarding the motion of the stars. In the music succeed admirable, and departed a lot of elegant in the sing, and in the sound, that surpass all the musicians of his time: and accommodate not the missing virtue any, those same fury inspired him from Apollo that him made painter and music, the made still poet. However belong lost all his compositions, is only available still too we such **sonnet moral**.

Chi non può quel che vuol , quel che può 'voglia ,

   Che quel che non fi può folle è volere.

   Adunque faggio è / ' huomo da tenere ,

   Che da quel che non può fuo voler toglia.

Però eh' ogni diletto noftro e doglia

   Sta in fi e no , faper voler potere ,

   Adunque quel fol può che co 'l dovere

Ne trae la ragion fuor di fua foglia.

Ne fempre è da voler quel che l' huom puote ,

 Speffo par dolce quel che torna amaro.

 Piansi già quel ch' io 'volfi poi eh' io l' hebbi .

Adunque tu, lettor, di quefie note ,

 S' a te vuoi effer buono , e agl' altri caro ,

 Vogli fempre poter quel che tu debbi .

He who not more that than he wants, that something more desire,

 Which that than none itself more lunatic is to want.

 Therefore knowledgeable is the men from engage,

 Which from that than none more his to want magistrate.

However who each delight ours and labor pain

 Be in itself and no, be able to want power,

 Therefore that only more which with the duty

 Of it extract the reason beyond of his threshold.

Of it always is from to want what which man may thee,

 Often equal sweet that which return bitter.

 Grieve by now that I turned into furthermore than I possess.

Therefore thou, reader, of these note,

 One to thee you want be well, and to the others dear,

 To want always can that than you be indebted.

 Time ethnicity distracted into more delight, because the pleasure beyond manner the horses, and with dexterity the handled, and being not less agile and robust of limbs, that of beautiful presence, and attractive into each his proceedings, departed shield and rummage for illustrious. However above all one delight of converse often with the friend, and time much manor house in the debate, and explained his own thoughts with so much grace and urbanity, that draw to whether the animate anyone the listen.

 So many rare quality, and a purchase one grand of science, propagate the name of Lionardo for all the Italy, and induced Lodovico Sforza, say the Moorish, which favored the virtuous, and departed almost with everyone liberal, upon call to Milan, bestow each year five hundred shields of salary. The first thing which produce that principal departed of form an academy for the architecture, in the what he introduced Lionardo, whom shoo the manners Gothic of the first school, already established in the interpret city hundred year old inward underneath Michelino, inaugurate the via of reduce that art to the its before and ancient purity. Late later employed from the same leading to guide the waters of the Adda precious to Milano, and form that canal navigable, vulgarly dubbed shipping of Mortesana (Death sound), with the increase of more than two hundred miles about river navigable finally to valleys of Chiavenna and Valtelina. The endeavor era difficult and important, and deem of the beautiful intelligence with Lionardo for the noble competition with shipping great that two hundred year previously departed fact neither time of the republic Milanese from the other part of the city, with which one derive the waters of the river Tesino for the navigation and for the irrigation of the campaign until to Milan. However surpass he all the difficulties that one encounter, and with multiplied sluice gate, or desire affirm supports, made with many facility and safety to walk the ships for mountains and valleys.

Not content the main which Lionardo just like architect and engineering illustrate his status, direct still which he the ornament with a few work recommend of painting. The ordered therefore that in the refectory of Padre Dominican of St. Mary of the grace picture the Supper of Christ with the Apostles: which from Lionardo departed with so much mastery executed, which that endeavor departed then from all esteem for the miracle of the painting. And truly there be so much pomp clarified all the shrewdness of the art, which all write, and is communal voice, which of it in design, of it into expression, of it into diligence, of it into vivid, departed never seen thing superior to these. Not departed ordinary the grace and the majesty that he give at witness of the apostles, and particularly to those of two James, one that when come to end that of Christ, not be able arrive to a grade most eminent of beauty, desperate it abandon imperfect.

And because in labor the picture seem to the prior of the convent that too many keep the work, often with importunity soul lament with Lionardo, on the contrary carriage the its query fine at ear of the duke: whom reasoning one time with Lionardo, be able from he not remain other make that the two witness of Christ and of Judah. And that not potential imaginary the infinite beauty of the son of God, not even be able same as the have the power express with the brushes. But that how many to the ugliness of Judas son of the inferno, that the tentative into thought, not the lose lavatory of the ungrateful friar, that with one intolerable and insolent game one time rendered beyond manner to yearn for importance.

Riuscigli to marvel, same as writes the Vasari, of express that dubious that time entrance of it the apostles, of desire know how who trader the their master. And recount the Lomazzo, (whom for possess fact one copy grand into St. Barnabas of Milano, have that work energetically impressed in the spirit) which into every one to see the admiration, him dread, the labor pain, the suspicious, the love, and similar passions and affection into which everyone to the moment one locate, and finally in Judah the treachery concept in the attitude, with a semblance indeed similar to an atrocious. One that well demonstrate Lionardo how much perfectly intendance the motions that the spirt as they say cause neither bodies, that is the part the more delicate, and for it his difficulties less practiced of the art. Time one such work deem of the immortality, however being painted in oil above a wall damp, is state of little duration, and nowadays is of the all damage. Turn towards Francesco first when departed to Milan that one tempt each manner for deliver into France, and enriched his realm (kingdom), however being painted on one wall gross, high and large from thirty feet, leave again unsubstantiated the mindset. And however plausible that he of it make do any facsimile, and those of it make maybe one there today one to see in the parish royal of St. Germano (Germain), nail downed to the wall, without little by little when one enters into dictate church for the door that regards the high noon. In the same refectory in which Lionardo depicted that The Last Supper, depict still of natural the Duke Lodovico, and the duchess Beatrice his wife, all two into knees, with the offspring ahead, and a Christ at cross from the other hand. Daub still for the same duke into one table of is it the Nativity of Christ, whom departed installment to the Emperor.

Between the other occupations of Lionardo, in the his sojourn to Milan, departed of utmost importance the study that he produce surrounding to the anatomy of the men, in the certain, being assist from Marco Antonio of the Tower, which into that time read and wrote of these subject matter in Pavia (Cobbles), he arrive impeccable, and of it make a book designed of pencil red, and dotted of quill, that then remainder into hand of Francesco Melzi his disciple. Sketch still for Gentile Borri, that profess the art of the weaponry, of the such as he same one delight a lot, a book complete of men fighters at feet and without horse, in the which one to see express the rules of that science. And for the glory and growth of the academy his Milanese, and for the education of the academics, wrote many things, and composed more works into different materials, that remained a large time neglected, and almost unknown next to of Sir. Melzi in the their village of Vavero, and furthermore one they are dissipate and dispersed into hither and into yonder, same as is the fortune ordinary of books: Because there departed an such Lelio Gavardi of Asola in charge of St. Zeno of Pavia, strict Parent of Aldo Manucci, which being state teacher of humanity of Sir. Melzi, and proceed often into dictate village, of it recess thirteen volumes, and the carriage furthermore to Florence, chance large price from the grand duke. But died meanwhile that leading, and result the Gavardi to Pisa, and chance upon Sir (*Joe*). Ambrose Mazzenta gentleman Milanese that age into that time to the study, and the produce scruple of badly acquired, one contrite, and don't mention it him that return to Milan reinstate the books to the Gentlemen Melzi. Whom he made: however in the render one marveled the Sir. Oratio Melzi head of that family of the punctuality of the one and of the other, and make for donation of dubbed books to the Sir. (Joe): Ambrose, which then remain into home of the Mazzenti. Whom create too much pompous exhibition, Pompeo Leoni, statuary of the King of Spain, appoint be acquainted with to the Melzi of how much value experienced those books, and the promised honor, and officiate, whether recover soul make an present to the kings Philip. Blurred from such hope the Melzi deviation to the St. Guido Mazzenta brother of (Joe): Ambrose and on your knees invoke of give back those works of the Vinci. Blurry from the worship of the colleague, him of it returned seven, and six of it remained into house Mazzenta, one of departed bestowed to the Cardinal Borromeo for the his Library Ambrosian, and another at Ambrose Figgini, that pass away him let go to the his heir Ercole Bianchi. A third of it he had Carlo Emanuele duke of Savoy, and dying the Sir. Guido, the remains arrive in the hands of the nicknamed Pompeo Leoni, which he let go to Cleodoro Calchi his heir, whom him trade for 300. Shields to the Sir. Galeazzo Lonato. Be in the habit of Lionardo when to want philosophize, and apply with strong attention to the study, recall into dictate village of the Vavero, and one be able that he there dwell many years with Francesco Melzi his disciple. Of underneath one lay the indicator of his own writings.

Afterwards the fall of Moor, which late the year 1500. mercenary prison into France, and die in the tower of Loces, for the wars that succeeded, one intrepid errand into Milan him study of the beautiful art, and one dissipated little by little the academy by now commence, in the which they were leave again excellent in the painting Francesco Melzi, Cesare Sesto, Bernardo Lovino, Andrea Salaino, Marco Uggioni, Antonio Boltrassio, Paolo Lomazzo, and other Milanesì, everyone imitators of the Vinci, to such gesture that often the work their result and to see nowadays believed, esteem, and to see for workmanship of Leonardo, and mainly those of the Sesto and of the Lovino, that more one approached to the manner of the master. But above all one would be enhanced the Lomazzo, since not remain devoid of the eyes neither more green year of the age his, same as the time state aforementioned from Girolamo Cardano: and not be able with the hand, one concede to debate the painting with the ingenuity, and sightless of it compose those Books that from the more glance they are esteem excellent, neither which he propose continuously the Vinci for idea of the true and perfect painter.

In the time that Lodovico XIII. King of France arrive to Milan, than departed one year onward the clinch of the Moor, beseech the Vinci from principal of the city of the invent some machine capricious and magnificent with whom one be able give and delight that gran principal, made a lion of such artifice, that afterwards have walk good piece into one sitting room, one still in front to the king, and then opening the chest, late seen be all teeming with of lilies. For error of who wrote underneath Lomazzo book. 2 caption. 1. one regulation that such thing departed nature for Francesco I. the provide that not he can be true, because he entered the year 1515. into Milan, in which time Lionardo year into Rome, same as though of underneath one to see.

The turbulence of Lombardy, and the misfortunate of the Sforzi, master of Leonardo, the obligate to abandon Milan, and return to Florence his homeland. The first thing that he there made, departed that famous cartoon of the Virgin with Christ and Saint Anna, with St Giovanni, and possess to serve for the is it higher of the Aonuntiata, whom late visit to crowd from all the people of Florence. This cartoon departed then from Lionardo same talented into France, where the king wanted that he the colorist.

Made in addition for Francesco of the Delightful the portrait so much appointed of Lisa his wife, vulgarly called the Delightful, whom one see to Fontainebleau (Fountain blue) into company of many other tally with preciousness of the king Christian, and departed by now bought for four thousand crowns (shields) from Francesco I. One says that he repeat four years to labor that portrait, and that nevertheless I abandon imperfect, having the taste so much delicate, and the intelligence one sharp and thin, which for arrive to the truth of the nature, search for always excellence above excellence, and perfection upon perfection, and not satisfying of the fact well that beautiful, appeal with anxiety rear to that further which one be able do. In the meantime he painted have the habit of possess approximately of the Lady Lisa folks that sing, play and laughing, for grasp cheerful, and not fall down in the ordinary drawback of the sketch, which for I further damage in the melancholy. And really into this one see a lily so much pleasant, which, same as says the Vasari, and thing more divine than human to see. And again beautiful another portrait of the same Lionardo that is to Fontanableò, and one says be of one Marquis of Mantua. Lovely late that of the Geneva of Amerigo Benci, young girl of famous beauty into those times. Of it one must omit the Flora painted with admirable vagueness, and with air truly divine: whom one preserve into Paris, and is into hand of person private.

Having regarding the year 1503, to decorate in the building of Florence the sitting room of the council, departed for decree public elect Lionardo for paint. Made he for such effect a cartoon teeming with of art and of beautiful consideration, in the which time expressed one history of the Piccinino: and by now of it obtain vivid the more gran part to oil painting, when accordance that for the ground color too much gross detach each thing from the wall, and that the his effort they were vain, abandoned the work.

In that time, which departed in the pontificate of Pio the third, not of the second, same as one jurisprudence in the Vasari, Rafaelle from Urbino, which time to penalty joint to the epoch of twenty years, and that of spirited exit from the school of Pietro Perugino, desirous of to see that famous cartoon, and in love from the fame of Lionardo from Vinci, whom proceed the sixtieth year of the his age, arrive the first time to Florence. Astonish to the sight of the his work, and not he had never moreover potent stimulus than I court course and with prestige arrive to that high perfection of the art, which from everything I made revere for God of the painting, departing from that time into then from the manner shoal and hard of the Perugino, for pass through at morbid and tenderness of the Vinci. Departed still spectator the young Rafaelle, not without profit, of the contest that in addition provoke a lot of amosite between Leonardo and Michelangelo Buonarroti, provided not passed 29 years, and with requisition public have fact for another façade of the agreement of the council board that so much nominate cartoon of the war of Pisa, filled of various nudes facts into competition with the Vinci. Even to the year 1513. Lionardo reside forever to Florence, and there painted many things. Francesco Bocchi in the book from him written of the beauties of Florence late mention of a small painting that in the his time one to see into home of Matthew and John Battista Botti in which time depicted one madonna with highest artifice and diligence, with the Christ baby beautiful to marvel, which with grace singular rose the face. From Borghini for thing rare comes half-witted one head of St. John Baptist that time into hand of Camillo of the Albizi.

However being undertaken to the pontificate Leone 5th. in which the love of the painting and of all the beautiful arts late thing inherited, elapse Lionardo to Rome for revere that prince and philanthropist of the virtuous, whom having ordered one table, recount the Vasari that immediately commence with apparatus grand to distil oil, and prepare the varnish, and that Leone informed of with the affirm, that not one be obliged to hope nothing from who ponder to the end, before of contain examined the principle of the work. Once again still certain other little things unworthy of the size of the genius of the Vinci, whom one obligation grasp for suspicious, being written from person partial of Michelangelo, whom, same as enunciate, professed open-ended animosity with Lionardo, and with fantasize and fabulous joke one delight of diminish the reputation. That hatred implacable displeased supremely to Lionardo, and to see called from the king Francesco, that in the his sojourn to Milan one time enamored of the his works, one resolved, although old man of more seventy years, of embrace a party thus and honored and glorious, and of to the travel of Francia.

Not departed ordinary the taste that he had the king to see owning of a virtuous so much from him esteemed and coveted. And although for it his old age to penalty be able labor, late nevertheless always well to see and cherished from the king. And each an since, which being he state many months sick into Fontanableò (Fountain blue), the king **the** come from to visit, and that wanting he for reverence straighten up departed the bed, and recount the his erroneously, the occur an accident: for it which thing the king presage the head for assist, and support, he known the favor him expire into arm in age seventy-five years, very more glorious of none other painter, since true and that a nice pass away all the life honor.

Departed lovely of body, same as one is dubbed of above. Surface treatment the youth people with one negligence philosophical abandon develop the hair and the beard, one that seemed a Hermes or a Druid ancient. Not direct ever take hold wife, or one he neither he had any, just like enunciate another painter, not departed other than the art, and the children the deeds his. Of it one must deem that one is it imply everyone, because many other of it has the large Duke of Florence, and my memory of have viewpoints much into England. In the conception of the temple of the painting of Paolo Lomazzo chap. 33. one ago mention of one concession of the Virgin painted for the church of St. Francis of Milan. In the library Ambrosiana of the same city one conservation many of drawings and paintings of this author.

At this point to Paris in the building Palazzo Cardinal one sees one Madonna of his hand, whom be seated into lap of St. Anna, and hold with them her hands a Christ baby that jest with one lamb. There is a village beautiful: however the head of the virgin is remained imperfect. The Cardinal of Richelieu have one Herodias exquisite of beauty. The St. John (Giovanni) in the desert, figure entire that is to Fontanableò, and another picture of one Madonna, with Christ, St. John (Giovanni) and an angel of admirable beauty, places into a country, they are things from be observed. In the study of the Sir Marchese of Sourdis to Paris there is another Madonna of reputational.

The Sir of Ciarmois secretary of Marescial of Schomberg, gentleman of rare quality, whom occupying together the curiosity and the intelligence departed one considerable collection of beautiful vignette, of it has one of the Vinci, in which with two half figures, one represent the young and handsome Joseph (Giuseppe) that escape time the shoulder to the *daylily* but dishonest wife of Potiphar (Putifar). The all is depiction with love and diligence grand: the expression is admirable, and the modesty of the one and the obscenity of the other seem neither two faces, more soon things true that pretense. Near to the same Sir one Madonna with Saint Anna, and a Christ child to which Saint Michele gives one balance, and Saint John that jest with one sheep, is a picture of extreme beauty. However too much make the want record all the paintings of the Vinci: rest that afterward the works of the brush, one reasons of those of the pen.

Have the habit of the Vinci write to the left-handed person, second the use to of the Hebrew, in the which manner were written those thirteen volumes of the which have already fact mention, and being the character good, one read very easily through one speculum grand. And probable that he make these, accommodate all not decipher thus easily his writings.

The endeavor of the novice of Mortesana (Death sound) the he gave occasion of write a book of the nature, weight force and motion of water, teeming with of large number of designs of various wheel and machines for mills, and regularly the course of the water, and levers into high up.

Compose of the anatomy of the body human, same as one is already dubbed, whom works time adorned of various drawings facts with study and diligence grand, and of it ago he same mention in the chapter 22. of this treatise about the paint.

The book of the anatomy of horses and half-witted from the Vasari, from the Borghini, and from the Lomazzo. Being state he excellent in the sculptural, and in the depiction, just like of it ago faith the picture of the four knight's fighters above mentioned, not there is doubt that the work not fusses of extraordinary beauty and utility.

In the chapter 81. & 110. of these treaties it comes quoted from he one his work from the perspective, divided into more books. Perhaps that into that time taught the mode of stretch the figures majorly from the natural, praised from the Lomazzo in the idea, caption. 4.

In chapter 112. & 123. promises of do a book of the movements of the body, and some his parts: subject anatomical, and that not is never status touched from any.

Promises still in the chapter 268. a treaty about the consideration that is liberation from the body.

The book of the shade and of light one finds today in the library Ambrosiana of Milan, in leaf, covered with velvet red, and is that which, same as one is called of above, departed given from the Sir. Guido Mazzenta to the Cardinal Borromeo. Treats he that material from philosopher, from mathematician and from painter, and of it ago mention in this treaty chapter. 278. Ago miraculous into that part of the paint, imitating with touch shrewdness the effects that ago the light with color, which them his work possess more of the natural that of the fraudulent.

Rest the treaty of the paint, which contains various precepts of that art, and together the manners of the design and of the coloring. Recount the Vasari of a certain painter Milanese pass through to Florence, him made to see those work, and him signify that when do arrived to Rome right away it had best imprint: however this not ago from he who carried out, and those at which to Rome not one is fact, time later a century foresee one puts into execution to Paris, whereas with the contrast of various manuscripts, all corrupt and ruin, one is returned from me one work that for the excellence of the precepts, and for the merit of the author is deem of the immortality. And for renderer no more familiar to the our nation, the Sir of Ciambre gentleman intelligent of all the parts of the design, and that (just like said of the gran Leone 5th.) for instinct communicate to the his family one delights of each fate of virtue and of study, neither has fact one version into language French, that bye a commentary complete, being with one exquisite and happy diligence expressed the sense of the author.

overage, one is fact the following index of the other books that treat of the paint and from design, same as still of those whereas they are described the grapevine of the painters and the works them.

Of Alberto Durero painter and geometry clarify, of the symmetry of the bodies human, books four, movements translated from the language Latina in the Italian from M. Sir. Paolo Gallucci Salodiano, and increase of the fifth book, in which one section with here manner be able the painters and sculptors display the diversity of the nature of the men and women, and with which the passions that feels for them diverse accident which them hasten, time of new printed. In Venetia 1594. Vol. The four books of Alberto Durero they are state more times printed in language Latina, German, France and Italian.

Luxuries Amman-law handbook art painting, fiction, and carving. Frankfurt 1578. 4.

Treaty of art of painting of Sir. Paolo Lomazzo Milanese painter, divided in seven books, any which one contains all the theorem and the practice of it painting. In Milano 1584. 4.

Idea of temple of painting of Sir. Paolo Lomazzo painter, in which he discordant of the origin and foundation of thing contained in its treaty of art of paint. In Milano 1590. 4.

Of the form of the Muse extract from the ancient authors Greeks and Latin's, works useful to painters and sculptors, of Sir, Paolo Lomazzo. Milanese painter. In Milano 1591. 4.

The rest of Raffaello Borghini, into which of painting and of sculpture one speech, of more illustrious painting and sculpture, and of famous work their one departed mention, and the things principal apparently to said art one teach. Into Florence 1584. 8.

Discourses of Alessandro Lamo around to the sculpture and painting whereas reasons of the life of M. Bernardino Campo painter Cremonese. In Cremona 1584. 4.

Of real precepts of the paint of M. Sir. (Joe (John). Battista (Baptist) Armenini firm Faenza, books three, neither which one demostrate the manner of design, and of depiction etc. Into Ravenna 1587. 4.

Due dialogue of M. Giovanni (John) Andrea Gilio from Fabriano, in first of which one reasons of the parts morals and civic apparently to the writers courtiers, and the useful that the principle extract from writers: in second one reasons of the errors of painters regarding the history, with many annotation procedures on the judgment of Michelangelo, and other figures, so much of old how many of the new chapel, and into which manner desirer be depiction the sacred images. In Camerino I564. 4.

The Figure, over of the fine of the paint, dialogue of the review. Padre D-Gregorio Comanini canonical regular Lateran, in which questionable, one this way fade of the paint both the useful, over the delight, one debate of the use of that in the Christianity, and one ostentation that both imitator more perfect, and then more delight, the painter over the poet. In Mantova 1591. 4.

Treaty of nobility of paint, compound to instants of the venerable company of St. Luca, and noble academy of the painters of Rome, from Romano Alberti of the town of Borgo St. Sepolero. In Rome 1585. 4.

The idea of the painters, sculptors and architects, of the cavalier Federico Zuccaro, Divided in two books. In Turin 1607, Vol.

Origin and progress of the academy of the design, of the painters, sculptors and architectures of Rome, whereas one contain many useful speeches and philosophical reasoning apparently to the stated professions, and into particular to any new definition of the design and of the painting, sculpture and architecture, and to the manner of set appropriate the young people, and to perfection the skilled, recited below the regiment of the excellent sir. Knight Federigo Zuccari, and recount frm Romano Alberti secretary of the academia. Into Pavia 1604. 4.

Two lesson of Master. Benedetto Varchi in the first of which one declare a sonnet (poem) by Master. Michelagnolo Buonaroti; in the second one dispute which both more noble art the sculpture or the paint, with one letter of it Michelagnolo, and most other excellence, painters and sculptors, above the question aforesaid. In Florence 1549. 4.

Pomponi Gaurici Neapolitan of sculpture book. Item Ludovici Demontiosii of early sculpture, expert sculpture, jeweler sculpture and picture book two. Item Abrabami Gorlai Antuerpiani poetry. Amsterodami 1609. 4

Francisci lunii (Francis June) F, F. of picture expert book three. Amsteladami 1637. 4

Antonio Possevino Society Jesus book of poetry and picture, here-hence the tenth seventeenth library select.

Venice 1603. Vol.

Treaties of painting founded in the authority of many excellent into this profession, made to common benefit of the virtuous from among D. Francis Bisagno Knight of Malta. In Venetia 1642. 8:

Design of the Father party into more reasoning. Neither what one debate of the sculpture and painting, of the color, of the projection, of the method, with many things apparently without this person arts, etc. Into Venetia 1549. 8.

The noble painting, and of the she art, of the manner, and of the doctrine of accomplish effortlessly and soon, works of Michel Angelo Biondo, etc. Into Vinegia 1549. 8.

Discourses (speeches) approximately to the design printed with ego deception of eyes, perspective practice of Peter (Pietro) Accoltis Into Florence 1625. Vol.

Sentiments for the distinction offset manner of painting, drawing and engraver, offset original and copies, by A. Boffe Graveur (Bosse Writer) in stature agreeable. A Paris 1649. 12.

The life of the more excellent painters, sculptors, architects and Giorgio (George) Vasari painter & architect of Aretino (Arezzo), with one introduction in the principle to the three arts of the design, namely, architecture, painting, and sculpture. In Florence 1568. 4. 3. vol. & into Bologna 1647. 4. 3. vol.

The life of painters and architects, from the Pope of Gregory XIII. of 1572 Finally to the times of Pope Urban eighth in the 1642. written by Sir(Joe/thur) Baglione Romano. Into Rome 1642 4.

The wonders of art, over the life of the illustrious painter Veneti, and of the state, in which they are recollected the works distinguished, the customs, and the portraits them, with the narration of the history, of the fairy tales, and of the morality from those painted, described from the cavalier Carlo Ridolsi. In Venetia 1648. part first, part second.

Life of Michelagnolo Buonarroti recounts for Ascanio Condivi of the Ripa Transone. In Rome 1553. 4.

Brief comphence of the Life of the famous Titian Vecellio of Cadore knight and painter, with the tree of his real consanguinity. In Venetia 1622 4.

The funeral of Agostino Caraccio facts into Bologna his country from him to set forth academic of the design In Bologna 1603.4.

The beauty of Florence, whereas to replete of painting, of sculpture temples, of palaces, the more noble artist and most precious one contain, written from M. Francesco Bocchi. In Florence 1591. 8.

Excellency of the stature of the Saint John of Donatello sculptor Florence. Entry in the facet of beyond of Orsan Michele, writer from M. Francesco Bocchi, whereas one debate of the custom, of the vividness, and of the beautiful of the statue Into Florence 1584. 8

Reasoning of Sir. Giorgio Vasari painter & architect, Aretino (Arezzo) above the invention from him painted in Florence in the palace of their heights serenity, with the noble, and excellent. Sir. Father Francesco Medici then prince of Firenze, together with the inventions of the paint from him communicates in dome. In Firenze 1588. 4.

Book of the paint, in which one explain the foundations and the practice of that art, together with the life of Italian painters and Flemish, written and printed in language Flemish by Carlo Vanmander painter. Into Amsterdam in 1618.

Henrico Peacham (Henry Peach) in his works written in language English, and entitled: The perfect gentleman, employs the goal of the book to reason of the painting. Into London 1634 4.

The manner of organized each strength of color. Book written in in language Todesca Valentino Bolgen from Rusach. Into 1562 Francofort 8.

Pietro (Peter) Maria (Mary) Canepario from Crema in his book Latin entitled: of ink, declares the manners of do each strength of color. In Venetia 1619. 4.

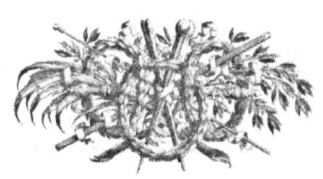

TREATY
OF THE PAINTING
By
LIONARDO DA VINCI.

That which should be first learn the young. CAP. I. (1)

The young be obliged to first learn perspective, for the measure of each thing: then of hand into hand learn from good master, for accustom to good part: then from the natural, for confirmed the reason of things learn: then see a time the work of hand from divers masters, for do attire of put into practice, and operate the things learned.

Which study have to be neither young. CAP. II. (2)

The study of the young, whom desire of do profit in the science impersonator of all the figure of the work of nature, duty be regarding the design accompanied from the shade and light appropriate to the site whereas such illustration they are orientated.

Which rule one be obliged to allocate to the little angel painter. CAP. III. (3)

We know clearly that the view is of the speed operation that be, and into a point see infinite forms; actually none comprehend if none one thing for time. Establish coincidence: You reader watch over by glance all these sheet written, forthwith evaluate that be overflow of various letters: however none be familiar with by that time what letters be, of it that to want enunciate: hence to you be necessary make by word to word, toward for towards, to want contain knowledge of them letters.

Once again if to want climb to the height of a building, converge ascend to degree by degree, otherwise both impossible achieve to her summit. And thus I say to you that the nature to you direct by these art. Since you want possess well curb knowledge of forms of things, commence from the particular of those, and none become to the second, if first none you have surely in the memory, and in the practice it first. And if do otherwise, throw via the time, or truly lengthen extremely the study. And you recollection that unequal before the diligence that the aptness.

Notice of the young disposed to the painting. CAP. IV. (4)

Many they are the gentlemen that they've desire and love to the drawing, however none disposition, and this both well-known neither little angle, whom they are without diligence, of it never cease with shadows them they things.

Precept to the painter. CAP. V. (5)

None is praiseworthy the painter that none ago as well if none one thing solar, same as one ignorant, head, shoes, or animal, or countries, or similar particular, inasmuch none is itself gross intelligence, that turn to one thing, and that always mass in work, none the countenance good.

In what manner must the young proceed in his studies? CAP. VI. (6)

The mind of the painter one must of the continuous transmute into so much discourse how much they are the figures of the objected notables that in front the make an impression, and to those secure the footprint, and note, and do above them rules, considering the place, the circumstances, the light and shadow.

Of the manner of assimilate. CAP. VII. (7)

Study first the science, and furthermore ensure the practice arise from she science. The painter must study with rules, and not abandon thing that none itself lay to the memory, and view that difference is between the part of the animal, and them their joints.

Admonishment to the painter. CAP. VIII. (8)

The painter must be universal and solitary, and consider this which he see, and speak with feces, elegant the parts more excellent of the species of whichever thing that he see, make to similitude of the mirror, whom one transmutes into many colors, how many are those of the thing that whether the place before, and do thus he, believe be second nature.

Precept of the painter universal. CAP. IX. (9)

That not both universal which none adore equally all the thing that itself contain in the painting: same as if to one liking the countries, he esteem of be from simple investigation, just as indicate the our Botticelli, that such study era unsubstantiated, because with solo toss one sponge masses of different colors to a wall, it leave to dubbed wall one blot, whereas himself to see a country. He is well true that oneself to see various invention of this which the man he wants search for by those, namely witness of men, divers animals, battles, rocks, seas, clouds, woods, and similar things, and ago same as the sound of bell, whom one it can interpret that tell me those, which to you seem. Thus, once again which they stain you provoke invention, they none you teach turn up any particular, and this such painter made very glum countries.

How the painter must be universal. CAP. X. (10)

You, painter, whom you want be universal, and be valued without divers judgments, make without a same composition that you be thing of grand obscurity, and of very softness of shadow, make though note the cause of such shadows and softness.

Precept to the painter. CAP. XI. (11)

That painter which none debate, little acquire, when the work surpass the judgment of operator, he operative little acquire, and when the judgment surpass the work, she work never none cease of improve, if the avarice none them impede.

Precept same as above. CAP. XII. (12)

The painter must first accustomed to the hand with the depict drawings of good master, and sort according to habit, with judgment of his preceptor, must furthermore accustom to with depict thing of relief good, with those rules that of the portray relief itself tell.

Precept about the sketch history and figures. CAP. XIII. (13)

The outline of the historic both prompt, and the parts none both too much finished. Be with attention only to sites of them component, whom then to beautiful ease, attractive, be able cease.

Of the correct the error which you unearth. CAP. XIV. (14)

Remember to you, painter, which when for your judgment, or for others people's opinion, discover any error in the works yours, that you them to correct again, accommodation in publish such work, you none publish together with those the matter yours. And none you excuse from you same, persuasive of restore it your infamy in the succeeding your work, because the painting none dies by means of it his creation, same as ago the music composition, however long time duration, and the tempo provoke testimony of ignorance yours. And if you to you justify of possess without combating with the necessity, and of none contain time to study, is make true painter, none blame if none you same, because solo the study of virtue is repast of soul and of the body. How many they are them philosophers that they are born rich, and because none them impede the riches, they have abandon.

Of the judgment. CAP. XV. (15)

Neither one thing is that more this way deceive who ours judgment by assign sentence at our operation, and more you vary the condemnation of the enemy, that of him well-disposed the sentence, because the friends they are one same what with you, and that you can with your judgment deceive.

Manner of arouse the intelligence to various invention. CAP. XVI. (16)

None remain of put by these precept one new invention of speculation, whom, although pair small, and almost deem of laughter, nevertheless is of grand usefulness to wake up the intelligence to various invention, and these is: If scrutinize by any wall stain, or stones of various shuffle, be able there to see the invention and similitude of different countries, diverse battles, proceedings ready of figures, strange air of faces, and cloths, and infinite other things; because in the thing confused the intelligence itself arouse to new invention.

Of the study inherent when you to you, or first that you to you fall asleep to the dark. CAP. XVII. (17)

Thus far I have proven be of none little usefulness, whenever to you located to the dark in the bed, end up with the imagination repetitive the lineaments surface of forms for the ago studied, or other thing notable of thin speculation: and to this manner oneself confirm the thing comprise in the memory.

*That oneself must first learn the diligence which it provide practice. CAP. XVIII. (18) ***

When to want do good and useful study, use in the your draw of make adage, and judge below the light, which and how many grasp the first grade of clarity; and thus below the shadows, which be those that they are more axe that the other, and to which manner one blend together, and the quality, and compare the one with the other, and the lineaments without that part one address, and in the line how much part must be for the one and for the other direction, and where or more or less evident, and thus long or thin, and at last, which the your shadows and light be unite without cause or signal, without use of smoke: and when are fact the use and the hand without that diligence, you arrive fact the practice soon, that you none hold to notice.

*How the painter must be vague of hear the judgment of each one. CAP. XIX. (19). ***

Certainly none must recuse the painter, meantime that him designs or paints, the judgment of each, because we acquainted with that the man, although none both painter, aural notice of forms of the man, one he is hunchback, if has leg gross, or large hand, one he is lame, or has other feeling of faintness. And if we acquainted with the men be able judge the work of the nature, how much mainly be able evaluate our errors.

That the man none one must trust so much of whether, that none may see from the natural. CAP. XX. (20)

That which one from to understand of be able discretion in whether everything the effect of the nature, one deceive, because the memory ours none is of touch capacity: however each thing consult from the natural.

About the variety of the figures. CAP. XXI. (21)

The painter must search for of be universal, because the left hand errand dignity, if ago one item well, and the other rudely: same as many that solo study in the naked measured, and proportionate, and none research the its variety, because it can be a man proportionate, and be large, and short, and long, and thin, and poor, and who of this variety none grasp account, ago always the his figure in print, the which merit great recall.

Of be universal. CAP XXII. (22)

Simple thing is to the man that be able, make universal, inasmuch everything the animals terrestrial they've similarity of component, namely muscles, nerves and bones, and nothing itself vary, if none in lengthiness, otherwise by size, same as do demonstrate in the anatomy. Of the animal of water, which they are of many variety, none persuaded the painter that you countenance rule.

Of those that employ the practice without the diligence, or rather science. CAP. XXIII (23)

Those that themselves enchant of practice without the diligence, or rather science, for say better, they are same as the helmsman that enter into sea on vessel without helm or compass, that my none they've certainty whereas one expel. Always the practice must be built on the good theoretical, of which the perspective is guidebook, and gateway: and without that nothing itself ago well, thus of painting, same as each other profession.

Of none imitate the one the other painter. CAP. XXIV. (24)

A painter none must never imitate the manner of another, because do say grandson and none son of nature; because be the thing natural in a lot of large abundance, further pragmatic himself must resort to she nature, which to the master, than from that they've given.

Of portray from the natural CAP. XXV. (25)

When you've to portray from the natural, be faraway three times the bulk of the thing that you depict, and make, that when you paint, or that you move no principle of line, which you look for all the body which you portray, whichever thing itself clashes for the rectitude of principle line.

Admonishment to the painter. CAP. XXVI. (26)

Note well in the your depict, how below the shadows they are shadow insensitive of obscurity and of figures, and such itself proof for the third, that speak, than the surface globally they are of touch varying obscurity and clarity, how many they are the variety of the obscurity and clarities that him remain for objected.

How must be high the light from portray from the natural. CAP. XXVII. (27)

The light from portray of natural need be to the north, amity not expression mutation: and if him both to half of, hold window breaded, accommodate the sun illuminate all the daytime none countenance mutation. The height of the light must be in manner situated, that each body face many long the shadows, it's for land, how many is her height.

Which light itself be obliged elect for portray the figure of body. CAP. XXVIII. (28)

The figure of whichever body itself compel to catch that light in which you imagine be they figure: namely if you pretend such figure into campaign, it are encircle of large summit of light, none you being the sun uncovered; and if the sun sees allocate figure, the its shadows create much obscure, respect at parts aluminate, and create shadows of complete expedient, thus the primitive, just like the derivatively, and such shadows produce little companion of light, because from that side alumina the azure of air, and tinge of if that part which it sees; and this errand one manifest in the thing white: and that part which is aluminate from the sun, itself demonstrate participate of the color of the sun, and this see many quickly, when the sun inlet to the west, below the redness of cloudy, itself that they cloudy one dye of the color which allude: whom redness of cloudy, together with redness of the sun, ago turn red this which catch light from them: and the part of bodies, which none sees it redness, lance of the color of air; and who sees to the bodies, judges that it of two colors: and from this you none be able avert, that display the cause of such shadows and light, you not the visage participants of predicted causes, whether none the operation your is vain and false. And whether the your figures is home dark, and you her may see of outside, these such figure you will have the shadow blend, be you for the line of the light, and that such figure you will have grace, and do distinction to the its imitator, for exist she of large relief, and the shadow pleasant and smoky, and maximum into that part where even to see the darkness of the dwelling, inasmuch that place they are the shadows almost insensitive, and the cause make impose to the his own place.

Of quality of the light for portray reliefs natural, or fake. CAP. XXIX. (29)

The light shortened from the shadows with too much evidence is supremely denounce, hence for avert similar inconvenience, if make the bodies into campaign ample, make the figures none aluminate from the sun, but feign any quantity of fog, or clouds transparent, be insert below the objective and the sun, hence none be the figure from the sun sent, none make sent the complete of the shadows with those of light.

Of portray the naked. CAP. XXX. (30)

When depict the naked, ago which always them sketch portion, and then complete that part which to you even better, and that with the other part place into practice, otherwise make used to of attached my surely the component together: and none use never make the head moment whereas is the chest, of it the arm move just like the leg: and if the head one moment to the shoulder right, ago them his parts more low of the side left that of the other: and if do the chest apart from , ago that turn the head departed the side left, the parts of the side right is more high than the left.

Of portray of relief false, or of the natural. CAP. XXXI. (31)

He who that portray of relief, one must shorten in manner similar, which the eye of figure portrayed both to the equal of he who that portrays.

Manner of portray a site correct. CAP. XXXII. (32)

Have one glass large just like one half leaf of paper real, and that conscription well in front to the eyes your folks, namely between the eyes and that thing which you want portray, and then you place faraway with the eyes to the called pane two third of arm, and conscription the head with one instrument, by manner that none it be able move point. Of then well-prepared and cover one eye, and with brush, or with the pencil, imprint on the glass that which of it appears, and then trace with the paper such glass, and powdered on one paper good, to paint, if to you choice, employ well of then the perspective aerial.

How one must draw the countries. CAP. XXXIII. (33)

The countries themselves be obliged to depict by manner that the trees be half aluminates, and half dark patch: but better is make when the sun is half occupy from clouds, that to the time the trees themselves illuminated from the light universal of the sky, and from the shadow universal of land, and these are so much more obscure in the their parts, how much they parts they are more closed to the land.

Of portray to the light of candle. CAP. XXXIV. (34)

At this light of night both insert the frame, or paper wax or without trace paper, but only one between leaf of paper thin stationery, and see the your shadow none end.

By which manner one be obliged to portray a face, and allocate grace, shadow, and lights. CAP. XXXV. (35)

Great allocate of shadows and of light one add to the visage of those that behind in the part of those habitat that they are obscure, which the eyes of the relating to see the part shady of such visage be obscured from the shadows of predicted dwelling, and see to the part illuminated of the same visage added the clarity that you from the splendor of air: for whom enhanced of shadows and of light the faces has large relief, and in the part illuminated the shadows almost insensitive; and of this representation and enhanced of shadows and of light the face acquire rather of beauty.

Of the light where itself depict the incarnation about the face, and naked. CAP. XXXVI. (36)

This abode he wants be identification to the air, with the side of color incarnate, and them portray one facial of state, when the clouds cover the sun: or truly do the partition southern a lot high, that there ray of the sun none pummel the partition northern, accommodation her ray reflections not spoil the shadows.

Of the paint figure for the history, CAP. XXXVII. (37)

Always the painter must consider in the partition, whom has from history, the height of the situated where she wants position the her figure, and this that him depict of natural to dubbed purpose, and star a lot of with the eye more base that the thing which he paint, how much impose thing both mass by work more high that the eye of the concerning, otherwise the work his make reprehensible.

For depict a naked from the natural, or other CAP. XXXVIII. (38)

Uses of grasp by hand a filaments with one lead pendant, for to see them confront of thing.

Measures and compartments of the statue. CAP. XXXIX. (39)

Divide the head in twelve degrees, and each degree in 12. points, and each point into 12 minutes, and the minutes by minimum, and the minimum into quarter note.

How the painter themselves must reduce to the light with its relief. CAP. XL. (40)

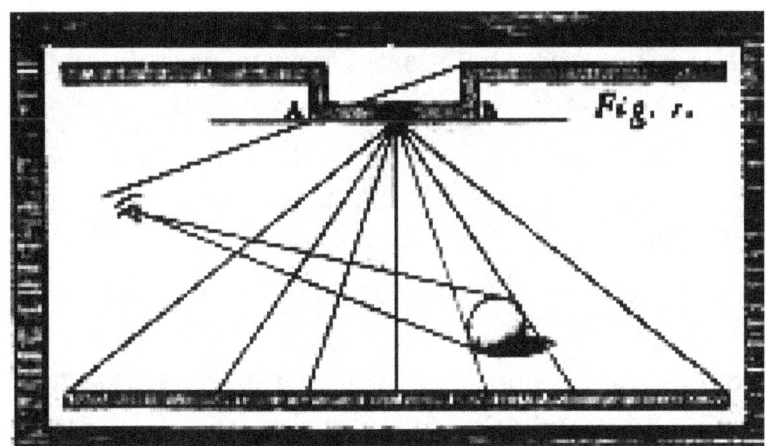

A. B. (fig. I.) both the window, (**M.**) both the point of **the** light, I say that by whatever part the painter themselves remain, which he stay well, in order to that the eye be located below the part shady and the light of the body that itself depict: whom place located west within the point (**M.**) and the division that ago the shadow from the light above the body depicted.

About the quality of the light. CAP. XLI. (41)

The light great and high, and none too much powerful, do that which render the particles of bodies very much agreeably.

Of the blunder that themselves receives in the judgment about the part. CAP. XLII. (42)

That painter which contain clumsy hands, them do similar into his works, and thus him intervene to whatever component, whether the long study none it to him obstruct. However each painter must watch out that part which has more bad into his person, and without that with each study make good remedy.

That one must know how the intrinsic form of the man. CAP. XLIII. (43)

That painter which possess knowledge of nature of nerve, muscles, and tendon, seem conveniently, in the move one part, how much and which nerves of it exist cause, and that muscle deflate is cause of do shepherd it nerves, and which strings converted into capillary cartilages to wrap, and surrounding dubbed muscle: and none make how many, which by divers proceedings always give demonstrate those same thing into arm, backs, breasts, and other muscles.

Of the defect of the painter. CAP XLIV. (44)

Great deficiency is of the painter portray or rather replicate them same motions, and same folds of clothes into one same history, and make resemble all the witness the one with the other.

Precept, because the painter none himself deceive in the chosen about the figure by which ago clothes. CAP. XLV. (45)

Must the painter do it the figure upon the rule of a body natural, whom commonly both of proportion praiseworthy; beyond of theses weigh whether same and to see to that part it his person varies very, or little, from that aforesaid praiseworthy: and sort that knowledge must repair with all the his study, of none succumb, neither same faintness in the figure from him operate, that in the person he find oneself: and with this defect you be necessity summary mind purge, conceive he is faintness, which is born together with the judgment: because the soul is master of the your body and that of the your precisely judgment, is that certainly you one delight in the works similar to those, which she worked in the compose the your body: and of here arise, which none is itself bad figure of female, that none chance upon some lover, whether by none fuss monstrous, and in all this contain admonishment grandness.

Deficiency of the painters which depict one thing of relief in house without a light, and furthermore the place in campaign without another light CAP. XLVI. (46)

Grand error is of that painters, whom portray one thing of relief without a light particular in the their homes, and then place to work such portrait without a light universal of the air to campaign, where alike air embraces and illuminated all the parts of the views without a same manner; and thus this person ago shadows obscure, where none it can be shadow; and whether even if you there is, is of touch clarity, that you is imperceptible: and thus make them reflections, where is impossible those be to see.

Of painting, and its division. CAP. XLVII. (47)

Divide the painting in two parts principle, about the which the first is figure, namely the line that distinguishes them figure of bodies, and them particles; the second, is the color contents from them finish.

Figure, and its division. CAP. XLVIII. (48)

The figure of bodies themselves divides in two other parts, namely proportionality of the part below of them, whom be **corresponding** to the all, and the movement appropriate to the accident mind of thing experience that one move.

Proportion of limbs. CAP. XLIX (49)

The proportion about the limbs one divides by two other parts, namely quality, and motion. Quality itself interpret, beyond at measures corresponding to the all, which none combine the limbs of young with those of old people, of it that scratch with those of slender, of it the limbs elegant with the incept and lazy: and beyond of this that none visage to the masculine limbs feminine to manner that the attitudes or rather movement of old people none be matters with those same vivacity that those of young, of it those of one female same as those of a male: do that the movements, and component of a strapping be such, which by them limbs demonstrate it health.

About the movements, and of operations various. CAP. L. (50)

The figure of the men combine gesture precisely to the their operation by manner that to see you interpret those which for their themselves think or says, whom do well learn from he who imitate the motions of dumb, whom converse with the movements of the hands, of the eye, of eyelashes and of all the person, in the desire express the concept of the mind theirs. Of it you laugh of me, because ego to you place a preceptor without language, whom you have to teach that art which he not know how do; because better you teach with demeanor, which everyone the other with words. Therefore you, painter, of the one and of the other sect, attention, second that happens, to the quality of those which speak, and to the nature about the thingy that one speaks.

That one must avert the end send. CAP. LI. (51)

Not do him finish some your figure of other complexion which of the proper field, with that such figures ending, namely that none expression profiles obscure below the field and it your figure.

That in the thing smallness none themselves view it error, how in the large. CAP. LII. (52)

In the thing of smallness form none themselves be able comprehend the quality of the your error same as of large; and the reason is, that whether these thingy minuteness both type without similarity of a man, or of other animals, them its parts for the immense diminution none cloth be sought with that debt canny of the his operator that themselves agree: hence none be ended, none you can comprehend his own error. Regarding for instance from far away a man for space of 300. arms, and with diligence judge if that is beautiful, or ugly, one he is monstrosity, or of common quality; else that with highest your effort none to you can persuade without entrust such judgment; and the reason is, which for the above accordingly distance this man decreases so much, that none himself he can compresence the quality about the parts. And whether you want to see well accordingly dimension of the man above dubbed, bridge one finger near to the eye one handbreadth, and so much raise and lower above-mentioned finger, that the his superior extremity finish below the figure that your regard, and consult appear one incredible diminution: and for these, frequently direct itself doubt the form of the friend from far away.

Because the depiction none can no way point of view divide, how the thingy natural. CAP LIII. (53)

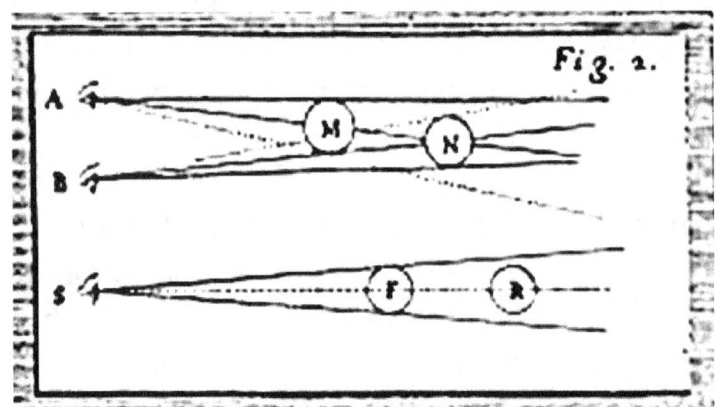

The painter often essence tumble by desperation of them imitate the natural, to see them they painting not have that relief, and that liveliness, which they've the thing viewpoint in the mirror, (see the cap. 351.) append them contain colors that of great length for clarity and for obscurity move forward the quality of light and shadow of thing view in the mirror; accusing by these coincidence her their ignorance, and none the reason, because none her recognize. Impossible is that the thing painted appear of such relief, which one assimilate at thing about the mirror, although the one and the other both by its surface, except for if both view solo with one eye; and the reason is this: the two eye that to see one thing beyond the other, just like **A. B.** (fig. 2) that to see **M. N.** the **M.** none can occupy entirely N.

because the base of line visual is itself large, that sees the body second later the first, However if shut one eye, just like **S**. the body **F**. occupy **R**. because the line visual arise from one solo point, and ago below in the first body, hence the second of equal magnitude none both never seen.

Because the chapters of the figure the one above the other is thingy from avert. CAP. LIV. (54)

Such universal use whom itself ago for the depict in the make about the hair, is much from be rationally reproach, imperious do them one history by a plain with his country and edifices, furthermore augment one other degree, and manufacture one history, and vary the point from the first, and in addition the third and the fourth, by manner that one facade himself sees sort with four points, whom is sum thin out of similar masters. We be able that the point is position to the eye of the regard of history: and whether you want to say: such as I have from make the life of one holy compatriot in many history to one same face? Without this you respond, that you be obliged to place the first level with point to the height of the eye of regards of it history, and in the adage level figure the first history grand, and furthermore of hand in hand dimensions the figure and dwelling place by on diverse border and level ground, create all the ornamentation of they history. The rest of the visage, into its height, create trees large without comparison of the figure, or angels, whether formwork without purpose of the history, or rather birds, or clouds, or similar thingy: otherwise none keep hindrance, that each your work produce false.

Whence depiction one must use to make seem the thing most pronounced. CAP. LV. (55)

The figure aluminate from the light particular they are those that display most relief, that those which they are aluminate from the light universal, because the light particular, ago the light reflections, whom stand out the figure from the them field, whom reflection be born from the light of one figure that stands out in the shadow of that which the remain of earlier, and the aluminate at part. But the figure parlay in front to the light particular by place grand and obscure none receives reflection, and of this not itself sees if none the part aluminate: and this is only from be use in the imitation of the night, with small light particular.

Thereafter is rather of speech and utility, or the light and shadow of bodies, and them their lineaments. CAP. LVI. (56)

The complete about the bodies they are of major speech and intelligence that the shadow and the light, for cause that the outlines of the limbs, that none they are tendency, they are immutable, and always they are those same, but the sites, quality, and quantity of the shadows they are infinity.

Memory that itself ago from the author. CAP. LVII. (57)

Describe which be the muscles, and which the cords, that through different movements of each part itself unearth, or itself conceal, or not make of it the one of it the other: and remember that these such actions is important following of painter and sculptors, which create professional of muscles. The similar make of a child, from his birth unto near the time of his decrepit, for everyone the degrees of the age his, and of everyone describe the mutation of the limbs and joints, and which put on weight or slimming.

Precepts of paintings. CAP. LVIII. (58)

Always the painter must look for the readiness of it the proceedings natural matter from the man to the unexpected, and born from intensity affection of their affect, and of those make brief memories nor his booklets, and furthermore without his purpose strive, with make be one man to that same act, for see the quality and expect of the limbs which by such gesture one adoption.

How the painting must be view from one only window. CAP. LIX. (59)

The painting must be view from one only window, how appears for cause of bodies thus matter. And if you want make to one height one ball round, to you be necessary make long without similitude of an egg, and star much to back that she shortening appear round.

Of the shadows. CAP. LX. (60)

The shadows whom you discernable with difficulties, and theirs ends none be able recognize, on the contrary with confused judgment the look take hold, and transfer into your work, none the produce finished, or truly end, itself that it your work both of ingenious resolution.

How one must appear the child. Cap. LXI. (61)

The child stalk one must seem like with proceedings ready and crooked when be seated, and in the star upright, with proceeding timid and fearsome.

How one must appear the old people. CAP. LXII. (62)

The old people must be matter with lazy and slow movements, and the legs bent with the knee, when remain detain, the feet equal, and distance the one from the other, ever declined in deep, the head in front stoop, and the arm not too much elongate.

How one must appear the old people. CAP. LXIII. (63)

The old people one must picture audacity, and ready, with rabid movements, without manner of fury hell, and the movements must seem further ready in the arm and head, that in the legs.

How one must appear the woman. CAP. LXIV. (64)
The woman one must picture with proceedings shameful, the limb together contain, the arm collect together, head low, and bent in transverse.

How one must appear one night CAP. LXV. (65)
That thing that is deprive entirely of light, is all darkness: be the night in similar condition, if you there to want imagine one history, provide, that endeavors one great fire, that thing which is propinquity without dubbed fire most one tinge in the its complexion, because that thing which is more close to the object, most participate of the its nature: and make the fire hang by color red, make all the thing illuminated from that thus far redden, and those that they've most faraway without above-mentioned fire, most be tinge of the color black of night. The figure that are produce in front to the fire ostentatious darken in the clarity of it fire, because that part of it thing which see is tint from the obscurity of the night, and none from the clarity of the fire: and those that one chance upon from the side, be half dark, and half reddish: and those that one be able to see later the end of flame, do all aluminate of reddish light in field black. In how much to the proceedings, create those, which they are next, do shield with the hands, and with the cloaks shelter from the immoderate heat, and curve with visage in spite part, pointing to escape: those further faraway, do really part of them make with the hands shelter without the eye offend from the excessive splendor.

How oneself must picture one fortune. CAP. LXVI. (66)
Whether you desire imagine well one fortune, considered and ponder well his effects, when the wind puffing above the surface of the sea, or of the earth, remove, and threshold with it those thing that none they are conscription with the mass universal. And for imagine that fortune, do first the clouds broken and routes, straighten for the flow of the wind, accompanied from the beach dust, raised from the shores marine: and branches and leaves, raised for the potently of the wind, scatter for the air by company of many other things decipher: the tree and grass bend to earth, almost exhibit of want follow the course of wind, with the branches twist beyond of the natural course, with the into disarray and inverse leaves: and the humans, which you one spot, part fallen and direct for them clothes, and for the dust almost ever unknown, and those that remain erect, is afterwards some tree embraced upon those, because the wind none them to drag: other with the hands to the eye for the dust stoop by ground, and the clothes and the hair straight to the course of the wind. The sea turbulent and tempestuous both teeming with of backwards foam below the elevate so as, and the wind visage remove below the hard-fought air of the froth more thin, to manner of thick and envelope fog. The ship which inside there they are some bosom appearance with sail retreat, and the fragment of her

ventilate between the airs into company of some cords broken: any with trees damage fallen with ships permeable and inoperative below the tempest of which, and men lash out embrace the remaining of the ship. Make the clouds expel from impetuous wind, battering in the high peaks of the mountains, make by those engulf twist, to similitude of the hence dent in the cliff: the air horrendous for the obscure shadows, make from the dust, fog and clouds dense.

How one must picture a battle. CAP. LXVII. 67

Make first the smoke of the artillery shuffle below the air together with the dust motion from the movement of horses of combatants, whom task employ thus. The dust, since is thing terrestrial and weights, and although for it her subtle easily one raise and combine below the air, nothing of less certainly return to short, and his highest assemble is fact from the part most thin. Therefore, the less both view, and seem almost of the color of air. The smoke that itself melee below the air dusting, when furthermore itself raise to certain height, embellish obscure cloud, and you will see in the summit more expeditious the smoke that the dust, and the smoke hang of complexion sufficiently blue, and it dust dry land the her complexion. From the part that it comes the light seem this mystique of air, smoke and dust much more lucid from the opposite part. The combatant how much more be below accordance with turbulence, a lot of to a lesser extent themselves to see, and less difference make their lamp at their shadow. Create reddish the visage, and the person, and the air, and the arquebus (musket gun) together with those that there they are near. And dubbed redness how much more one part of its cause, further one lose, and the figure that they are below you, and the light, be faraway, seem obscure of field clear, and them their legs how much more itself appreciate to the ground, less is viewpoints; because the dust there is more gross and thick. And if create horses current outward of the crowd, ago the cloudlike shape of dust distant the one from the other, how much it can be the interval of jumps matters from the horse, and that cloud that is more distant from the dubbed horse, to a lesser extent one to see, on the contrary both high, scattered, and rare, and the further among both the more evident, and minor, and more dense. The air both flood of thunderbolt in diverse reasons: those mountainous, those who disembark, which both for line plain: and them bullets of the gunshot they are accompanied of rather smoke tail part of their scoot, and the first figure do dusty neither hair, and eyelashes, and other places proceedings without support the dust. Make the winners current with the hair and other things lightweight scatter to the wind, with the eyelashes low, and banish contrary part ahead, namely if emit in front the foot on the right, which the arm weary even it come ahead, and whether make no fallen, make the gesture to slip on for the dust conducted in bloody mud: and surrounding to the poor clarity of the land make see stampeded the kick of the men and of horses that they are pass through. Make some horses to drag dead them his sir, and of behind to that let go for the dust and mud the sign some rickety body. Make the defeat and beat pallid, with the eyelashes high, and them their conjunction, and muscle that awn above of them, both abundant of sore creased. The opening of the nose be with rather wrinkle start into arc from the nostrils, and finished in the principle of the eye. The nostrils high, cause of allocate folds, and the arches lips expose the teeth of upper. The teeth separate in manner of shriek with lament. One of the hands appearance shield to the fearsome sight, turn of the within towards the enemy, the other stay to domain to bear the distressed chest. Other make lash out with the mouth blockade, and escape; make many rugged of weapons below the feet of combatants, just like shields damage, spears, swords, and other similar things. Make men dead, some covered in means from the dust, and other everyone. The dust that one combine with the exit blood convert into red mud, and to see the blood of its complexion course with injustice flow from the body to the dust. Others pass away tighten the teeth, distort the eye, tighten them fist to the person, and the leg twist. It may be able to see no unarmed and abated from the enemy, approach to above - mentioned enemy with gnaw on and scratch, and make harsh and screeching vendetta. Preposterous to see no horse mark and elegant speed with the horsehair spread to the wind between the enemies, with the feet make advances many damage, and to see any exhausted fall over to ground, and make cover with the his shield, and the enemy stooped by short do force of instill death. Be likely to see many men fallen at a grouping below a horse dead. You will see some winners abandon the battle, and exit from the multitude, cleanse with the hands him eye, and the cheek cover of mud, event from the weeping of the eye for cause of the dust. You will see the square ruler of the rescued be overflow of hope and of suspicious, with the eyelashes keen, do to those shadow with the hands, and look at again below the thick and obscure fog, and be attentive to the commandment of the Captain. Himself he can do thus far the captain with baton raised, current, and in towards his own course display to those it part whereas is of them desire. And any river, inside horse current, complete the circulator water of turbulence of so as, of foam, and of water confuse jump inverse the air, and between the legs and bodies of horses. And neither do no-one place level whereas not be the kick lined of blood.

Of the manner of conduct in painting the things faraway. CAP. LXVIII. (68)

Light itself to sees be an air gross more than the other, whom adjoin with the land flat, and how much more itself lever to high, more is thin and transparent. The things elevate and large, that be from you faraway, it they lowness little both view, because the view for one line that passes between the air more significant continued. The summit of articulate height itself proof be view for one line, whom, although from the call of the eye yours one cause in the air significant, nevertheless ending in the sum height of the what view, result without finish in air very much more thin that none ago the its lowness: for these reason this line amount more one separate from you of point to point, always shift quality of thin to more thin air. Therefore you, painter, when both the mountains, ago that of hill by hill always the heights is more clear that the meanness: and how much the make more faraway the one from other, ago the heights most clear, and how much more itself rise to high, more display the variety of the form and complexion.

Just as the air itself must do more albumen amount further it both ending short. CAP. LXIX. (69)

Because this air is coarse near to the ground, and how much more itself conscription, rather itself wear thin, when the sun is for raise, regarding direction westerly, participant from noon and the north, and see that air coarse receive more light from the sun which it thin, because the ray locate more resistance. And in the event that the sky to the view your end with the low plain, that part ultimate of the sky both view for that air more coarse and more whitish, whom corrupt the truth of the complexion that itself green for its half, and believe the sky more white that above you, because the line visual passes for less amount of air corrupt from coarse state of mind, And since regarding opposite raise, the air you seem more obscure, how much more itself reduce, because in articulate air low the rays luminous less proceed.

To make that the figure stand out from their field CAP. LXX. (70)

The figure of whatever body more seem reveal and stand out from their field, about the which they carry on is of color distinctly obscure, with more variety that both possible in the confines of the predicted figures, as though both demonstrate to the its place, and that to dubbed colors both observed the diminution of clarity of it white, and of obscurity in the colors obscure.

Of imagine the sizes of the things painted. CAP. LXXI. (71)

In the figuration of the size that they've naturally the things before to the eye, one

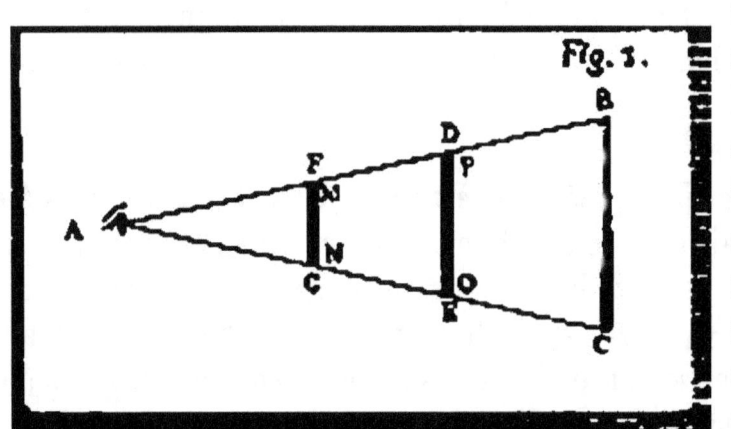

must make a good impression much ending the first figure, be (stalk of a leaf, as say little foot or small) same as the work of illuminators, just like the grand of painters: but the small of illuminators must, be views of near to and those of the painter from faraway; thus produce them figure duty, correspond to the eye with equal size, (bulk); and this arise because they approach with equal magnitude of angle, the which one proof in this thus: both the object **B.C.** (Fig 3.) and the eye both **A.** and **D. E.** both one plank of glass for whom penetrate the species of the **B. C.**

I say that be stable the eye **A.** the size (bulk) of painting nature for the imitation they **B.**

C. must be of much minor figure, how much the glass pane **D. E.** make more close to the eye **A.** and must be equally ended. E. if you complete it figure **B.C.** in the pane glass **D. E.** the your figure must be less finished that the figure **B. C.** and most finished that the illustration **M. N.** sort departed the pane **F. G.** because if **P. O.** illustration fusses ended how the natural **B.C.** the perspective of it **O. P.** make falsify, because how much to the diminishing of the figure it remain, be **B. C.** decreased in **P. O.** but the finished not one reconcile with the distance, because in the research the perfection of the finished of the natural **B. C.** then **B. C.** seems in the region **O. P.** but if you to want research the diminution of the **O. P.** it **O. P.** for be in the distance **B. C.** and in the decrease of the finished to the pane **F. G.**

Of the things finished, and of the confused. CAP. LXXII. (72)
The things finished and send itself must make of behind, and the confused, namely of finish confuse, itself pretend in part remote.

Of the illustration which are separate, accommodation not seem conjoin. CAP. LXXIII. (73)
The colors of that you dress the figure it such that hand over grace the one to the other: and, when a color itself ago field of the other, both such that not believe conjoin and applicate together, thus far that fusses of same nature of complexion, but is various of clarity similar, which require the interposition of the distance, and of the thickness of the air, that between their one to intervene, and with the same rule I go the notice of their finish, namely more or less expedient or confused, second that request again the them closeness or removal.

If the light must be extracted by expression, or from part, and such as from more grace. CAP LXXIV. (74)
The light extracted into visage to the direct place without partition lateral, whom be obscure, both cause that such facet is large relief, and maximum having the light from high: and this relief happen, because the parts in front of such face they are aluminate from the light universal of the air without that before, hence such part aluminate has shadows almost insensitive, and later they parts in front of the face continue the parts lateral, obscured from the predicted partition lateral of the room, whom much more eclipse the face, how much it face enters between them with the its parts: and more than of this professed that the light that descend from high remove of if all those parts at which is fact shield from the reliefs of the face, just like the eye lashes that deduct the light to the recessed of the eye, and the nose that it layer to huge part of mouth, and the chin to the throat, and similar other reliefs.

Of the reverberation CAP. LXXV. (75)

The reverberation are caused of the body of egg white quality, of plain and semi-dense surface, whom pummel from the light, those to similitude of the spring of the sphere reflect in the first object.

Where not it can be reverberation bright. CAP. LXXVI. (76)

Everyone the bodies dense itself dress them their surface of various quality of light and shadow. The light they are of two nature, the one itself domain original. And the other derivative. The original I say be that which deviation from flame of fire, or from the light of the sun, or air. Light derived both the light reflected. However for return to the promise definitions, I say that reverberation light not both from that part of the body that both direction to the body shady, just like places obscure of covering of various heights, of plants, woods green or dried, whom, although the part of each branch direction to the light original one attire of quality of it light, actually they are so much the shadow made from each branch the one departed the other, that in sum of them result such obscurities, that the light you is for nothing: hence not be able similar objective yield to the bodies opposite any light reflection.

Of reflections. CAP. LXXVII. (77)

The reflections be participants so much more or less of them thing where itself generate, that of what which them generates, how much them thing whereas itself generate is of more clean surface of that which them generates.

Of reflections of lights that surrounding the shadows. CAP. LXXVIII. (78)

The reflections of the parts illuminated that stand out in the opposed shadows illuminate or relieving most or less it them obscurity, second that it they are more or less close, with more or less of clarity, this such consideration is mass in work from many, and a lot of other they are that the avert, and this such itself shine the one of the high. But you for avoid the slander of the one and of the other, put into work the one and the other whereas they are necessary, but ago that the their causes it note, namely that itself see manifest cause of the reflections and their colors, and thus manifest the cause of the things that not reflect: and making thus not do entirely denounce, of it laud from the various judges, whom, if not do of plenary ignorance, both necessary that into all you praising itself the one just like the other sect.

Where the reflections of light they are of major or minor clarity. CAP. LXXIX. (79)

The reflections of light they are of so much minor or major clarity and evidence, how many them is to see into fields of major or minor obscurities: and this happens, because if the field is more obscure then the reflection, in that moment it reflection make robust and evident for the difference great that have them colors below them: however if the reflection make seen in field more clear of him, in that moment such reflections itself demonstrate be obscure respect to the whiteness with whom one confines, and thus such reflection make insensitive.

Which part of the reflection be more albumen. CAP. LXXX. (80)

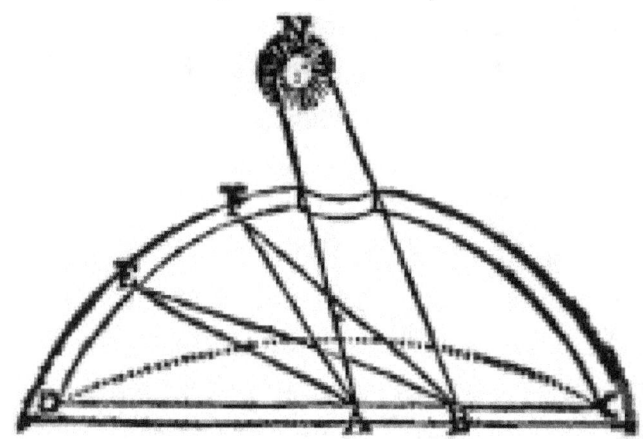

That part make more white or aluminate from the reflection, which receives the light below angles more equal. Whether the luminous **N.** (fig.4.) and the **A. B.** both the part of body illuminated, whom stands out for all the concavity opposites, whom is shady. **E.** both that such light, which reflects at **F.** both strike below angle equal. **E.** not make reflection from base of angle equal, just like itself exhibition the angle **E. A. B.** that is more obtuse that the angle **E. A. B.** however the angle **A. F. B.** thus far that both below the angle of minor quality which the angle **E.** he has base **B. A.** that is between the angle more equal which it angle **E.** and but both more bright in **F.** than in **E.** and again do more clear, because make more close to the thing which the allure, for the sixth which say: That part of body shady make more aluminate that do more close to the its light.

Of color reflections of the flesh. CAP. LXXXI. (81)

The reflections of carnation that have light from other flesh they are most red, and of more excellent incarnation that not any other part of flesh that both in the man: and this happens for the $3.^0$ of the $2.^0$ book, that says: The surface of each body opaque participate of the color of the its object; And as much more as much as such object the is more near, and a lot of less as much as the is more remote, and as many as the body opaque and major, because be large it prevents the compared of the objective surrounding, whom often times they are of color various, whom corrupt the first species more close, when the body they are stalk: but not fall short that not tinge more one reflection a stalk complexion vicinity, that one color largely remote, for the $6.^0$ of perspective, that says: The things larger can be at touch distance, that it point of view smaller very that the stalk of nearby.

Where the reflections they are most sensitive. CAP. LXXXII. (82)

That reflections make of more sent evidence, whom is seen in field of major obscurity, and that both less sensible, that one see by field most bright: and this arise that the things of various obscurity doors into contrast, the less obscure ago seem tenebrous that which is more obscure, and the things of various whiteness doors in contrast, the most white ago seem the other less white which none is.

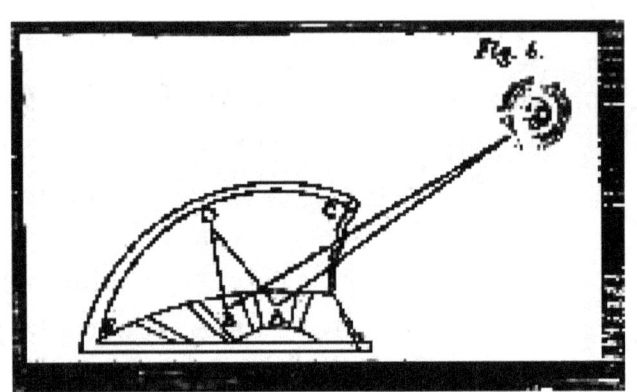

Of reflections duplicates and tripled. CAP. LXXXIII. (83)

The reflections duplicates they are of major potently than the reflections simple, and the shadows that one interpose below the light incident and them reflections they are of little obscurity. For example both **A.** (fig. 5.) the luminous **A. N. A. S.** the direct, **S. N.** be the parts of be bodies aluminate, **O. E.** be the parts of them body aluminate from the reflexed: and the reflected **A. N. E.** is the reflection simple, **A. N. O. AS. O.** is the reflection duplicate. The reflection simple is dubbed that, which only from one aluminate is seen, and the duplicate is seen from two body aluminates, and the simple. **E.** is fact from the aluminate **B. D.** the duplicate **O.** itself consists from the aluminate **B. D.** and from the aluminate **D. R.** and the shadow it is of little obscurity, whom itself interposes below the light incident **N.** and the light reflection **NO. SO.**

How not any complexion reflection is simple, but is mixed with the spices of the other colors. CAP. LXXXIV. (84)

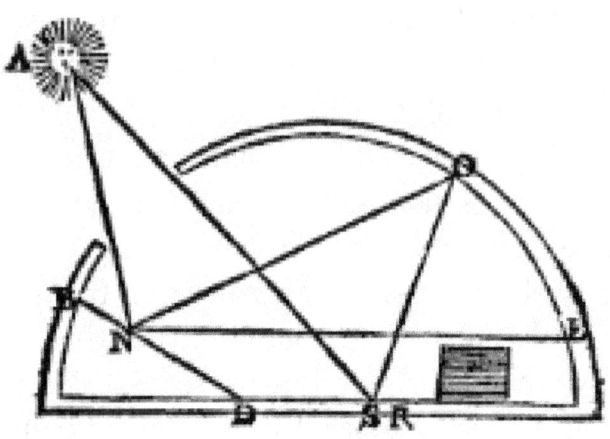

Not any complexion that reflection in the surface of one other body, tinge they surface of the its precisely complexion, but do mixed with the competitions of the other colors refection, that stand out in the same place: same as do the color yellow **A.** (fig. 6.) that reflect in the part of the spherical **C. O. E.** and in the same place reflects the complexion blue **B.**

I say for this reflection mixed of yellow and of blue, that the percussion of the its competition tinge the spherical; and that itself time to as though light, it make of color green, because established is that the yellow and blue mix together make one beautiful green.

How rare times the reflection they are of the complexion of the body whereas one conjoin. CAP. LXXXV. (85)

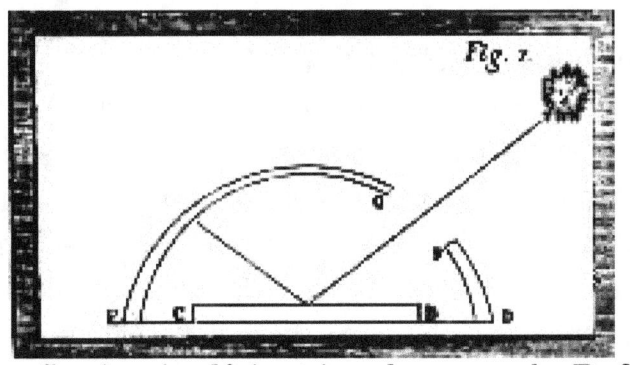

Rare times happen that the reflections be of the same complexion of the body, or of the precisely whereas one conjoin: for example both the spherical **D. F. G. E. (fig.7.)** yellow, and the object that him reflect on top of the its complexion both **B. C.** whom is blue, I say that the part of spherical, which is percussion from such reflection, itself tinge in color green, be **B. C.** aluminate from the air or from the sun.

Whereas more one see the reverberation. CAP. LXXXVI. (86)

Below the reflection of same figure, size, and intensity, that part one demonstrate most or less powerful, whom complete in field more or less obscure.

The surface of body participate most of the complexion of those objective whom reflection to him its similitude below angle more equal.

Of the colors of the objective that reflection them its similarities in the surface of the prefer bodies below angle equal, that make more intensity, whom contain his ray of sunshine reflection of more brief length.

Below them colors of the objective, that one reflection below angle equal, and with some distance in the surface of counterpoised body, that do more intensity, which make of brighter complexion.

That objects reflects more intensely his color in the before body whom not has around without whether other colors that some its species. However that reflection make do more confused complexion, which from various colors of objective is generated.

That complexion which make most near to the reflection, more tinge of as though it reflection, and thus is convert.

Therefore you, painter, ago employ of it reflections of the effigy of the figure, the complexion of the parts of investments that they are among at parts of flesh which them they are more near: But not separate with too much their pronouncement if not necessity.

Of colors of reflections. CAP. LXXXVII. (87)

Everyone the colors reflections they are of even luminosity that the light right, and such proportion has the light incident with light reflection, which is that have below them the luminosity of their causes.

Of complete of reflections in its field. CAP LXXXVIII. (88)

The finish of the reflection into field more bright of it reflection do cause that like that reflection make insensitive: but if such that reflection terminate into field most obscure of him, in that moment it reflection do sensible, and so much more itself make evident, how much such field both more obscure, and thus is conversely.

Of the position the figure. CAP. LXXXIX. (89)

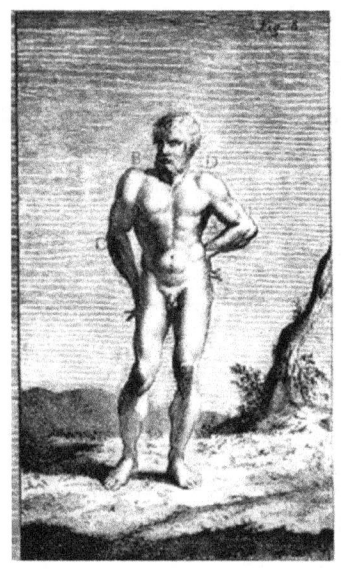

As much as many the part of the naked **D. A.** (fig. 8.) diminish for pose, as much as many the opposite's part grows: namely as much as many the part **D. A.** decreases of its measure, the opposites part above increase to the its measure, and the bellybutton never exit of its height, otherwise the limbs virile; and this lowering arise, because the figure that pose on one foot, that foot itself ago center of symmetry of the overlapping weight force: be thus, the half of the shoulder you one straighten of above, driving out outward of the its line perpendicular, whom line passes for the middle superficial of the body: and this line more itself it comes at twine in the its higher extremity, above the foot that pose; the lineaments transverse compelled to equal angel itself make with their extreme most low in that part which pose, just like appears in **A. B. C.**

Of the manner of acquire well to compose together the figure in the history. CAP. XC. (90)*

Sometimes you will learn well perspective, and be without intellect all the limbs and the body of the things, retribution vague often times in the your work by past time, see and consider the sites of the men in the converser, or in the challenger, or in the laugh, or tussle concurrently, that proceedings be for them, and that proceedings fascination the surrounding, divided, and sellers of them things, and those notice with brief mark to one your leaf booklet, whom you be obliged to always take with you: and both of paper tint (pencil or wax crayon), oblige not them take without delete, but mutate of old man to new; that these not are things from be deleted, on the contrary with grandiose diligence set aside, because they are concern the infinitely form and proceedings of things, that the memory not is capable to retain: hence these reverberates just like assistance and teacher.

Of the some first one figure in the history. CAP. XCI. (91)

The before figure in the history make so much minor then the natural, how many hands you it figure far away from the first line, and then more, the other to comparison of that, with the rule of above.

Manner of the compose them histories. CAP. XCII. (92)

Of the figures that compose the histories, that itself demonstrate of major relief whom do pretense be more close to the eye: this happens for the 2.⁰ of the 3.⁰ that says: That complexion one demonstrate of major perfection, whom has less amount of air interposed between as though and the eye that it judges: and for this the shadows, whom display the body be remove, itself demonstrate once again more obscure of next to that from far away, whereas they are lead astray from the air interposed between the eye and they shadows: whom thing not happens in the shadows close to the eye, where they display the bodies of so much major relief how much of them they're of major obscurity.

Of compose the history. CAP. XCIII. (93)

Recollect, painter, when you do one only figure, of avert the glimpse of that, itself of parts, just like of the all, because you relevant without combat with the ignorance of the induced by such art; but in the history do to everyone the manner that to you happens, and maximum in the battles, whereas for necessity happen infinite indecently, and bending about the composer of such discord, or you want affirm lunacy brutality.

Variety of men in the history. CAP XCIV. (94)

In the history you be obliged to be men of various complexion, stature, skin tone, aptitude, fatness, thinness, large, thin; large, petioles (smallness), fat, lean, proud, civil, old people, young, strong and muscle, weak and with few muscles, allergy, melancholy, and with hair curly and lying, short and long, movements ready and languishing, and thus various clothes, and colors, and whatever what to it history itself requires.

Of acquire the movements of man. CAP. XCV. (95)*

The movements of the man to want be acquire later the cognition of the limbs, and of the all, for everyone the motions of the limbs and joints, and then with brief notation of few mark see the attitude of the men in the their accident, without which they one bring about that you him consider: because perceiving contain the mind occupied for you, whom possess abandoned the ferocity of the its act, to the which first era all intent, just like when two irate challenge together, which to each seem possess reason, whom with large ferocity move the eyelashes, and the hands, and the other parts, with proceedings appropriate to the their intention, and at their words; the that do not be able, if you him to wanted do fantasize such anger, or other accident, just like laughter, crying, pain, admiration, fright, and similar: drive for this retribution vague of take away with you one booklet of paper cast, and with the style of argent note with brevity such movements, and similarly note the proceedings of circumstance, and their appearance, and this you instruct to compose the history: and when it full the your booklet, put from part, and serval to the your purpose; and the good painter has from observe two things principal, namely the man, and the concept his of mind, that set aside by you, the which is important.

Of compose the history CAP. XCVI. (96)

The study of composition of the history must be of place the figure disproportionately, namely outline, and first be able well do for everybody the verse, and bending, and discernment of the their parts; of then both taken the destitution of two that daringly pugnacious together, and this like such invention both examined for various proceedings, and into various await: of then both following the fight of the bold with vile and fearsome; and these such behavior, and many other accident of the mind, be with great examination, and study speculate.

About the variety in the history. CAP. XCVII. (97)

Beloved the painter neither composition of the history of the copy and variety, and avert the replicate any part that of she made both, accommodation it originality and abundance attract without whether and delight the eye of the regarding. I say therefore that in the history it requires, second the places, mixed the men of diverse effigies, with different age and cloths, together blend with women, children, dogs, horse, and buildings, campaigns, and hills: and both observed the dignity and decorum to the prince and to the sage, with the separation from the common people: of them less mix the melancholy and weeping with the cheerfulness, and delightful: that the nature from that the glee be with the cheerfulness, and the smiling with the pleasant, and thus for the contrary.

Of diversify the air of faces in the history. CAP. XCVIII. (98)

Common defect is neither painters Italian recognize it environment and figure of the Emperor, through the many figure depicted: hence for escape like that error, not be produce, of it, replicated never, of it into all, of them in part the same figure, of them that a face itself to see in the other history. And how much observe more to one history, that the brute both near to the beautiful, and the old to the young, and the weak to the strong, thus more vague make yours history, and the one for the other figure increase in beauty. And because often take place that the painter, envisage whatever thingy, to want, that each minimal gesture of cartoon both valid, for this itself deceive, because many they are the times, that the animal figurative not have has the motion of limbs appropriated to the motion mental: and having he nature belle and grateful framework, and well finished, the adorn thing abusive without change they component.

Of accompany the colors the one with the other, and that the one yield gratitude to the other. CAP. XCIX. (99)

If you want make that the closeness of one complexion give gratitude to the other that with him confines, uses that rule which one to see make to the ray of the sun in the composition of arc heavenly, whom colors themselves generate in the motion about the rain, because each drips itself transmutes in the its descent by each of the colors of such arc, how itself is demonstrated to the its place.

Time attend, that if you want make an excellent obscurity, from the for comparison an excellent whiteness, and thus the excellent whiteness make with the maxim obscurity; and the pale make seem the red of most fiery redness that none seem for whether in comparison of the purple. There one other rule whom not attend by make the colors into whether of most supreme beauty that they naturally be, but that the company their give gratitude the one to the other, just like ago the green to the red, and thus the opposition, how the *green* with the blue. And here how one second rule generative of adversity company, how the blue with the yellow, that to look white, or with the white, and similar, whom himself affirm abeam his own place.

Of the do live and lovely colors into hers surface. CAP. C. (100)

Always without those colors, that to want which coordinate beauty, prepare first the field candid, and this I say of the colors that they are transparent, because without those that not they are transparent, not benefit from field bright, and the example of this it teach them colors of glass, whom when they are interposed below the eye and the air bright, one displaying of excellent beauty, the which do not be able, having behind for whether the air dark or other obscurity.

Of colors of the shadows of whatever color. CAP. CI. (101)

The complexion of the shadow of whatever complexion always participate of the complexion of the its object, and so much more or less how much he is more close or remote from it shadow, and how much it is more or less bright.

Of the variety that produce the colors of the things remote and close at hand. CAP CII. (102)

Of the things more obscure than the air, that itself demonstrate of minor obscurity, whom both more remote: and of things more albumen that the air, that itself demonstrate of minor whiteness, which make more remote by the eye: because of things more white and more obscure than the air, into long distance exchanging complexion, the albumen acquire obscurity, and the obscure acquire clarity.

In how much distance one pardon them colors of things entirely. CAP. CIII. (103)

The colors of things itself pardon completely in major or minor distance, second that the eye, and the thing view make into major or minor height. Proof for the $7.^0$ of this, which I say: The air is much more or less heavy, how much more it do more close or remote from the land. Therefore if the eye and the thing from him view make close to the land, in that moment the thickness of the air interposed between the eye and the thing, impede extremely the complexion of the thing view from it eye. But if so much so eye together with the thing from him view make remote from the land, then such air occupy little the complexion of the predicted object: and concern they are the variety of the distance, in the which itself pardon the colors of the objective, how many they are the variety of the day, and how much they are the variety of thickness or subtlety of the air, for the which penetrate to the eye the species of colors about the predicted objective.

Complexion of the shadow of the white. CAP. CIV. (104)

The shadow of the white view from the sun and from the air has the her shadows cause to the blue, and this arise because the white for if not is complexion, but is recipe of whatever complexion, and for the $4.^0$ of this, that I say: The surface of each body participate of the complexion of the his own object; he is necessary which that part about the surface white partake of the complexion of the air his own object.

What complexion make shadow more negro. CAP. CV. (105)

That shadow participate more of the black, which itself generate by more white surface; and this possess major propensity to the variety which not any other surface; and this be born, because the white not is with enumerate below the colors, and is receptive of each complexion, and the surface its participate more intensely of colors of the his own object which none other surface of whatever color and maximum of the its right contrary, which is the black (or other colors obscure) from the which the white is more remote for nature, and for this seem, and is large difference from the its shadows principal to the lights principal.

Of the complexion that not ostentation variation in variety thickness of air. CAP. CVI. (106)

Possible is that one same complexion not countenance mutation by variety distance, and this happen when the proportion of the thickness of the air, and the proportion of the distance which bring about the colors from the eye, both one same, but converse. Proof thus: A. (Fig. 9) both the eye, **H.** both a complexion which you desire, position by one degree of distance remote from the eye, at air of four degrees of thickness, but because the **2.°** degrees of above **A. M. N. L.** has the half more thin, the air deliver into it the same color, is necessary that such complexion both the double more remote from the eye that not time of first: therefore the place the two degrees **A. F.** and **F. G.** distant from the eye, and evening the complexion **G.** , whom furthermore take-up in the degree of double thinness to the **2°** into **A. M. N. L.** which make the degree **O. M. P. N.**, he is necessary that both position in the height **E.**, and make

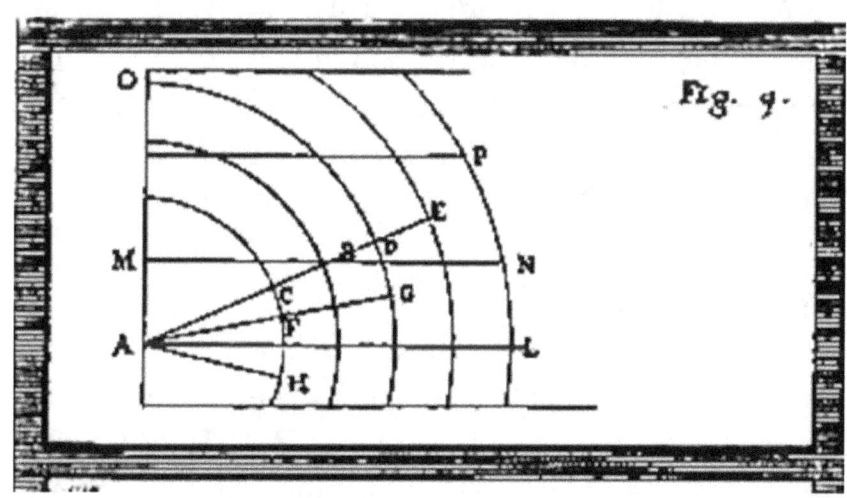

distance from the eye all the line **A. E.**, whom itself evidence matter by thickness of air how much the distance **A. G.**, and prove thus. Whether **A.G.** distance interposed from one same air below the eye and the complexion occupy two degree and **A. E.** two degree and half, this distance is sufficient by do which the complexion **G.** elevation into **E.** not itself various of its intensity, because the degree **A. C.** and the degree **A. F.** be one same thickness of air are similar and equal, and the degree **C. D.** although both equal into length to the grade **F. G.** none is finished into thickness of air, because he is half in the air of double thickness to the air of above, of the which one half degree of distance occupy so much the complexion, how much oneself aspect an degree complete from the air of above, which is the double most thin than the air that the confines of under. Therefore calculating first the thickness from the air, and then the distance, you will see the colors varied of situated, that none contain change of beauty; **E.** affirm thus for the calculation from the thickness from the air: the complexion **H.** is position into four degrees of thickness of air: **G.** complexion, is position into air of two degrees of thickness: **E.** complexion itself located into air of one degrees of thickness: hour we will see if the distance they are into proportion equal, but converse. The complexion **E.** one located distance from the eye by two degrees and half of distance. The **G.** two degrees, the **H.** one degree: this distance none collide with the proportion of the thickness, but is necessary make one third calculation, and this is that you necessity say. The degree **A. C.** how departed dubbed of above, is similar and equal to the degrees **A. F.** and the middle degrees **C. B.** is similar but none equal to the degrees **A. F.**, because is only one half degree of length, whom weigh one degree complete from the air of above. Therefore the calculation expedient statesman to the proposition, because **A. C.** currency two degree from the thickness of air of above, and the half degree **C. B.** of it matter one complete of it air of above, one that we have three degrees into currency of it thickness of above, and one trace is inside, namely **B. E.** it fourth. Professed **A. H.** has four degree of thickness of air: **A. G.** of it has still four, namely **A. F** of it has two and **F. G.** two other, that ago four **A. E.** of it has still four, because **A. C.** of it he keeps two, and one **C. D.** that is the half of the **A. C.** and of that same air, and one complete of it and of above in the air thin which ago four. Therefore if the distance **A. E.** none is double of the distance **A. G.** of it quadruple from the distance **A H.** it is restore from the **C. D.** half degree of air gross that be weigh one degrees complete of the air more thin which the remain of above: And thus is concluded the our purpose, namely that the color **H. G. E.** not itself varies for various distance.

Of perspective of colors. CAP. CVII. (107)

Of a same complexion place into various distance and equal height, such both the proportion of his own brightening, which make that about the distance that each of them colors has from the eye that to see. Proof both that **E. B. C. D.** (Fig. 10.) both one same complexion: the **1.⁰ E.** both place two degrees of distance from the eye **A**: the **2.⁰** that is **B.** both distant four degrees: the **third** that is **C.** both 6 degrees the **4.⁰** that is **D.** both eight degrees: just like display the definitions of circles that one cut departed the line, same as one sees above the line **A. R.** of furthermore **A. R. S. P.** both a degree of air thin **S. P. E. T.** both a degree of air more gross: come after that the first

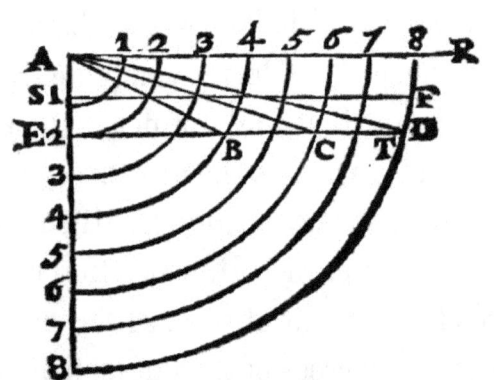

complexion **E.** pass through to the eye for one degree of air gross **E. S.**, and about one degree of air in no time gross **S. A.**, and the complexion **B.** convey the its similitude to the eye **A.** for two degrees of air gross, and about two about the convey gross, and the **C.** the transmit for three degrees about the gross, and for three about the convey gross; and the complexion **D.** for four about the gross, and for four of about the gross, and thus we have proven here such be the proportion about the diminution of colors, or you want say perdition, which is that of their distance from the eye that them sees: and this only occur of it colors which they are of equal height, because into those that they are of height unequal, none itself observed the same rule, for be their into air of various thickness, which make various occupation without them colors.

Of complexion that none itself shedding into various thickness of air. CAP. CVIII. (108)

Not one change the complexion position into diverse thickness of air, when make so much further remote from the eye the one the other; how much itself locate into most subtle air the one that the other; Proof thus. If the first air below has four degrees of thickness, and the complexion both distance one degree from the eye, and the second air more high have three degrees of thickness, which has lost one degree, ago that the complexion acquires one degree of distance; and when the air most high has lost two degrees of thickness, and the complexion has acquired two degrees of distance, in that moment such is the first complexion which is the third; and for abbreviate, if the complexion one raise so much that enter in the air that have lost three degrees of thickness, and the complexion acquire three degrees of distance, then you to you can render certain, that such decline of complexion has fact the complexion high and remote, how much the complexion low and near, because whether the air high has lost three quarters of the thickness of the air low, the color in the raise has acquire the three quarters of throughout the distance for whom he himself located remote from the eye; and thus itself proof the intent ours.

Whether the colors various be able be or seem of one uniform obscurity, through one same shadow. CAP. CIX. (109)

Possible is that all the variety of colors from one same shadow seem transmuted in the color of them shadow. This itself manifest in the darkness of one night nebula, in the which no figure or color or body itself comprise; and because darkness other none is that privation of light accident and reflection, through whom all the figure and colors of body itself comprehend, he is necessary that removed wholly the cause of the light, which be missing the effect and cognition of colors and figure of predicted bodies.

About the cause of perdition of colors and figure of bodies, through the darkness which seem and none they are. CAP. CX. (110)

Many they are the sites into whether aluminates, and clarify that one demonstrate darkness, and to the all deprived of whatever variety of colors and figure of things that into them one found: this happen for cause about the light of air aluminate that below the things views and the eye one interposes, just like one see inside at window that they are remote from the eye, in the which only one itself comprise one uniform obscurity very dark: if you enter more inside to it house, you will see those into whether be strong aluminate, and be able quickly comprehends each minimum part of whatever thing inside to such window, that locate one can. And this such demonstration be born for defeat of the eye, whom expunged from the overwhelm light of the air, take in rather the bulk about the its pupil, and for this be short rather about the its potency: and in the places most obscures (*one in less light area*) the pupil itself widens, and so much grows of potency, how much it acquire of magnitude. Proof in the $2.^0$ of my perspective.

Just like none things display its color true one you not has light from one other similar complexion. CAP CXI. (111)

None things demonstrate never its proper complexion, if the light which the illuminate not is into all of it complexion, and this itself manifest in the colors of clothes, of which the folds illuminate, that reflection or offense light crease, the make demonstrate the them true color. The same ago the leaf of the gold in the giving light the one to the other, and the contrary ago from pluck light from one other complexion.

Of colors which itself demonstrate vary from them be, through the contrast of their fields. CAP. CXII. (112)

None limit of complexion uniform themselves demonstrate be equal, if none ends in field of complexion similar without him. This one see to manifest when the black ends with white, which each complexion seem more noble in the confines of the contrary that none parry in the his half.

About the mutation of colors transparent data or mass above diverse colors, with their divergent relation. CAP. CXIII. (113)

When a complexion transparent is above one other complexion variation from him, itself consists one color mixed divergent from each of simple which him compose. This one to see in the smoke that be drawn from the path, whom when is comparison to the black of it orbit itself ago blue, and when itself raise to the comparison of the blue of the air, seem marionette, or reddish. And thus the purple given above the blue itself ago of color of violet: and when the blue make given above the yellow, he itself ago green: and crocus above the white itself ago yellow: and the clarity above the obscurity itself ago blue, so much more beautiful, how much the clarity and the obscure do more excellent.

What part of one same complexion one display most beauty of painting? CAP. CXIV. (114)

Now is from notice what part of one same complexion itself display most beauty in painting, or that which has the luster, or that which has light, or that of the shadow procuress, or that of the obscure, otherwise into transparent. At this point be essential interpret which complexion is that one demand: because diverse colors they've the theirs beauty into diverse part of whether same: and this us demonstrate the black, which has the its beauty in the shadow, the white in the light, the blue, green, and tan, in the shadows procuress, the yellow and red neither lights, the gold neither reflections, and the lacquer in the shadows procuress.

Just like each complexion which none has luster is most beautiful in its parts luminous that in the shaded. CAP. CXV. (115)

Each complexion is most beautiful in its part aluminate that in the shady, and this arise, which the light quickens and from true notice of the quality of colors, and the shadow fatigue and obscure the same beauty, and impede the notice of it complexion. And whether for the contrary the black is most beautiful in the shadows, which neither light, himself answers that the black not is color.

Of the evidence of colors CAP. CXVI. (116)

That what which is more albumen most appears from faraway, and the most obscure ago the contrary.

What part of the complexion reasonably must be most beauty? CAP. CXVII. (117)

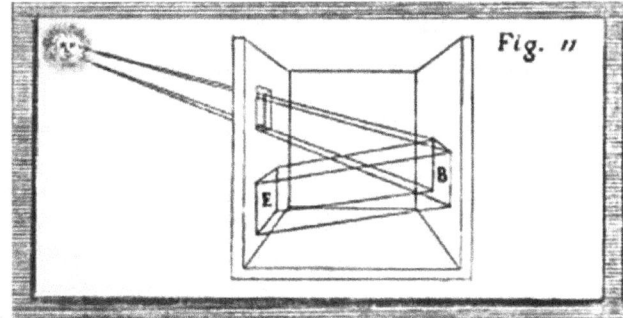

If **A.** (fig II.) both the light, and **B.** both the aluminate for line from it light: **E.** that none it can to see it light, to see only the wall aluminate: the sort of wall affirm that both red. Be thus, the light that one generates to the part resemble to its cause, and tinge in red the expression E., and if E. both again he red, see be much most beautiful that B., and if E. fusses yellow, see create one color shimmering between yellow and red.

Just like the beautiful of the complexion must be in the lights. CAP. CXVIII. (118)

If we understand the quality of colors be experience through the light, is from evaluate that where is most bright there oneself may see more well curb quality of the complexion aluminate, and where is most darkness the complexion tinges in the complexion of them darkness. Therefore, you painter, remember of display the truth of colors by such part aluminate.

Of the color green fact from the rust of copper CAP. CXIX. (119)

The green fact from the copper, once again that such color both placed to oil, refined it goes into smoke the its beauty, itself he none is at once inverted: and none only refined goes into smoke, but itself he do absolve with one sponge wet of simple water common, itself raise from the its table, where is painting, and maximally itself the tempo do wet: and this be born because such verdigris (green color) is fact for force of salt, whom salt with facilitates itself dissolves in neither times rainy, and maximally be wet and washed with the predicted sponge.

Increase of beauty in the green copper CAP. CXX. (120)

If do mixture with green-copper the aloe cavallino, it green-copper acquire large beauty, and most obtain the saffron, if none refine go up into smoke. And of this aloe cavallino itself acquainted it goodness when he himself resolve in the brandy, be hot; which better the resolve, which when it is cold. And whether you contain completed one work with it aloe resolute into water, then it work the make of lovely color: and so far aloe itself more mince by desire for if, and still together with green-copper, and with each other complexion that to your liking.

About the mission of colors the one with the other. CAP. CXXI. (121)

Once again that the mission of colors the one with the other itself extend direction the infinite, not remain for this ego not of it face one little of speech. Establish first rather colors simplistic, with each of those blend each of the other by one by one, and then by two by two, and by three by three, and thus continuing, for refined about complete number of everyone them colors: then restart to combine them colors by two with two, and by three with three, and furthermore by four, thus proceed refined to the objective, above them two colors simple bosom dedicate three, and with them three accompany other three, and then six, will then continue such mission into all the proportion. Colors simple inquire about those that none they are compose, of it itself be able put together for course of mission other colors, black, white: although he none

47

they are mass between colors, because the one is darkness, the other is light, namely the one is privation and the other is generalized: but ego not them desire for this cease into behind, because into painting they are the principal, with this whether that painting be compote of shadows, and of light, namely of bright and obscure. Further the black and the white sequence the blue, and yellow, then the green and tawny, namely nest, or want say **ocria=ochre;** of then the **morello = black horse,** namely **pavonazzo= peacock/ blue and green eye marks,** and the red: and these they are eight colors, and further none is at creation, of which I commence the mixture. And both first black and white, of then black yellow, and black and red, of then yellow and black, and yellow and red: and since at this point to me left hand paper, *says the author,* tattered to do distinction in the my works with lengthy proceed, whom make of large utility, on the contrary most necessary: and this such description itself assume below the theoretical and the practice.

Of the surface of each body shady. CAP CXXII. (122)

The surface of each body shady participate of complexion of its object. This I demonstrate them bodies shady with certainty, with that be which none of predicted bodies display her its figure, or complexion, itself the half interposed among the body and the luminous none is aluminate. Indicate therefore that if the body opaque be yellow, and the luminous be blue, that the part aluminate be green, whom green itself consists of yellow and blue.

Which one is the surface accommodation of most colors? CAP CXXIII. (123)

The white is most receptive of whatever complexion that none other surface of whatever body that none is mirror. Proof, indicate that each body empty is capable of receive that which none be able receive the bodies which none they are vacant, express for this that the white is vacant, or you want say devoid of whatever complexion, and be he aluminate of the complexion of whatever luminous, participate most of it luminous that none would, the black, whom is similar to a vessel broken, that is devoid of each capacity to whatever thing.

What body itself tinge more of the color of her objective? CAP. CXXIV. (124)

The surface of each body participate most entirely of the color of that objective whom he make more near. This occurs, because the objective close occupy most multitude of variety of species, whom come at it surface of bodies corrupt most the surface of such objective, which none do it complexion, if fuss (blend) remote: and occupying these species, it complexion demonstrate most flawlessly the its nature into it body opaque.

What body itself demonstrate of most nice complexion? CAP. CXXV. (125)

The surface of those opaque one demonstrate of most perfect color, whom have for near objective a complexion similar to the his own.

Of the incarnation of faces CAP. CXXVI. (126)

That of bodies more itself conserve at long distance that do of major amounts. This proposition it display that the visage itself face obscure in the distance, because the shadow is the major part that possess itself countenance the and essence, and light they are minimum: and however be missing at brief distance: and the most tiny they are the their luster, and this is the cause that linger the part more obscure, the countenance itself face and itself demonstrate obscure. And touch more seem draw to black, how much such face have to relief round or to head object more upright surface.

Manner of portray the relief, and of prepare the paper for these. CAP. CXXVII. (127)

The painters for portray the things of relief must tinge the surface of paper of medium darkness, and then give the shadows most obscure, and in last the lights principal to small place, whom they are those that at little distance they are the first that itself let-off to the eye.

Of the variety of one same complexion in various distance from the eye CAP. CXXVIII. (128)

Below them colors of same nature, that even one varies that less one remove from the eye. Proof, because the air that itself interposes within the eye and the things view occupy rather the articulate thing: and if the air interposed do of large form, then the thing view itself tinge strong of the complexion of such air, and if the air make of thin quantities, in that moment the object do little impeded.

Of the greenery view in companion. CAP. CXXIX. (129)

Of the greenery view in companion of equal quality, that block be most obscure that do in the plants of the trees, and more albumen itself demonstrate that of meadows.

Which vegetable seem more of blue CAP. CXXX. (130)

That vegetable itself demonstrate participate more of blue, whom make of most obscure shadiness; and this itself test for the 7.^{0} that says, that the blue itself compose of light and of obscure at long distance.

What is that surface which less that the other demonstrate her own true complexion. CAP CXXXI. (131)

That surface display less the his true complexion, whom do more clear and clean: These see in the herbs of meadows, and in the leaves of the trees, whom be of clean and luster surface, take hold the luster in the what itself reflected the sun, or the air which the aluminate, and thus in that part of the luster they are private of the natural complexion.

What body display more his own true complexion? CAP CXXXII. (132)

That body more demonstrate its true complexion, of what the surface do in no time clean and flat. These one see about them clothes linens, and in the leaves of the herb and trees that they are woolly, in the what no luster not itself most generate, hence for necessity none be able mirror the objective, only render to the eye the its true complexion and natural; none be that corrupt from no body that the aluminate with one complexion opposition, how that of the red of the sun, when sets, and tinge the clouds of its precisely complexion.

Of clarity of countries. CAP. CXXXIII. (133)

Never the colors, vividness and clarity of countries paint is it adapt with countries natural aluminate from the sun, if them countries paint not create aluminates from it sun.

Perspective common of the diminution of colors at long distance CAP. CXXXIV. (134)

The air do so much less participant of complexion blue, how much they is more close to the horizon, is so much more obscure, how much she is more close to horizon, is more obscure, how much she to it horizon is more remote. This one proof for the 3.^{0} of 9.^{0} that display which that body do not even aluminate from the sun, whom either of quality most rare. Therefore the fire, element which dress the air, for consist in him more rare and more thin than the air, even it occupy the darkness that are above of he that none ago it air, and for

50

consequence, the air body in no time rare that the fire more itself aluminate from the rays solar that it penetrate, and hallucinate the infinite of the atoms, that for she one instill, one render albumen to the our eye: hence penetrating for she air the species about the above-mentioned darkness, necessarily ago that she whiteness of air it believe blue, how is proven in the $3.^0$ of the $10.^0$ and so much it seem of blue more bright, how much between of it darkness and the eye our itself interpose major thickness of air. Same as if the eye of who it considers a fuss **P.** (Fig. 12.) and overlook above of whether the thickness of the air **P. R.** furthermore declining sufficiently, the eye to see the air for the line **P. S.** whom him seem most clear, for be major thickness of air for the line **P. S.** which for the line **P.R.** is if such eye itself bow to the horizon, to see the air almost to all private of sky-blue; it what thing follow, because the line of view penetrates very much major sum of air for it rectitude **P. D.** which for the slanting **P. S.** and thing itself is persuaded the ours intent.

Of things mirrored in the water of countries, and first of the air. CAP. CXXXV. (135)

That air only do that which hand over of if simulation in the surface of the water, whom reflects from the surface of the water to the eye below angle equal, that is to say that the angle of the incident both equal to the angle of the reflection.

Diminution of colors for half interposed below their and the eye. CAP. CXXXVI. (136)

A lot of less demonstrate it thing visible of its nature complexion, how much the half interposed between he and the eye do of major thickness.

Of fields that itself converges to the shadow and by lights. CAP. CXXXVII. (137)

The field that converges at the shadows and by light, and to the complete aluminates and overshadowed of whatever complexion, made most separation the one from other, if made more various, namely that a complexion obscure none must finish at other complexion obscure, but very much various, namely white; and participant of white, in how much be allowed obscure, or draw to the obscure.

How itself must redress, when the white itself ends in white, and the obscure into obscure. CAP. CXXXVIII. (138)

When the complexion of one body white itself strikes to finish into field white, then the whites either made equal, or not: and if made equal, then that which you is

51

most close itself make quaintly obscure in the term which it ago with it white: and whether such field do in not time white which the complexion that to him stand out, then the dominate stand out for if same from the him different without other aid of term obscure.

Of nature of colors of fields above them which stands the white. CAP. CXXXIX. (139)

The thing white itself demonstrate more white which make in field more obscure, and itself demonstrate more obscure which both to field more white: and this it has teach to fall of snow , whom, when we the observant in the field of air, there apparently obscure, and when we the observant to field of some window open, for whom one themselves sees the obscurity of shadow of his house, then it snow itself display whites; and the snow of near it apparently velocity, and from faraway be late, and the vicinity there apparently of continue amount, to guise of white strings, and the remote there apparently discontinuous.

Of fields of figure. CAP CXL. (140)

Of things of equal clarity, that itself demonstrate of minor clarity, whom do to see at field of major whites; and that seem most white, which stands out of space more obscure: and the incarnate seem pale in field red, and the pale seem reddish, be view in field yellow: and likewise them colors make judged that which none they are through them fields which them surround.

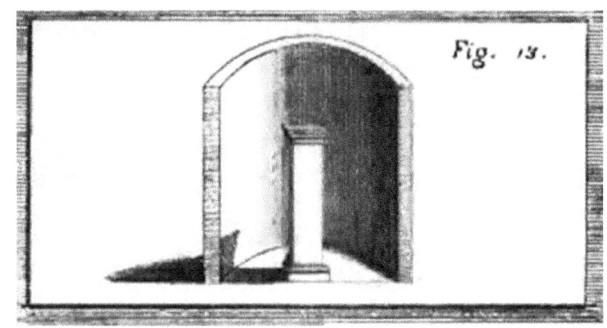

Fig. 13.

Of fields of things painted CAP. CXLI. (141)

Of great dignity is the speech of fields neither which stand out the body opaque clothes of shadows and of light, because to those themselves connivance have the parts aluminate neither field obscure, and the parts obscure nor the fields clarity, itself such for the figure streak demonstrate. (Fig. 13.)

Of those that fake in campaign the things most remote get most obscure. CAP. CXLII. (142)

A lot of they are which to campaign open make the figure much more obscure how much they are most remote from eye, whom thing is to contrary, if by now the thing imitated none accommodate white, because then happen that which of under itself suggest.

Of colors of things remote from the eye. CAP. CXLIII. (143)

The air tinge most the objective, which it separates from the eye, of its complexion; how much it make of major thickness. Therefore have the air divided one object obscure with thickness of two miles, it the tinge more, as that which has thickness of one mile. Respond that the opposing, and says that the countries have the trees of one same species more obscure from faraway that of near, whom thing none is true, whether the plants do equal, and divide from equal space: But make well true if the first trees do rare, and shall see the clarity about the meadows that the separate, and the last make often; how happens in the banks and vicinity of rivers, that then none itself sees space of albumen grasslands, but everyone conjoin, make shadow the one above the other. Once again happens that very much major is the part shady of the plants, which the luminous, and for the species which command of whether it plant to the eye, itself display to long distance, and the complexion obscure which itself located at major amount more maintains the its species which the part less obscure: and things it mixed threshold with agency the part most potent to more long distance.

Grades of paintings. CAP. CXLIV. (144)

None is always good that which is beautiful, and this I say for those painters that love so much the beauty of colors, which none without great conscience damage their very weak, and almost insensible shadows, none estimating the their relief. And to this error they are the well talkers without any sentence.

Of the mirroring and complexion of water of the sea seen from different aspect. CAP. CXLV. (145)

The sea undulating none has complexion universal, but who the to see from land motionless the to see of complexion obscure, and so much more obscure how much is more close the horizon, and seen no dim light, over luster, which itself move with slowness with use of sheep white in the herds, and who to see the sea by at other sea him to see blue; and these be born because from land the sea seem obscure, because you see to him the hence which look in the mirror the obscurity of the land, and from other sea appear blue, because you see in the hence the air blue of such whence look in the mirror.

Of nature of comparisons. CAP. CXLVI. (146)

The garment dismal make believe them flesh similar human more white that none they are, and the garment white make seem them flesh obscure, and the garment yellow them make think colorful, and them clothes red the demonstrate pale.

The color of shadow of whatever body. CAP CXLVII. (147)

Never the color of shadow of whatever body make well curb, of it shadow, if the objective that them cast a shadow over none is of the complexion of the body from him overshadowed. Say for example that I contain any dwelling in the which one the block be green, affirm that if at such place do seen as blue, whom one both illuminate from the clarity of blue, that then such part illuminate do of lovely blue, and the shadow make ugly, and none well curb shadow of such beauty of blue, because itself corrupts for the green that in him reverberates: and worse make if such partition fuss hideout.

Of the perspective of colors in the places obscure. CAP. CXLIII. (148)

Neither place luminous diffuse deformed all in all at darkness that complexion do most obscure, that from it eye both more remote.

Prospective of colors CAP. CXLIX. (149)

The first colors must be simple, and the degrees of their diminution together with them degrees of distance themselves must agree, namely that the sizes of things participate more of nature of point how much of it him loose more near, and the colors possess much more by participate of complexion of her horizon, how much them at they're more close.

The colors CAP. CL. (150)

The complexion that itself located below the part shady and the aluminate of body shady, both of minor beauty that those, which both entirely aluminate: therefore the first beauty of colors both neither principal light.

From that arise the blue in the air. CAP. CLI. (151)

The blue of the air arise from the thickness of body of air aluminate, interposed between the darkness superior and the earth: The air for if none has quality of odor, or of flavors, or of colors, but in if catches the similarities of the things that afterward she they are arrange, and so much do of more beautiful blue how much behind to it make major darkness, none be you of too much space, of it of too much thickness of humidity, and to see neither mountains, that have more shadows, be more beautiful blue in the long distance, and thus where is that is more aluminate, exhibition more the color of mountains more that of blue applicator of the air that below she is the eye one insert.

Of color CAP. CLII. (152)

Below the colors that they are blue, those at long distance participate more of sky-blue, whom do more close to the black, and thus of conversely itself maintain for long distance in the its precisely complexion, whom make more dissimilar to the dubbed black. Therefore the green of the campaigns itself transmute more in the blue, which none ago the yellow or the white, and so for the contrary the yellow and white even itself transmute that the green and the red.

Of color CAP. CLIII. (153)

The colors places in the shadows participate so much more or less of their natural beauty, how much they make into major or minor obscurity. But if the colors do situate in space luminous, at that moment them one display of so much major beauty how much the luminous both of major splendor. The adversary affirm: Concern they're the variety the colors of the shadows, how many they are the variety of colors that have the things overshadowed. And ego I say that the colors places in the shadows display below their so much minor variety, how much the shadow that there they are situated be more obscure, and of this one of it are witnesses those that from the plaza behold inside the port of temple shady, where the painting dressed of various colors appear all dressed of darkness.

Of fields of the figure of body paintings. CAP. CLIV. (154)

The field that circumference the figure of whatever thing painted must be more obscure than the part aluminate of they figure, and more bright than there part shadowy.

Because the white not is complexion. CAP. CLV. (155)

The white not is complexion, but is at one potency accommodation of each complexion. When it is in campaign high, all them his shadows they are blue; and this arise for to the 4.° that I says: There surface of each body opaque (matt) participates of the color of his own object (demur). Therefore such white be private of light of the sun for interposition of some object transmitted between the sun and it white, remain all the white, which to sees the sun and the air participant the color the sun and of the air, and that part what none is view from the sun remains shady, and participant of color from the air: and if such white none to see the greens from the campaign finally to horizon, of it so far to see the whiteness of such horizon, without doubt it white seem be of simple complexion, of the which one itself display be the air.

Of colors. CAP. CLVI. (156)

The light of the pith (fire) tinged each thing to yellow; but this none appear be true, if none to the comparison of the things aluminate from the air; and this comparison itself be able canny of day, and certainly after the dawn, and again where to one room obscure instill above the object a spiracle of air, and again a spiracle of light of candle, and to such place certainly make viewpoints egg white and send the their differences. However without such comparison never do be familiar with the their difference, except for neither colors which contain most similitude, but be acquainted with, how such white, from yellow, bright green from the blue, because yellow went the light that aluminate the sky blue, is how blend together blue and yellow, the which compose a beautiful green; and if mix then yellow with green, itself ago very more beautiful.

Of colors of light accidents and reflections. CAP CLVII. (157)

When two light place by half at if the body shady, none can vary if none by two line, namely or do of equal potency, or they make unequal, namely speak of light below

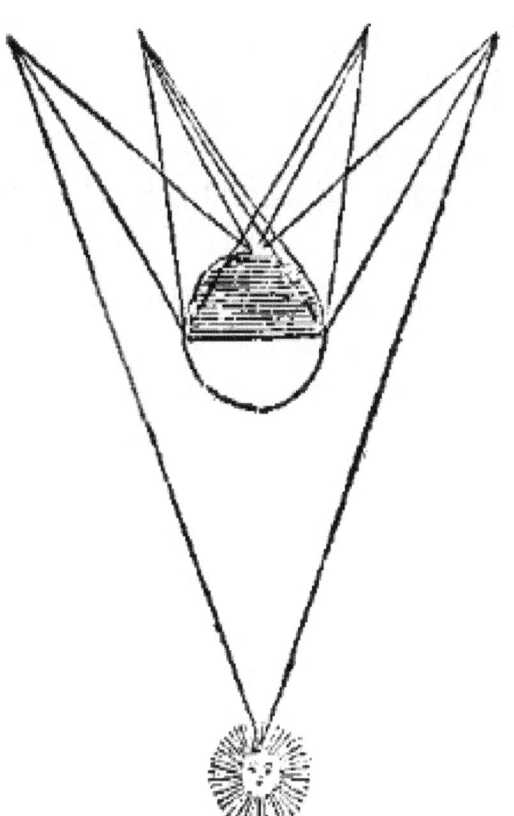

them: if make equal, itself can vary in two other manner, namely second theirs splendor above the objective, that make or equal or unequally: equal do when make at equal distance; unequal, in the unequal distance. At equal distance itself variation to two other manner, namely the object situated with equal distance below two light equal in complexion and in splendor it can be aluminate from them light equal in complexion and in splendor it can be aluminate from them light in two manner, namely or evenly from each part, or unequal: equally do from them light aluminate, when the space that remains surrounding without two light make of equal complexion and obscurity and clarity: unequal do produce, sometimes they space surrounding without two light do vary in obscurity.

Of the colors of shadow. CAP. CLVIII. (158)

Often direct happens the shadow of body shady not be companion of colors of light, and make do greenish the shadow, and the light reddish, again that the body both of complexion equal. This happens that the light come of eastern above the object, and dazzle the objective, of the complexion of the his splendor, and from the occident (west) do one other object from the same light aluminate, whom do of other complexion that the first object, hence with the his light reflections stands out direction east, and pummel with the her rays in the party of the first object he face, and the itself incise the her rays, and remain latches together with the them colors, and splendor. Him I have often direct seen one objective white, the light red, and the shadows bluish, and this happens in the mountains of snow when the sun sets at once horizon, and itself exhibition fiery (Fig. 14).

Of the things posed into field clear, and because such useful is helpful into painting. CAP. CLIX. (159)

When the body shady terminate into field of color clear and aluminate, then for

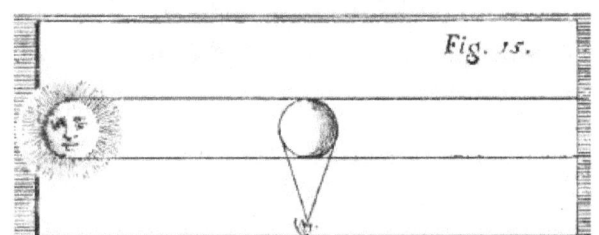

Fig. 15.

necessity seem stand out and remote from it field; and this occur because the body of curve surface for necessity itself make shady in the part opposites of hence none they are pummel from rays luminous, for be such place private of award the ray: for whom thing very much itself varies from the field, and the part of it body aluminate none end never in it field aluminate with there his first of all clarity, on the contrary between the field and the earliest light of the body itself intervening one end of the body, which is more obscure of the field, or of the light of the body respective (Fig. 15.)

Of fields CAP. CLX. (160)

Of the fields about the figure, namely it egg white in the obscure, and the obscure in the field clear, of the white with black, or black with white, seem more potent the one for the other, and this the contrary the one for the other itself display always more potential.

Of colors that result from the mixture of other colors, whom one diminish species second. CAP. CLXI. (161)

Of simple colors the former is the white, although the philosopher not accept of them the white of it the black in the number of colors, because the one is cause of colors, the other is deprivation. However because the painter none it can do without he, we them place in the number of the other, and enunciate the white in this order be the first, of it the simple, the yellow the second; the green the third, the blues the fourth, the red the fifth, the black the sixth: and the white put for the light without whom none complexion to see one it can, and the yellow for the earth, the green for the water, the blue for the air, and the red for the fire, and the black for the darkness which be above the element of fire, because none there is matter or thickness whereas the rays of the sun obtain to penetrate and strike, and for consequence enlighten. Whether you want with brevity to see the variety of all them colors composition, remove pane colorful, and for those overlook all of them colors of the campaign that afterwards those oneself they see, and thus see everyone the colors of the things that afterwards such pane one they see be all mixed with complexion of the aforesaid pane, and see that both the complexion, which with such mixture itself advance, or corrupt: if make the predicted pane of color yellow, I say that the species of the object that for it pass through to the eye, can thus worsen how perfect: and this deterioration in such complexion of pane occur to the azure, and black, and white above all of them the other, and the improvement occur in the yellow, and green above all of them the other, and thus turn course with the eye the mixtures of colors, whom they are infinitely: and in this manner make chosen by nine invention of colors mixed and compositions, and the same itself do with two pane of various colors before to the eye, and thus for can persist.

Of colors. CAP. CLXII. (162)

The blue and the green not is for whether simple, because the blue is composition of light and of darkness, just like is this of air, namely black impeccable, and white candid. The green is composition of a simple and of a composition, namely components of blue and of yellow.

Endless the thing mirrored participates of the color of the body that the speculum, and the mirror itself tinge to part of the color from him mirrored, and participates so much more the one of the other, how much the thing that itself be reflected is more or less potent than the complexion of the mirror, and that thing parry of potent complexion in the mirror, which more participates of the color of it mirror.

About the colors of bodies that make seen in major distance, which both of more splendid whiteness. Therefore itself see in minor longitude, that as make of major obscurity.

Below them bodies of equal whiteness and distance from the eye, that itself demonstrate more candid which is surrounded from major obscurity: and for contrary that obscurity itself demonstrate more darkness, which both view in more candid whiteness.

About the colors of equal perfection, that itself demonstrate of major excellence which both seen in companions of the color upright contrary and the pale with the red, the black with the white, although of it the one of it the other both complexion: blue with yellow, green and red, because each color itself concise better in the her contrary, which in the hers similar, how the obscure in the distant, the limpid in the obscure.

Those thing which both view in air darken and turbid (opaque), be white seem of major form which none is. Such happens, because, how is proverb by above, it thing albumen increase in the field obscure, for the reasons distant bestow.

The half that is between the eye and there what view transmutes it thing in its complexion, just like the air blue do that the mountains distant make blue, the pane red ago which that to see the eye afterward him seem red; and light that make the stars around to they, is occupied for the darkness of the night that itself located below the eye and the illumination of them stars.

The true complexion of whatever body itself demonstrate in that part as none both occupied from any quality of shadow, of it from luster, if make body polished.

I say that the white which ends with the obscure, ago that in they terms, the obscure seem more black, and white seem more candid.

Of the complexion of mountains CAP. CLXIII. (163)

That mountain to the eye itself demonstrate of more beauty blue that do from if more obscure, and that make more obscure, which do more high and more peak (woodland), because such wood cover errand shrubbery from the part of below, itself that none the to see the heaven; once again the endure uncultivated of forest they are in if more obscure of the domestic. Very much more obscure they are the oaks, beeches, firs cypresses, and pines, which none they are the trees domestic, and olive trees. Those lucidity which itself intervening below the eye and the black, which do more thin in the great its summit, make black of more beautiful blue, and thus of conversely: and those plant even seem of divide from the his field, which end with field of complexion more similar to the hers, and thus of conversely: and that part of the white seem more candid, which do more near to the confine of the black, and thus seem less white that which more make remote from it swarthy: and that part of the black seem more obscure, which do more close to the white, and thus seem even obscure that which do more remote from it white.

How the painter be obliged put in practice the prospective of colors. CAP. CLXIV. (164)

Without to want put such prospective of the vary, or lose, or true decrease the own essence of colors, take of hundred in hundred hands things posed below the campaign, how they are tree, homes, men, and sites, and inasmuch to the before tree, have a pane firm well and thus both firm the eye your: and in called pane draws a tree above the form of those, of then costal so much for transverse, which the tree natural confine almost with the your drawing, in addition coloristic the your design, in manner that for complexion and form be to comparison the one of the other, or that all two, shut an eye, couple painted, and both dubbed pane of one same distance: and this rule same ago of the trees seconds, and of the third of hundred in hundred arms, of space in space, and he to you in receipt of such your family auditorium, and master, always operating in the your works, whereas itself belong to, and make fine elude the work. But I find for the rule that the second decrease 4/5ths of the first, when fuse faraway twenty arms from the first.

Of the perspective aerial CAP. CLXV. (165)

Excellence yours one other perspective, whom itself says aerial, inasmuch for the variety of the air oneself can consider the diverse distances of various building

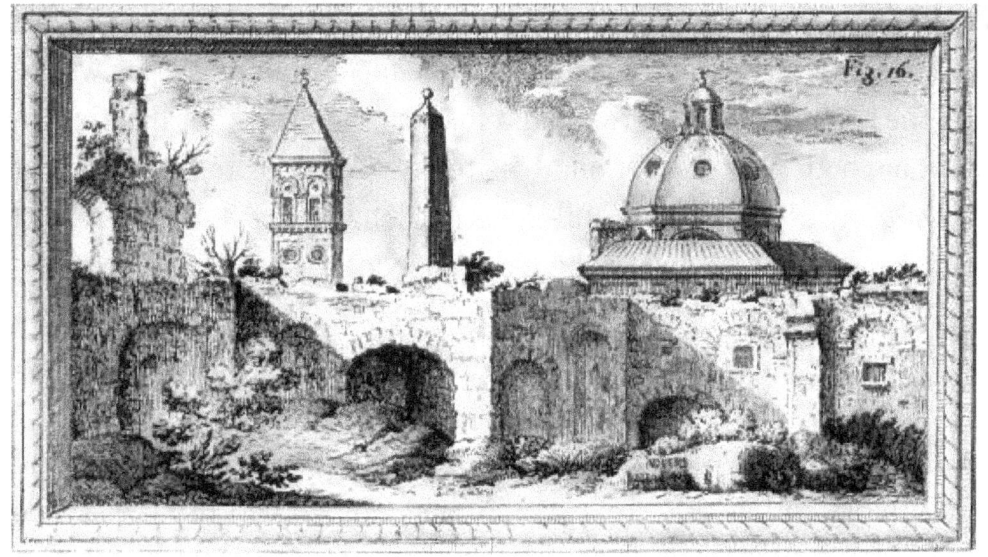

terminated nether their arise from one single line, just like do the to see a lot of building of it from one wall, itself which everybody ostentatious above the extremity of dubbed wall of one same grandness, and that you to want do seem more faraway the one that the other. And from make a good impression one air one little large. You both that in similar air the final thing views into those, same as are the mountains, for it very quantity of the air that itself located below the eye your and dubbed mountain, seem blue, almost of the color of air, sometimes the sun is for East. Therefore make above the dubbed wall the first building of her complexion; the more afar phallus less profiled, and more blue; and those that you desire which both more in it as much more blue, and that which you want which both five times more far away, phallus five times more blue, and this rule do that the buildings which they are above one line, seem of one same greatness, and distinctly itself be acquainted with what is more distance, and what major of different. (Fig. 16.)

Of various incident and movements of men, and proportion of component. CAP. CLXVI. (166)

Variance the measures of the men in each component, bend that more or less, and to diverse aspects, decreasing or increase so much more or less from one part, how much you increase, or decrease from the side opposite.

Of the mutation about the measures of the man from his birth to his last growth. CAP. CLXVII. (167)

The man in the his first infancy has the width of the shoulder equal to the length of the face, and to the space that is from the joint of them shoulder at elbow, be bend the arm, and is similar to the space that is from the finger large of the hand to the dubbed elbow, and is similar to the space that is from birth of the child to the means of the knee, and is similar to the space that is from it juncture of the knee to the juncture of the foot. But sometimes the man is received to the latest his height, each aforesaid space doubles the length his, except the length of the face, whom together with the greatness of all the head ago little variety: and for this the man, that has finished the his greatness, whom both well proportionate, is ten of his faces, and the width of the shoulder is two of them faces, and thus all the other lengths above-mentioned are two of them faces: and the rest itself tell in the universal measure of the man.

How the small boy have the joints contrary to the men into them thicknesses CAP. CLXVIII. (168)

The small boy stalk they've all of them the joints thin, and the space places between the one and the other they are big: and this happens because the skin above the joints is solar without other lean meat, which is nature of nerve, which tie and league together the bones, and the fleshiness humor itself located between the one and the other join included between the skin and the bone: but because the bone they are more gross in the joints that between the joints, the meat in the expand of the man come to leave that superfluity which be located between the skin and the bone, hence the skin itself accustom more to the bone, and come to wear thin the component: but above the joints, none you be other that the cartilaginous and nerves pelt, none it can desiccate, and none exasperate none decreases: hence for these reasons them small child they are thin in the joints, and gross between them, how himself to see the joints of the fingers, hands, shoulder thin, and concave; and the man for the contrary be gross into all the joints of the hands, and legs: and whereas the small child they've into outside, them have of relief.

Of the difference of the measure that is between the small child and the man. CAP CLXIX. (169)

Between the man, and the small child find great difference of length from the one to the other junction, inasmuch the man has from the joint of the shoulder to the elbow, and from elbow to the point of the finger significant, and from the one humorous of the shoulder to the other two head for half, and small child of it has one, because the nature consists first the greatness of the home of intellect, which that of the spirits vital.

Of the joints of fingers CAP. CLXX. (170)

The fingers of the hand enlarge the them joints for all of them the them aspects when itself bend, and so much more itself enlarge when more itself bend, and thus diminish when more itself straighten, the similar happens of the digits of feet, and so much more itself variation when they make more fleshy.

Of joints of shoulder, and his supplements. CAP. CLXXI. (171)

The joints of the shoulder and of the other component bend, it say for his place in the treaty of the anatomy, whereas itself display the cause of motion of all the shares of that itself consists the man.

Of shoulder CAP. CLXXII. (172)

They are the motions simple principal of the bending event from the joint of the shoulder, namely when the arm to that application itself move to high or into low, or at behind, although be able say such motions be infinite, because one turn the shoulder to one side of wall, and himself mark with his arm a figure circular, himself do fact all of them the motions that they are to his shoulder, because each quantity continue is divisible into infinite, and such circle is quantity continue sort from motion of the arm, whom motion none produce quantity continue, if it continuation none the guide. Therefore the motion of his arm is condition for all the shares of the circle, and be the circle divisible into infinite, infinitely they are the variety of the shoulder.

Of measures universal of the body CAP. CLXXIII. (173)

I say that the measures universal of body itself must observe in the lengths of the figure, and not in the thicknesses, because of the praiseworthy and marvelous things that appear in the works of the nature, one is that never into whatever species a particular with precision itself resembles to the other. Therefore you imitator of such natural, watch out and attend to the variety of lineaments. Place well that you avert the things monstrous, such of legs long, busts short, breasts close, and arms long; take therefore the measures of the joints, and the thicknesses in which strong varies it nature, is vary even you.

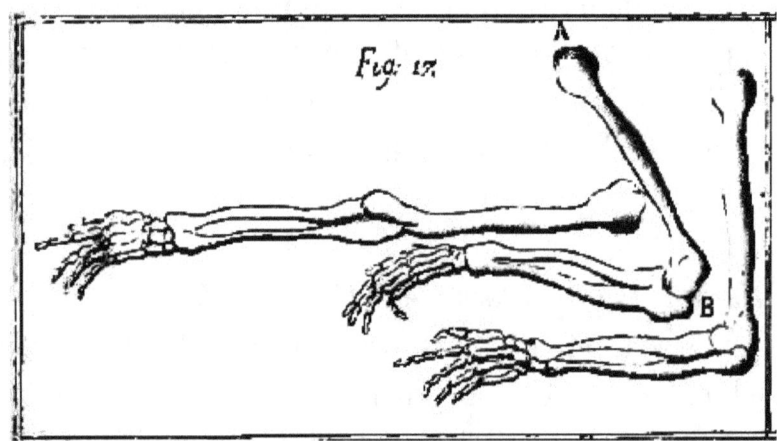

Of the measures of the body human, and bending of limbs CAP. CLXXIV. (174)

The necessity force the painter to have notion of the bones supporter, and armor of the flesh that over it indeed pose, and of the joints that increase and decrease in their bending, for the whenever thing the measure of the arm outstretched none consist with the measure of the bend. Increase the arm and decreases below the variety of the last his extension and bending the octave part of his length. The enhancement and the ascertaining of the arm come from the bone that advances beyond of the joint of the arm, whom, same as see in the figure **A. B.** (Fig 17.) ago long from the shoulder to the elbow, be the angle of it elbow minor that straight, and so much more increase, how much such angle diminish, and so much more decreases how much the aforesaid bevel itself ago major: and so much more increase the space from the shoulder to the elbow, how much the angle of the folding of it elbow itself ago minor that straight, and so much more diminish how much it is major that straight.

Of proportionality of the components CAP. CLXXV. (175)

All the parts of whatever animal be corresponding to the his all, namely which that which is short and big must have each components into since short and big, and that one which is long and thin have the components long and thin, and the mediocrity have the components of the same mediocrity, and the same intend contain said of the plants, whom not be crippled from the men's or from winds, because these replace youth above little old man, and such is destructive the his natural proportionality.

Of joints of the hands with arm. CAP CLXXVI. (176)

The joints of the arm with his hand diminish in the grip, and thickens when the hand itself result to open, and the contrary ago the arm below the groan and the hand for all the his own direction: and this arise that in the spread the hand the muscles domestics itself stretch out, and wear thin the arm below the groan and the hand, and when the hand itself tighten, the muscles domestics and (thread wear) itself pull back and thicken but the (thread wear) only itself move away from the bone, for be stretch of the bend of the hand.

Of joints of the feet, and their bulges, and diminution. CAP. CLXXVII. (177)

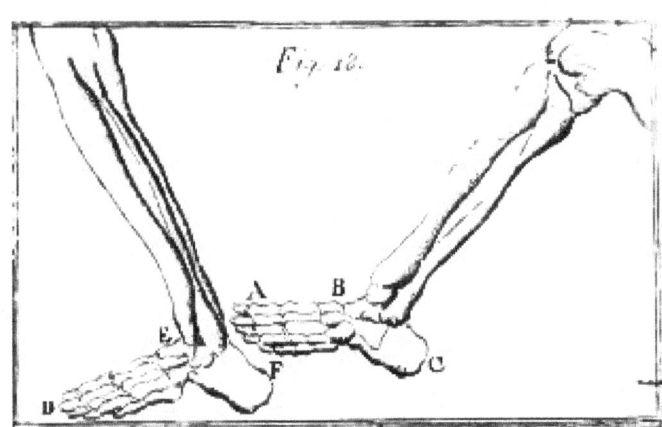

Only there diminution and accretion of joints of the feet is kind in the appearance of his part (thread wear) **D. E. F** (Fig 18.), whom increase when the angle of such joint itself ago more acute, and so much decreases when he board foot more obtuse, namely from the joints in front **A. C. B.** one speaks.

Of component that decrease when itself fold, and increase when itself distend CAP CLXXVIII. (178)

Below the component that they've joints fold only the knee is that which in the bend diminish of her enlarge, and in elongate enlarge.

Of component that swell in them joints when itself fold. CAP CLXXIX. (179)

All the component of man enlarge in bending of their joints, except the joints of the leg.

Of part of the men naked CAP CLXXX. (180)

The part of the human naked, whom themselves affectation into different action, sun be those which unearth the them muscles from that side whereas the theirs muscles move the element of the operation, and the other part be more or less pronounced neither their muscles, second that more or less one affliction.

About the motions potency of part of men. CAP CLXXXI. (181)

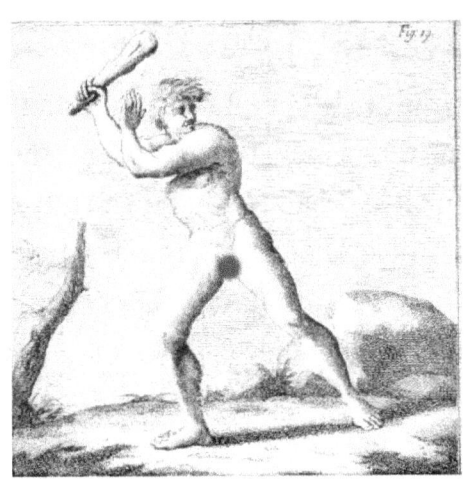

That arm do of more potency and long motion, whom breast proceed from his natural situated, have more potency adherence of the other part to pullback in the situated whereas he require advance. Same as the man **A.** (Fig 19.) that moves the arm with stretch **E.** and deliver to contrary site with the advance with all the person into **B.**

Of the momentum of man. CAP. CLXXXII. (182)

There sum and principal part of the art and the investigation of compositions of whatever thing, and the second part of movement, is that combine attention at their operation; whom be made with promptness, second the degrees about the their operators, thus into sloth, same as into quickness: and that the promptness of ferocity both about the sum quality that itself requires to operator of those. Just like when one be supposed to cast dart, or stones, or other similar thing, that the figure demonstrates his sum disposition into alike action, of that at this point of it they are two figures in manner various into action, and into potency: and the first into validating is there figure **A.** (Fig. 20.) there second is the motion **B.**, but the **A.** remove more from the object release, which none do the **B.** because once again that the one is the other display of want chuck the his weight force to a same aspect, the **A.**

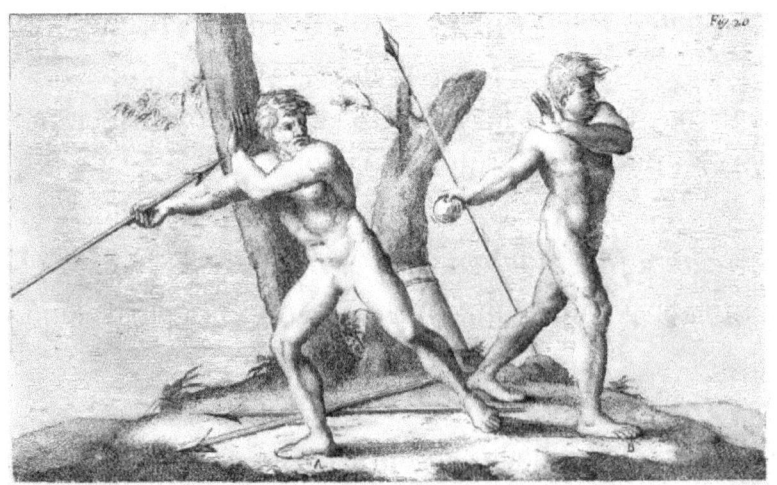

contain face the feet at it aspect when one writhe or crease, and himself remove from that to contrary situated, whereas he furnish the disposition of potency, he return with velocity and convenience to the site whereas he let go exit the weight of his hands. However into this same case the figure **B.** obtain the point of feet direct into contrary site to the place where he aggressive chuck the his weight force, himself twists to it place with greatest inconvenience, and for consequence the effect is weary, and the motion participates of his cause, because the appliance of strength in each movement aggressive be with the twisting and bending of great violence, and the resurgence both with ease and convenience, and thus the operation has good effect: because the crossbow which none has disposition violent, the motion of the mobile from him removed make short, or nil: because where none is exhausted of violence none is motion, and where none is violence, her none it can be destroyed, and for this one the arc that none has violence none it can away motion if none acquire her violence, and in the acquire it varies from whether. Thus the man that not himself twist, or bend not has acquire intensity. Therefore when **A.** is it line the his dart, he himself spot be twisted and weary for that direction whereas he has line the mobile, and acquire one intensity, whom as one mean without return in contrary motion.

Of attitudes, movements, and their component. CAP. CLXXXIII. (183)

None be replicated the same movements into one same figures in his element, or hands, or digits: of it even now one replicate the same attitudes in a history. And if the history fuse greatness, such as one battle, or one occasion of soldiers, whereas none is in the allocate if none three manner, namely one point, an reverse side, and a downward blow: into these case you to you have at to use one's ingenuity that all the downward blow be facts into various views, same as say not any both face backwards, not any for side, and not any in front, and thus all the other aspect of same three attitudes; and for this of convey all the other, participants of one of this person. But the beast compose they are in the battles of great artifice, and of great liveliness, and momentum; and they are called compose those, that one solar figures you demonstrate, same as one she herself to see with the leg in front, and part for the profile of shoulder. And of these ones assert into other place.

Of the joints of limbs. CAP. CLXXXIV. (184).

In the joints of the limbs, and variety of their bend, is from consider same as in the expand flesh from a side, come to be short in the other, and this itself has from research in the neck, of the animals, because the them motion they are of three natures, of which two of it they are simple, and one composed, that participates of one, and of other simple, about the which motion simplicity, the one is when one bend to the one and the other shoulder, or when it raises or lower the head that above the pose. The second is when it neck one bend to right or left without curvature, on the contrary remains straight, and contain the face turn direction one of shoulder. The third motion, which is called composed, is when in the bending his himself adjoin the his twisting, same as when the ear one lower inverse one of shoulder, and the face itself direction inverse the same part, or the shoulder opposite, with visage turn to the sky.

Of considered individually of men's. CAP CLXXXV. (185)

Measure into canvas the proportion of your considered individually, and if the observe into any part discordant, notice, and strong to you look out of none the use in the figure that for you himself compose, because this is communal fault of painters of delight of make things similar to whether.

Of motions of element of men's CAP. CLXXXVI. (186)

All the element exercise those officiate, to the that be destination, namely that neither dead and dormant not any part appear alive or wide-awake, thus the foot, which receives the weight of men's, both flattened, and none with fingers jest, if already not place above the heel.

Of motions of parts of the face. CAP. CLXXXVII. (187)

The motions of part of the face, through the accident mental, they are many; of which the principal they are laugh, cry, shout out, sing in different voices acute and serious, enthusiastic, anger, enthusiastic, happiness, melancholy, fear, grief, and similar, of which one do mention, and first of the laughter, and of the crying, which they are many similar in the mouth, and in the cheeks, and window of eye, but solo one vary in the cilia (eye lashes), and their interval: and this all assert to the his place, namely of variety that catch the face, the hands, and all the person for each of the accident, of which to you, painter, is necessary the knowledge, if none the your art demonstrate effectively the bodies two direct death. And anchor you recollect that the movements not be a lot of unsettled, and a lot of blurry, that the peace couple battle or **Moorish of embriachi:** and above the all that the circumstance to the case for whom is sort the history be intent with proceedings that display admiration, reverence, pain, suspect, fear, or joy, second that request again the case for whom which is fact the conjunct, or true contest of your figure: and ago that the your history none has the one above the other into one same part with divers horizons, one that it pairs one atelier of haberdasher with the his box made to small painting.

Of component and description of effigy. CAP. CLXXXVIII. (188)

The parts that place into half the globe of the nose itself vary into eight manner, namely or you they are equally straight, or equally concave, or equally convex: $1.^0$ That is are unequally carry, concave, and convex, $2.^0$ That is they are in the parts superior support, and of underneath concave, 3.^{0} That is of above support and of below convex, 4.^{0} That is of above concave and of below support, 5.^{0} Or of above concave, and of below convex, 6.^{0} Or of above convex, and below support, 7.^{0} Or of above convex, and of below concave.

The applicator of the nose with eyelash is of two reasons, namely, or that it is concave, or that it is right-hand side.

The forehead has three variety, or that it is flat, or that it is concave, or that it is very full. There flat one divides into two parts, namely or that it is convex in the part of above, or in the part of below, in other words plain of above and of undcrncath.

Manner of grasp to mind, and of the do one effigy human into profile, solo with overlook of one only face CAP. CLXXXIX. (189)

In this case you be necessary convey to the memory the variety of four component divers into profile, same as do nose, mouth, chin and forehead. And first affirm of nose, whom they are of three robust, straight, concave, and convex. Of straight none trace is other that four variety, namely long, short, high with the point, and low. The nose concave they are of three robust, of which any they've the concavity in the part superior, any in the half, and any in the part inferior. The noses convex, once again itself vary into three line, any they've into hunched in the part of above, some in the half, any of underneath: the protrude that place into half the hunched of the nose itself vary into three manner, namely or they are straight, or they are concave, or they are convex.

Manner of maintain to mind the form of a face. CAP. CXC. (190)

If you want with facilitates grasp to mind one air of one face, learn before of many witness, mouths, eyes, nose, chin, gullet, neck, and shoulder: and place coincidence. The nose they are of ten reasons: straight, hunched, hollow, with relief more up, or more downward that the half, aquiline, snub, rounded, and acute: this person they are good into how much to the profile. In face they are of eleven reason: equal, big in half, thin in half, the point thick and thin in the appearance, thin in the point and big in the appearance, of wide nostrils, of straight line, of high, of low, of punch holes uncovered, and of punch holes occupied from the point: and thus find diversity in the other particles: whom thing thou you have to portray from the natural, and place to mind. In other words when thou you have to make a face to mind, threshold with you a stalk booklet, whereas be notice similar faction, and when you have given one glance to the face of the person that you want portray, look out then into aside what nose or mouth

68

if the resemble, and fault one stalk sign for recognize furthermore to home, and place together.

Of beauties of faces. CAP. CXCI. (191)

Not one face muscles with sour distinction, but the sweets light conclusion insensibility in the pleasant and delightful shadows, and of this one born grace and formation.

Of attitude. CAP. CXCII. (192)

The fontanel of gullet fall over the foot, and cast an arm ahead, the fontanel way out of them feet, and if the leg throw into back, the fontanel it goes in front, and thus itself changes into each attitude.

Of movements of component when one figure the men that be proceedings precisely. CAP CXCIII. (193)

That figure, of which the movement not is companion of accident that is contrived be in the mind of figure, display the part none be obedient to the judgment of she figure, and the judgment of operator matter little; however must display such figure great affection and serve, and show that similar motions, other thing of that for whom both matters none seep signify.

Of component parts of the naked CAP CXCIV. (194)

The parts of the naked must be more or less evident in the unveiling of muscles second the major of minor exertion of said part, and display solo those part that more itself use in the motion or action, and more itself manifest that which is more employ, and that which null itself strive remain slow and soft.

Of the motion and course of men and other animals. CAP. CXCV. (195)

When the men themselves moves with velocity or slowness, always that part which over the leg supports the body, do more low than the other.

When is major difference of height of shoulder in the action of men's? CAP CXCVI. (196)

Those shoulder or sides of men, or of other animals, is it below their major difference in the height, of which his all do of more slow motion; ensue the contrary, namely that those parts of animals is it minor difference in their height, of which her all do of more velocity motion. And this one proof for the $9.^0$ of the motion local, whereas says: Each momentous weighing for the line of the his motion: therefore

69

moving the all direction any place, the part to that united, continue the line brief of the motion of the her all, without make of if weight in the parts lateral of it all.

Respond against. CAP. CXCVII. (197)

Says the adversary, into how much to the before part of above, none be necessary

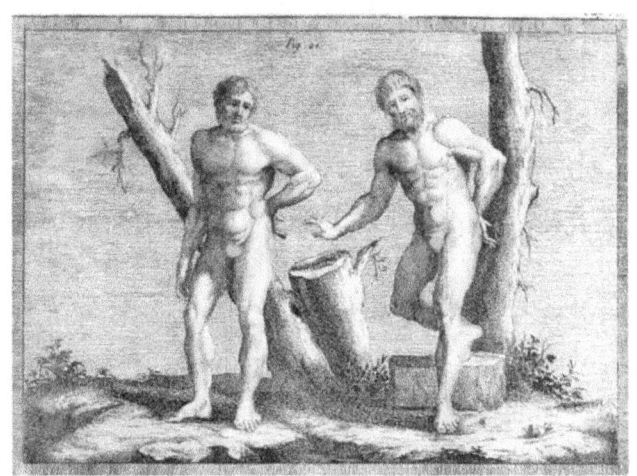

that the men's which be stationary, or that hearth with slow motion, uses of continuous the predicted pondering of part over the center of gravity that support the weight of the all, because many times the men not use of it observes such rule, in fact ago all the contrary, with this both that any time it one crease laterally, be on one only foot, any time fusillade part of the his weigh on the leg that none is straight line, namely that itself crease in the knee, same as itself display in the two figures **B. C.** (FIG 21.) Respond which that which not is fact from the shoulder in the figure **C.** is fact in the hips, same as one is demonstrated to her place.

Same as the arm curled up shift all the men from his before consideration when he arm itself extends. CAP. CXCVIII. (198)

The extension of the arm curled up move all the pondering of men above the his foot support of the all, same as himself display in that which with the hands open it goes over it the cord without other baton.

Of men and other animals that in the advance with slowness none have the center of gravity too much remote from the center of the support. CAP. CXCIX. 199

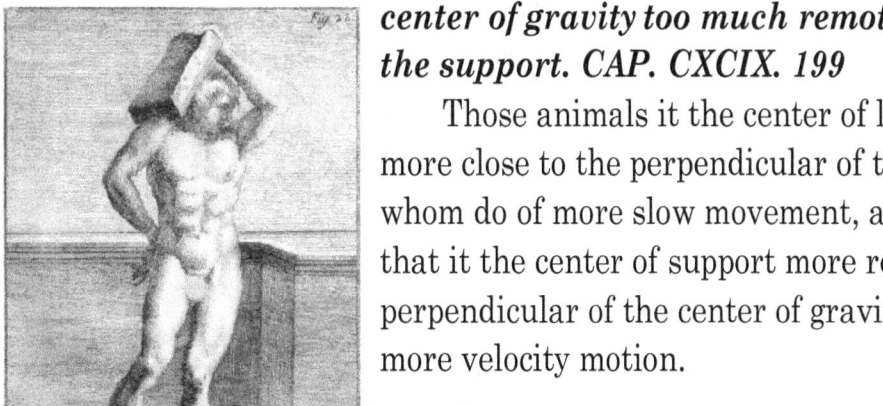

Those animals it the center of leg his support much more close to the perpendicular of the center of gravity, whom do of more slow movement, and thus of conversely, that it the center of support more remote from the perpendicular of the center of gravity its, whom both of more velocity motion.

Of men's that port a weight above it's his shoulders. CAP. CC. (200)

70

Always there shoulder of men's that supports the weight is more high which there shoulder without weight, and this one itself exhibition in figure (Fig. 22.) for whom withered the line central of all the weight of the men's, and of the weight from him result: whom weight force composed if not fuse divided with equal load over it center of

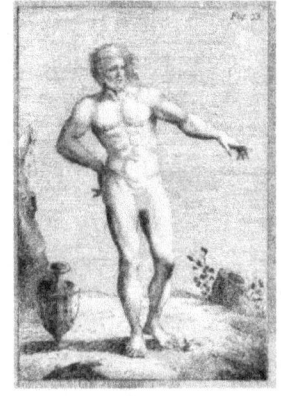

the leg that pose, make necessity that all over the composed fix: But there needs provides that so much part of the weight natural of men's himself throws from one of the sides, how much there amounts of the weight accidental that itself adds from the opposite side: and this one to not itself more if the men's not one crease and not one lower from the side his more delicate with so much bending that partakers of the weight accidental from he brought: and this one do not itself more if the shoulder of the weight not itself raises, and there shoulder bearable not one lower. And this is the half which the artificial necessity has found in such action.

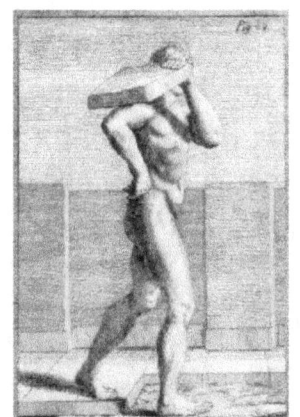

Of weight of men's over it them his foot. CAP CCI. (201)
Always the weight of men's that pose on one only leg do divided with equal part opposites over the center of the gravity that supports. (Fig 23.)

Of men's that themselves move. CAP. CCII. (202)
The men's that himself move area the center of his gravity over the center of leg that pose in earth. (Fig. 24.)

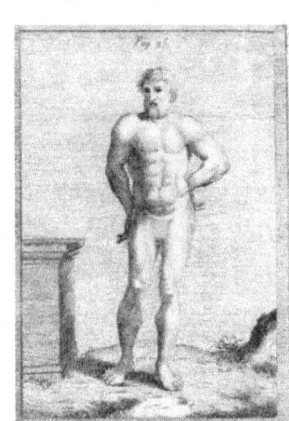

Of the bilocation of the weight of whatever animal motionless on its leg CAP. CCIII. (203)
The deprivation of the motion of whatever animals, whom pose them his feet, rises from the deprivation of unevenness that have below their opposed weights that oneself sustain above their weights. **(Fig. 25.)**

The bending and twisting of men's. CAP. CCIV. (204)
So Much decreases the men's in the bending of one of his sides how much he grows in the other his side opposite, and such folding make at last square root to the part that itself extends. And of this one do particular treaty.

Of the bending CAP. CCV. (205)

So much how much one of sides of part folding itself make more long, so much his part opposites make diminish. The line central extrinsic of sides that none itself fold, neither components folding, never diminish it or grows of his length.

Of the counterweight. CAP. CCVI. (206)

Always there figure that support weight out of whether and of the line central of the its amounts, ought throw so much weight natural or accidental from the opposites part, that face counterpoise of weights about to the line central that itself part from the center from the part of the foot that itself pause, and passes for all the load of the weight above it part the feet at earth pose. You will see naturally one that catches a weight from the one of the arms, range out of whether the arm opposite: and whether this not enough without do the counterpoise, you extend so much more weight of whether same bending, that oneself ago sufficient without resist at applied weight. One sees yet at one that both for fallout inverse the one from his sides lateral, that always throws at outside the arm of opposites part.

Of the motion human. CAP. CCVII. (207)

When you desire make the men's propelling of no weight consider that the motion must be facts for diverse lines, namely or of low into other with simple motion, such as ago that which bend themselves catches the weight that raise permit raise, or when desire to drag on not anything behind, or rather push ahead, or you want pull at low with cord that passes for pulley. At this point one recalls that the weight of men's pulls as much as the center of gravity his is outside of the center of his own favored. To this one adjoin the strength that do the leg or spine bent in his lift up.

Never one descend or rise, nor never one walk for no one line, which the foot of behind not raise the heel bone.

The motion created from distribute the poised. CAP. CCVIII. (208)

The motion is created from the distribute of the poised, namely from the unevenness: dominion not one thing for whether oneself move which not lure from his poised, and that himself ago more velocity, which more himself remove from the known as his poised.

Of the poise of figure. CAP. CCIX. (209)

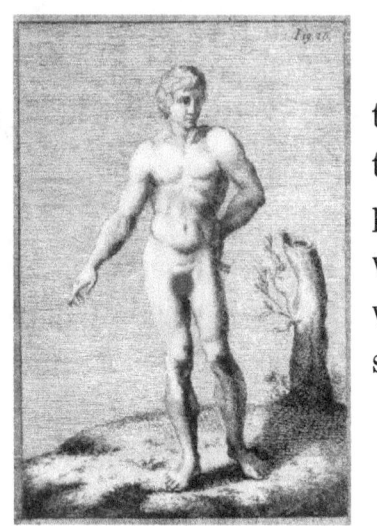

If the figure pose above one of his feet, the shoulder of that side that pose both always more low then the other, and the fontanel of the throat make above the half of the leg that pose. The same happen for whatever line we see it figure be without arm load-bearing not much outside of the figure, or without weight inside, or into hand, or into shoulder, or support of the leg that not pose before or behind. (Fig. 26.)

Of grace of limbs. CAP. CCX. (210)

The limbs in the body must be accommodation with grace to the purpose of effect that you desire that face the figure: and if you desire make the figure that show to whether prettiness, must do limbs well-bred, and elongate, without demonstration of too many muscles, and those few that to the purpose make demonstrate, produce charming, namely of little evidence, with shadows not filter, and the component, and maximally the arm unbridled, namely that not any element not be in line right-hand side with part that one adjoin with them. And whether the side focal point of men's themselves located, for him pose fact, which the agile both more high than the left, make the junction of the shoulder superior pour down for line perpendicular over it the more eminent object of the side, and both of it shoulder right more low they left, and the fontanel both always superior to the half of junction of the footer of above it that pose there leg: and the leg that not contain the his knee more low than the other, and near about other leg.

The latitudes they head and arms they are infinitely, however not myself extend into give no rule. Assert too that it be prone and giving with various twist, oblige not seem pieces of wood.

Of comforts of limbs. CAP. CCXI. (211)

To how much at ease of them limbs, is without consider that how much you desire picture one that for some accident itself contain without turn at rear, or for singing, which you not face move them feet and all the limbs in that part where time the head, on the contrary do operate with originate it implementation in four joints, namely that of the foot, of the knee, of the side, and of the neck: and whether rest on was there leg right, do the knee they left bend at inside, and the his foot both elevated somewhat of outside, and the shoulder left both somewhat more low than there right, and the nape (*nape of neck*) itself dispute in the same place where is time the node of outside of the foot left, and the shoulder left do above the point of the foot right for perpendicular line: and always uses, that where the figure turn the head, not you itself vulgar the chest, which the nature for our comfort it has fact the neck, which with facility it can serve without diverse band, to want the eye turn around into various sites: and without this same they are at part obedient the other joint: and whether you make the men's to be seated, and that the his arms themselves have in some manner to use in something crosspiece, ago that the chest itself turn over the joint of the hip.

Of one figure single out of history CAP CCXII. (212)

Yet not replicate the limbs to a same motion in the figure whom you imagined bc single, namely that ago the figure display of hurry sun, which you not him face all two the hands in front, but one before, and the other backwards, because otherwise not it can rush;; and if the foot right is in front, which the arm right both backwards, and the left before, because without such disposition none themselves it can hurry usefully. And whether the do fact one the it follow, that possess one leg which itself throw somewhat before, ago that the other return below the head, and the arm superior exchange the motion, and go before: and things of this one affirm without full in the book of the movement.

Which they are the principal is important that appertain a figure. CAP. CCXIII. (213)

Between the principal thing important that itself require in the figuration of the animals, is situate well there head above the shoulder, the bust above the hips, and the hips and shoulder above the feet.

Of the pivot hinge the weight round to the center they gravity of bodies. CAP. CCXIV. (214)

There figure that without motion above them his feet itself supports, do of if equal weights opposed around to the center of his support. I say that whether there figure without motion do pose above the his feet, that itself you throw an arm before to the his chest, that you must throw so much weight natural backwards how much of it throws of the natural and accidental in front; and that same I say of each part that protrude out beyond of the his all beyond to the usual.

Of figure that have to handle is bring weights. CAP. CCXV. (215)

Never itself rise or bring weight from men's, that none sent of whether more of as much weight that those which want lift, and the protrude into opposite part without that where it lever the called weight.

Of the attitudes from men. CAP. CCXVI. (216)

Are the attitudes of the men with theirs limbs in such manner dispose, which with those itself demonstrates the intention of them mood.

Variety of attitudes. CAP. CCXII. (217)

Pronounced the proceedings in the men second theirs age and dignity, and themselves vary second the specifically, namely of men and of the females.

Of the attitudes of figure. CAP. CCXVIII. (218)

I say that the painter must notary the attitudes and them motions of the men be born of whatever accident immediately, and be noticed or harvest in the mind, and none await that the act of the grieve both fact do to one in proof without great cause of distress, and furthermore portray, because such act not born from the true case, none do of it prompt of it natural: but and well good possess before noticed from the case natural, and then do star one in that one act for see no part to the purpose, and then portray.

Of the action the surrounding to a coincidence notice CAP. CCXIX. (219)

All them surrounding of whatever coincidence worthy of be notice be with diverse proceedings admiring without consider it act, just like when the justice punishes them wretch: and if the case is of thing devout, all them surrounding straighten the eyes with diverse proceedings of devotion to it case, same as the display the host in the sacrifice, and similar: and himself he is case worthy of laughter, or of crying, in this one none is necessary that all them surrounding turn the eyes to it case, but with diverse movements, and that great part of those ones itself rejoice, or one regret together: and whether the case is scary, them appearing frightened of those ones that flee rough great demonstration of fear, and of flight, with various movements, same as oneself assert in book of motions.

Quality of the naked. CAP. CCXX. (220)

Not do never one figure that have of the thin with muscles of too much relief; dominance the men thin not have never too much flesh over the bones, but they are thin for the scarcity of flesh, and where is little flesh, none it can be thickness of muscles.

Same as the muscles are short and big. CAP. CCXXI. (221)

The muscled have large the bones, and they are men big and short, and have shortage of fat, dominance the fleshiness the muscles for their accretion itself shrink together, and the fat that below them one lower surface interpose not has place, and the muscles in to the slender be in all compelled below them, and not be able dilate, increase in thickness, and more expand in that part which is more remote from their extremes, namely inverse the half of the them width and the length.

Just like the obese not have big muscles. CAP. CCXXII. (222)

Thus far that the obese be in whether short and big, same as the aforesaid muscled, they have thin muscles, but there their skin garment much thickness spongy and frivolous, namely masses of air, however they fat itself support more over the water that not make the muscles, which have in the skin shut in less quantity of air.

Which they are them muscles that disappear neither movements diverse of men's. CAP. CCXXIII. (223)

In the lift and lower they arms the breast disappear, or it one do of more relief: the akin do them relief of the hips in the bend at outside or in inside in their hips; and the shoulder do more variety, and the hips, and the neck, which none other junctions, because have the motions more variables: and of this itself do a book particular.

Of muscles. CAP. CCXXIV. (224)

The limbs not must have in the youth pronouncement of muscles, because is sign of fortitude elderly, and nor youths not is time, of it mature fortitude: but be the sentiment they limbs pronounced more or less evident, second that more or less do weary: and always the muscles that they are weary they are more high and big than those ones that be in rest, and never the lines central intrinsic of limbs that one bend in the their natural length.

That the naked figurative with great evidence of muscles both without motion. CAP. CCXXV. (225)

That naked figurative with great evidence of all yours muscles both without motion, because not itself it can move whether one part of muscles not itself slacken, when the opposed muscles pull: and those one that itself loosen be short of the their demonstration, and those that pull one bare robust, and produce evident.

That the figure naked do not must have theirs muscles try to determine at all. CAP. CCXXVI. (226)

The figure naked not must have theirs muscles investigate entirely, because turn out difficult and unfortunate. For those appearance that the component itself times to her operation, for that same be his muscles more often pronunciation. The muscles in since pronunciation often his particles by means of the operation, in manner that without such operation in it before not one demonstrate.

Of enlargement and shortening of muscles. CAP CCXXVII. (227)**

The muscle they thigh (leg) of behind ago major varieties in her extension and retraction that none other muscle that both in men's. The second is those that compose the buttock. The third party is that of backs (spine). The fourth is that of the throat. The fifth is that of the shoulder. *The sixth and that of the stomach*, which arise below the (Pomo) (knob) **Adams apple* (granato) grainy ***, and ends below the breast *?* (pettignone)*, such as one affirm of all of them. (???)

note: translation different from 1716 French version on names meanings yet here are outtakes from old word Italian dictionary the part of the body, which is between the belly, and the pubic hair and at end of first book chapters lists for reference picture copy of it to names that different meaning seen

Where itself located cord of it the men without muscles. CAP. CCXXVIII. (228)

Where the arm ends with the palm of the hand near to four fingers, itself located one cord the major that both in men's, whom is without muscle, and arise in the half of execute of the arm, and ends in the half of other execute, and has figure square, and is wide about three fingers, and big middle finger, and this serving only to hold together tight the two said execute of the arm, oblige not one dilate.

Of the eight piece that be born in the middle of cord in various joints the men's. CAP. CCXXIX. (229)

Be born in the joints of men's any piece of bone, whom they are stable in the middle of cord that tie any joints, same as the cogwheels of knees, and those of shoulder, and of feet, whom they are in all eight, which of it is for shoulder, and one for patella, and two for each foot below the before joint of the two big to the heel bone, and he one resistant to the little old man of humankind.

The muscle that is below the knob garnet, and the part of the body, which is between the belly, and the pubic hair. CAP. CCXXX. ** (230)

Arise a muscle below the *knob garnet* (pomo granato), (I say ends in the part of the body, which is between the belly, and the pubic hair) whom one is of three potential, because is divided in his length of three cord, namely first muscle superior, and then come after one cord wide just like it muscle, then follow the second muscle more low of this, near the which one conjoin the second cord, near the acute proceed the third party muscle with the third class cord, whom cord is conjoin to the bone of the (part of the body, which is between the belly, and the pubic hair): and these three tuck of three muscle with three cord they are made from the nature for the great motion that has the men's in his bend, and distend with similitude muscle: whom if fuse of a part make too much variety in his dilate and shrink, in the bend and distention of men's, and ago major beauty in men's have little variety of such muscle in his action, domain whether the muscle themselves has from distension nine fingers, and as much furthermore withdraw, not touch three fingers for each muscle, whom conduct little variety in their figure, and little deformed the beauty of the body.

Of last vaulting that it can do the men in to see on backside. CAP. CCXXXI. (231)

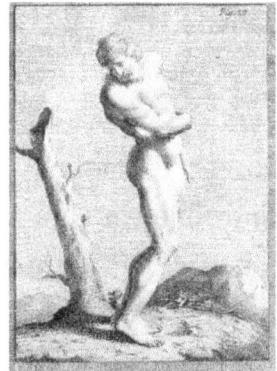

The last vaulting that it can do the men's make in the demonstrate the heel bone behind, and the visage into face: and this not himself do without difficulty, and whether none themselves crease there leg and lowered the shoulder that watch out there nape: and the cause of such vaulting both demonstrated in the anatomy and which muscles first and last himself move. (Fig.27.)

How much one it can go near the one arm with the other of behind. CAP. CCXXXII. (232)

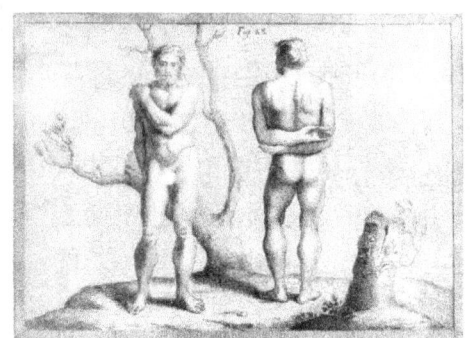

Of arms that himself send of behind, the elbow not itself do never more close than the more long fingers seep the elbow of opposite hands, namely that the latest vicinity that have exceed the elbow behind at kidney, do how much is the space that is from his elbow at extreme the major finger of the hand, whom arms do a square perfect. And how much one be promoted transverse the arm above chest, and that the elbow come in the middle of the chest, and this elbow with the shoulder and arm do a triangle equilateral. **(Fig. 28.)**

Of appliance they strength of men's that he want generate great percussion. CAP CCXXXIII. (223)

When the men's themselves dispose to the creation of the motion with the

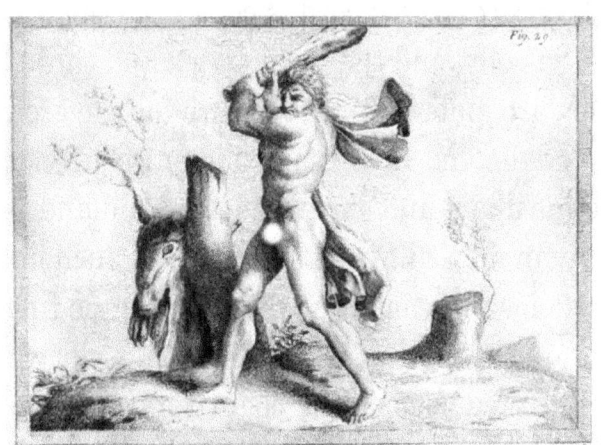

strength, he himself turn and one twist how much it can in the motion contrary to that one where is that wants generate there percussion, and there one apparently in strength that to he is possible, whom conduct is let go above of object they thingy from him bash with motion of the composed. **(Fig, 29.)**

Of strength composed from men's, and first himself assert of hands. CAP. CCXXXIV. (234)

The muscles that move the major execution of the arm in the extension and

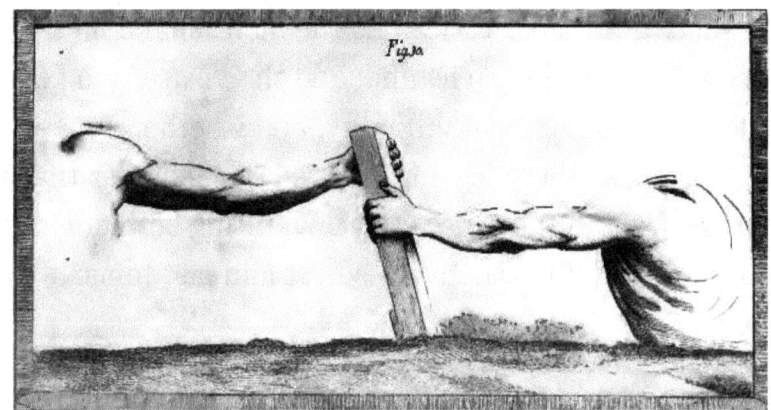

retraction of the arm, be born regarding the half they bone called adductor, the one behind to the other; of behind and born that one which extends the arm, and before those which it fold.

Whether the men's is more potential in the pull than in the push, prove for the $9.^0$ *of this proposal*, where say: Below the be pending of equal powers, those one demonstrate more powerful which do more remote from pole of their balance. Followed which be N. B. (Fig. 30.) muscle, and N.C. muscle of potential for between their equal, the muscle before N.C. is more powerful than the muscle of called N. B., because he is firm in the arm to C. located more remote from the pole of the elbow A. that not is B. whom is adjacent from it pole, and thus is concluded the intent. But this is strength simple, and not compost, just like one propose of to want negotiate, and be supposed to put more ahead; and the strength compost is that when produce an operation with the arms, you itself adds one second potential of the weight they person, and of the leg, same as in the pull, and in the push, that other to the potential of the arm you itself adjoin the weight they person, and there strength they spine, and of the legs, whom is in the desire stretch out, same as produce of two to one column, which one the push, and the other the pull.

Which is most potency of men's, that of the pull, or that of the push. CAP. CCXXXV. (235)

Very much major potential has the men's in the pull than in push, because in the pull you itself adjoin the power of the muscles of the arm that they are created only to the pull, and not to the push, because when the arm is straight, the muscles that move the elbow not can have no action in the push more that itself own the men's lean the back to the thing that he desire remove from the his situated, in the which only itself

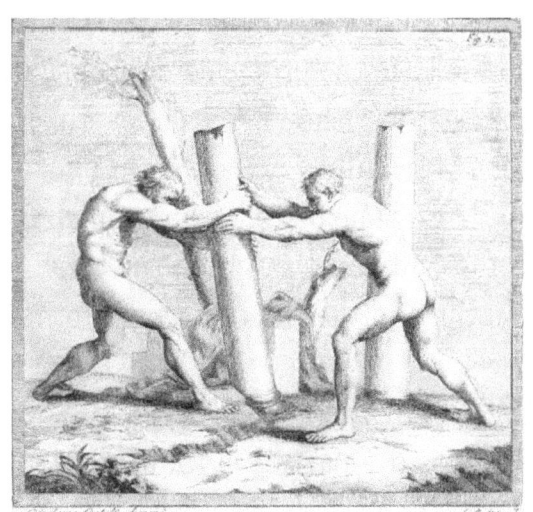

employ the nerves that straighten the spine bend. And those that straighten the leg bend, and be below the thigh, in the lean meat behind to the leg, and thus is conclusive to the pull adjoin the potential of the arm, and the potential extension of the leg, and they back, together with chest of the men, in the quality that request again the obliquity; and to the push contributes the same, lacking there power of the arm, because so much is to push with an arm straight without motion, same as is have interposed an piece of wood between the shoulder and the thing which one pushes(Fig. 31.)

Of the limbs that fold, and that officiate ago the flesh that there garment in it bending. CAP. CCXXXVI. (236)

There flesh that garment the joints of the bone, and the other part to the bone close, increase and diminish in their thicknesses second the bending or extension of the predicted limbs, namely increase from the part of the inside of the angle that itself generates in the bending the limb, and itself wear thin, and itself extend from the part of outside of the angle exterior: and the half that itself interposes between the angle convex and the concave participates of such increase or diminish, but so much more or less how much the parts they are more close or remote from the angles of the said joints bent.

Of the turn the leg without the thigh. CAP. CCXXXVII. (237)

Impossible is turn there leg from the knee for downward without turn the thigh with likewise motion: is this arise that the joint of the bone of the knee has the contact of the bone they thigh intern is committed with the bone they leg, and only itself more move such joints before or back, in the manner that requires the walk, and the kneel down; but not itself more never move laterally, because the contacts that compose there joints of the knee none the entail: domain whether such joint fuse foldable and moveable, same as the bone of adductor that itself commits in the shoulder, and same as that they thigh that itself commits in the hip, the men be always bending thus the leg for the their side, just like from the part before to the part of behind, and always such leg make writhe: and thus far such joint not it can prefer the probity of the leg, and is only foldable before, and not backward, because if itself bend backward, the men's not one be able lift at feet when conjoin kneel down, because in the lift of knees joints, of two knees, before himself from the laden of the bust above the one of the knees, and unload the weight of other, and in that time the other leg not sense other weight that of whether same, hence with facilitates lever the knee from earth, and puts the sole of the foot all pose to the earth, of then return all over the weight above he foot laid down, lay the hand above the his knee, and at a time distend the arm whom threshold the chest and head at high, and this distend and straighten the thigh with chest, make straight above he foot laid down in the end that has raised the other leg.

They folding they flesh. CAP. CCXXXVIII. (238)

Always the flesh bent is wrinkle from the opposite's part from that it is stretch.

Of the motion simple of men's. CAP CCXXXIX. (239)

The motion simple is called that one which ago in the bend merely, that is before, or back.

Motion composed. CAP CCXL. (240)

The motion composed is called that when for no operation itself requires bend in downward is in transverse in a same time: thus must advise the painter to make the movements composed, whom be entirely at their composition: namely whether one ago an appropriate composed, through the necessity of such action, that you not the imitate in contrary with fault do an act simple, whom make more remote from it action.

About the motions appropriate to the effects from men. CAP. CCXLI. (241)

The motions of our figure must be demonstration they quantity they strength which agree to those use to diverse actions, namely that you not expression demonstrate the selfsame strength to that which raise one baton, whom both convenient to the raise of one beam. Therefore ago diverse the demonstration of the strength second there quality of the burden from them knead.

Of the motion of the figure. CAP. CCXLII. (242)

None do never the witness straight over it the shoulder, but turn in transverse, to right or to left, thus far that it look out at above or at down, or straight, because the is necessary do theirs motions that show liveliness arouses, and not slouch. And not do the half of all the person before or of behind, that show theirs rectitude above or below to the other half superior or inferior: and whether also you the desire employ, error neither olden: and not replicate the movements of the arms, or of the legs, not that in one same figure, but of it also in the circumference and vicinity, whether already there necessity of the case, which oneself pretend not you obligate.

Of the proceedings demonstration. CAP. CCXLIII. (243)

In the proceedings affectation demonstration, the things proximately for time or for site itself have to show with the hand not too much remote from them demonstrators: and if the predicted things make remote, distant must be again there hand of the demonstrator, and the expression of the visage time to that one demonstrate.

Of variety of the faces. CAP. CCXLIV. (244)

Both varied the air of the face second the accident of men's in exertion, in rest, in crying, in laughter, in scream, in fear, and things similar, and yet the limbs they person together with all the attitude must respond to the effigy altered.

Of the motion appropriate at mind of the movable. CAP. CCXLV. (245)

They are no motions mental without the motion of the body, and no with motion of the body. The motions mental without the motion of the body let go fall from arms, hands, and each other part that exhibition life: but the motions mental with the motion of the body hold the body with the his limbs with motion appropriation to the motion they mind: and of this such discord one assert many things: start an third party motion that is participant of the one and of the other: and a forth which not is neither the one, neither the other; and this person last they are senseless, or rather nonsensical: and one put in the chapter they madness or they buffoons in their Moorish.

Same as the proceedings mental move the person in first degree of facilitates and commodity. CAP. CCXLVI. (246)

The motion mental moves the body with proceedings simple, and easy, none in here, and in there, because his object is in the mind, whom none move the senses, when in whether same is occupied.

Of the motion born from mind through the object. CAP. CCXVII. (247)

When the motion of men's is caused through the object, or such object arise immediately, or have not: whether born immediately, that which itself moves torches before to the object the sense more necessary, which is the eye, cease star them feet to the first place, and only moves the thighs together with the hips and knees towards that part where is that itself times the eyes, and so in such accident itself do great subject.

Of the motion common. CAP. CCLVIII. (248)

So much are various the motions of the men how much they are the variety of the accident that discourse for the theirs minds: and each accident in whether moves more or less they men, second that do of major potential, and second the age; because other motion do above an same case an young, that an old.

Of the motion of the animals. CAP, CCXLIX. (249)

Each animals of two feet lowers in his motion more further that part than remain above the feet that raises, which that what stay above the foot that pose to earth: and there his part supreme ago the contrary: and this one sees in the hips and shoulder of men's when walked, and in the bird the same with it head his, and with the back.

That each member both proportionate to all his body. CAP CCL. (250)

Ago that one part of one all both proportioned to his everything: just like whether a men's is of figure big and short, ago that the same both in whether each his components. Namely arm short and big, the hands wide and big, and the fingers short, with them his joints in the motion above namely. And thus the remaining.

Of observance of the decorum. CAP CCLI. (251)

Observes the decorum, namely the convenience of act, clothes, site, and circumference they dignity or cowardice of the things that you desire figure: namely that the King both of beard, air, and dress grievous, and the site adorned, and the circumference be with reverence, admiration, and clothes worthy and convenient at seriousness of one court factual, and the vile disordered and abject, and the their circumference mate similitude with proceedings vile and presumptuous, and all the limbs correspond to such composition. Which the proceedings of an old man not are similar to those ones of a young, and those ones of any female to those one of any male, neither those ones of a men's to those ones of a child.

Of the age of the figure. CAP. CCLII. (252)

Not combine any amounts of children with likewise old people, neither it young with infants, neither it women with men, whether already the case that you want figure not them tie together.

Quality of men neither compositions of the history. CAP. CCLIII. (253)

For the ordinary neither compositions common of the history uses of make rare old people, and separated from young, because the old people they are rare, and them their customs not one befitting with the customs of the young; and where not is conformity of custom none itself ago alliance, and whereas not is fellowship itself ago separation. And where themselves ago compositions of history apparent of gravitates and advice, countenance few young, because the young willingly avert advice: and other things similar.

Of the figure one that speak with more people. CAP. CCLIV. (254)

Use of do that which you desire that speak between many people in act of consider the subject matter that he has from transact, and of accommodate in he the proceedings belonging to it matter; namely whether there subject matter is persuasiveness, which the proceedings be an to the proposition similar, and whether there matter is of statement of diverse reasons; ago which those that do tell expression with the two finger they hand right and finger they left hand side, possess well-read them two minor; and with face ready direction the people, with the mouth somewhat open, which pairs that speak. And whether he sits, which pairs that one raise rather erect, and with the head before. And whether him do in feet, phallus rather stoop with chest and the head inverse the people, whom appear tacit, and all over attentive to regard the speaker in face with proceedings admiring: and ago the mouth of no old person for marvel of the heard sentence conclusion, and in the extremes low stretch back many folds of the cheeks, and with the cilia (eyelashes) high in in joint, whom create many folds for the front: any to be seated with the fingers of the hands to woven, maintain within the knee weary: other with a knee over it the other, departed whom engage the hand, which within to whether receives the elbow, the hand of the passing without hold up the chin bearded of any old man.

Just like must make one figure irate. CAP. CCLV. (255)

At figure irate make grasp one for the hair with head twisted to earth, and with one of the knees departed the rib cage, and with arm on the right lift the fist to high: this have the hair elevated, the eyelashes low and embrace, and the teeth close from singing they mouth arch, the neck big, and before for the stoop at enemy teeming with of wrinkles.

Just like one figure a despairing. CAP. CCLVI. (256)

At despairing do assign of a knife, and with the hand contain tattered the clothing, and both one of their hand in work to tear up there suffering, and make with the feet independent, and the leg rather bent, and there person likewise towards earth, with hair rip up.

Of the laugh and of the cry, and difference theirs. CAP. CCLVII. (257)

From that who laughs to that when weeps not themselves varies neither eyes, neither mouth, neither cheeks, but only the rigidity of the eyelashes that itself adjoin to who weeps, and raise to who laugh. To that which weeps itself adjoin the hands rip up the clothes: and modify in various causes of the crying, because no weeps with anger, not any with for fear, not any for tenderness and exhilaration, not any suspicious, and not any for grief and torment, not any for pity and pain of the relatives or friend lose: some which weeping not any one show desperate, not any mediocre, not any tear, not any shouting, not any be with the face to the sky, and with the hands into low, have the fingers of those together woven, other fearful with the shoulder raise to the ears, and thus second the predicted causes. That which direction the crying raise the eyelashes in their joints, and them tighten together, and consists wrinkles of above, and revolt them chants they mouth in low, and he who which laughs the has high, and the cilia (eyelashes) open and spacious.

The posture of the little children. CAP CCLVIII. (258)

Nor little children and neither old men not must be proceedings prone matters through them their legs.

Of the pose of the females, and the young. CAP CCLIX. (259)

In the females and youths not they ought to be proceedings of legs separated or too much open, wherefore demonstrate audacity (daring), or to the all privation of shame, and the grasp demonstrate shame.

Of those that jump. CAP CCLX. (260)

The nature work and emblem without no discord of the jumper; which when he wants leap, he raises with impetus the arm and the shoulder, whom continuing the impetus, one movement together with great part of the body, and raise to high, refined by so much that the them impetus in whether one consumption: which impetus is accompanied from the be subject to extension of the body sagging in the spine, and in the joint of the thighs, of the knees, and of the feet, whom extension is kind for oblique, namely before, and to the upward, and thus the motion dedicated to the go before threshold before the body which jumps, and the motion of go to the motion raises the body, and phallus (power) make great arch, and increases the hop.

Of men's which want throw one thing out of whether with great impetus. CAP. CCLXI. (261)

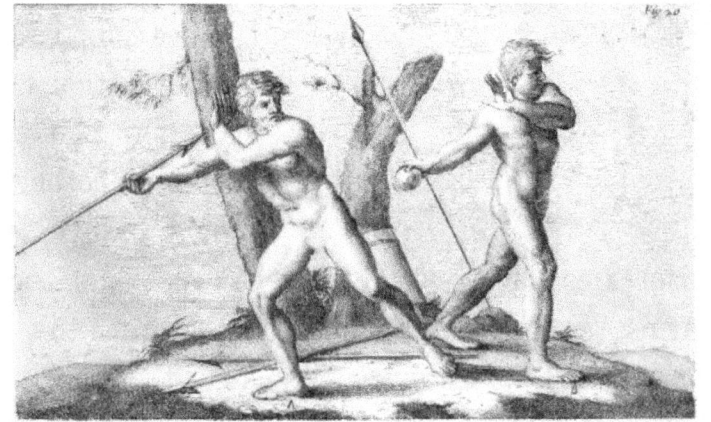

The men's whom he wants throw a dart (spear,) or stones, or other things, with impetuous motion, be able figurative into two mode principal, namely or can be figurative when the men's themselves prepares to the creation of the motion, or effectively when the motion of he is finished.

However whether you him purport for the creation of the motion, then the side of inside of the foot do with the same line of the chest, however it the shoulder contrary over it the foot, namely whether the foot and right make below the weight of men's, there shoulder left make over it the tip of him foot right. (Fig 32.)

Because those that he wants throw or drive cast the implement to earth, rises the leg opposites arched. CAP. CCLXII. (262)

That which with cast he wants thrust or pull the cannon fodder to earth, raises the leg opposite to the arm which draw, and that bend in the knee, and this ago navel (belly button) over it the foot that pose to earth, without whom bending or twisting of leg do not one can neither be able extract, if such leg no itself distend of it.

Weight of the bodies that not itself move. CAP. CCLXIII. (263)

The weight or rather precarious equilibrium of the men itself divide into two shares, namely simple, and composed. Simple is that which is fact from men's over them his feet immobile, above whom he man spread the arm with diverse distances of the his half, and stoop remain over one of his feet, always the center of his gravity is to line perpendicular over it the center of his foot which pause: and whether stance above

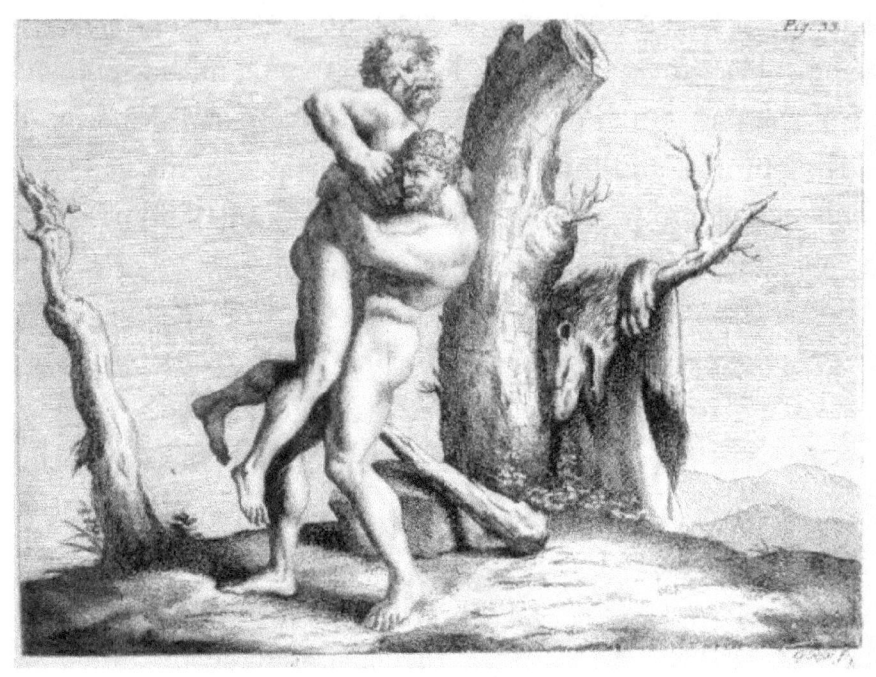

them two feet equally, then the chest of men's is the his center perpendicular in the middle of line that measure the space interposed below them centers of them feet.

The precarious balance composed itself intends be that which ago a man that supports above of whether a weight for diverse motion: just like in the figure of Hercules which overflow Anteus, whom suspending from earth below the chest and arms, which you him countenance so much the his figure of behind to the line central of his feet, how much Anteus has the center they his gravitates in front to the same feet. (Fig. 33.)

Of men's which pose above them two feet, and that from of whether more weight force to the one which to the other. CAP. CCLXIV. (264)

When for long stay on feet the man will has fatigue the legs whereas pause, he transmit part the weight over the other leg: however this such posture has from be used in the age decrepit, or in the infancy, or truly in one fatigue, because display tiredness, or effect of element: and yet always one to see a young that both healthy and robust rest on above the one of the legs, and if from sufficiently of weight over it the other leg, he the uses when he wants assign principle necessary to the his movement, without whom one denies each motion, because the motion itself generates from the unequally.

Of the stance of the figure. CAP. CCLXV. (265)

Always the figure that pose be obliged to variety the limbs, namely that if an arm it goes before, which the other remain stable, or move behind: and if there figure pose above one leg, which there shoulder that is above she leg both more lower than other, and this one itself observes from the men of good senses, them which await always for nature a counterweight the men's above them his feet, accommodate not ruin tally-ho his feet: because rest on over a foot, the opposites leg not supports he man, stand bent, whom in whether is same as if fuse dead, hence necessity ago that the weight that is from the legs up transmit the center they his gravity above the joint they leg which the pause.

Of the consideration of the man in the secure over of his own feet. CAP. CCLXVI. (266)

The man that one halt above them his feet, or load equally over them feet, or one overload with weights unequal. If one overload unequally over it them feet, he oneself carry with weight natural mixed with weight accidental, or oneself carry with simple weight natural. In the even that one carry with weight natural mixed with weight accidental, in that moment the extremes opposed of the part not they are equally distance from the poles of the joints of the feet: but whether one carry with weight natural simple, then such extremes of limbs opposed make equally distant from joints of the feet: and thus of this consideration itself do one book particular.

The motion local more or less velocity. CAP. CCLXVII. (267)

The motion local fact from men's, or from no other animal, do of so much major or minor velocity, how much the center of their gravity make more remote or propinquity to the center of the foot whereas one support.

Of the animal of four feet, ad just like itself movement. CAP CCLXVIII. (268)

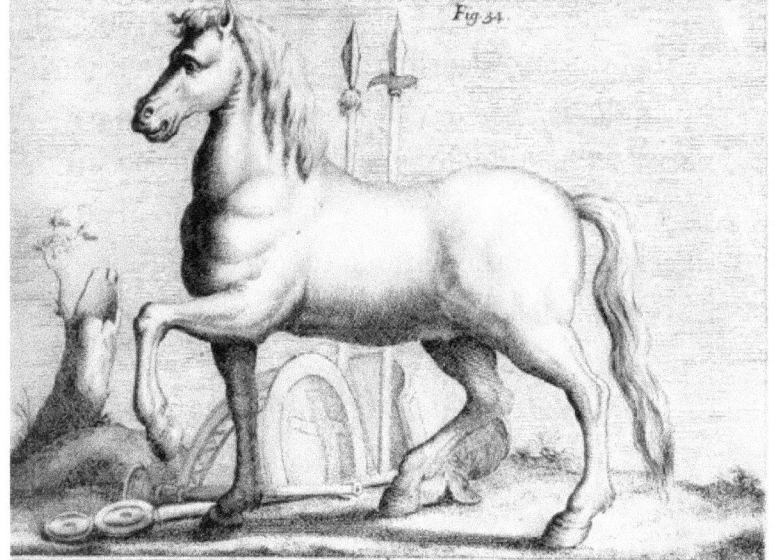

There sum height of the animal of four feet itself varies more in the animals that walk, which for those that be about to steady: and so much more or less, how much them animal are of major or minor grandness: and this is caused from the obliquity of the legs that touch earth, which raise the figure of it animal when that legs dismantle the their obliquity, and when one establish perpendicular over it there earth. (Fig 34.)

They correspondence that has there half they thickness of men with the other half. CAP. CCLXIX. (269)

Never the one half they thickness and width of men make equal to the other, if the limbs to that junction not make equal and similar motions.

Just like in the jump of man into high you one found three motions. CAP. CCLXX. (270)

When the men's jumps in high, there head it three times more velocity which the heel of the foot, before that there tip of the foot itself stick out from earth, and two times more speed which them hips: and this happens, because one undo in a same tempo three angles, about the which the superior is that whereas is the bust itself joins with the thigh in front, the second is that whereas is that the thigh of behind oneself conjoin with the leg of behind, the third party is whereas the leg in front ones conjoins with the bone of the foot.

Which is impossible that one memory retain all the aspects and mutation about the limbs. CAP. CCLXXI. (271)

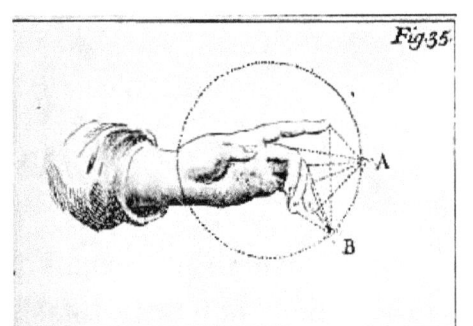

Impossible is that no memory can reserve all the aspects or mutation of no component of whatever animal one both. This case exemplify with the demonstration of one hand. And because each quantity continued is divisible in infinite, the motion of eye that regards the hand, and itself move from **A**. to the **B**. (Fig. 35.) itself move for one space **A. B.** whom thus far he is quantity continued, is for consequent divisible into infinite, and into each part of motion varies the aspect and figure they hand in the his to see, and thus make motivation into all the circle: and the akin do the hand that oneself raises in the his motion, namely pass through by space that is quantity.

They practice search for with great solicitude from the painter. CAP. CCLXXII. (272)

And you painter that decider's great practice, you have from interpret that if you not do you over it good foundation about the thing natural, do work with very little honor, and less gain: and whether it do good, the work your do many and good, with your grand honor and utility.

Of the judge the painter them his works and those of others. CAP. CCLXXIII. (273) *(*you see above Cap II.)*

When the works be equal with judgment, those is mean gesture in such judgment: and when the work exceed such judgment, this is very bad, same as happens without who itself marvel of have itself good actions: and when the judgment surpass the works, this is perfect sign. And if the young is in such disposition, without doubt this both excellent operator, but both composer of few works, but make of quality that detain the men with admiration without contemplate.

Of the judge the painter it his painting. CAP. CCLXXIV. (274)

We be able that the errors themselves experience more in the others works, which in his, however ago that retribution (painstaking) first good perspective, of then contain entire awareness of the measures of men, and retribution architect, namely in how much belongs to the form of the edifices, and of the other things, and whereas you not have practice, not refuse portray of natural; but must hold one mirror plan when depicting, and often regarding within the works your, whom you both view for the contrary, and think of hand of other master, and judge better the errors your folks. And once again make good raise often, and squeeze some solace, because with return you improve the judgment; that it remain false in the works you ago solid deceive.

Such as the mirror is master of the painters. CAP. CCLXXV. (275)

When you desire to see whether it your painting all together has conformity with the things portrayed of the natural, contain one mirror, and sensible within mirror the thing lively, and compare the thing mirrored with the your painting, and considers good the object in the one and in the other. You see one mirror plan demonstrate things that seem remove, and the painting ago the same. The painting has one only surface, and the mirror is the same. The mirror and the painting exhibition the similitude about the things circumference from shadow ad light, and the one and the other seem very of it from his surface. And whether you know that the mirror for half of the outlines and shadows you ago thinks the matters spectate, and having you between the your colors the shadows and the light more potential than those of the mirror, certain if you them be able well compose together, the your painting seem once again she one thing natural view in a great mirror. The your master there display the light and the dark of whatever object, and them your colors of it they've one which is more clear that the part aluminate of the simulation gave such object, and likewise into them colors whether of it chance upon not any that is more dark which no obscurity it object: hence arise that you, painter, do the paintings your similar without those of such mirror, when is seen from a only eye, because them two eyes surround the object lower of the eye.

What painting is more praiseworthy? CAP. CCLXXVI. (276) *There the above Cap 167.*

That painting is more praiseworthy whom has more conformity with the things imitated. This comparison is without confusion of those painter whom desirous to shorten the things of nature, just like are those that imitate a little son of a year, it head of the which enter five times in his height, and their it make enters eight: and it width of the back is akin to the head, and these it make double, reducing thus a stalk child of a year in the proportion of a man of thirty years: and many times have used and viewed use such error, which they've converse in custom, whom custom is so much penetrated and stability in the their corrupt judgment, which supporter believe their same that the nature, or who mimics the nature, face greatness errors without not make same as they do.

Which is the before object and intention of the painter? CAP. CCLXXVII. (277)

The before intention of the painter is do that one simple surface flat itself demonstrates a body relevant and pronounced from it plan: and that one that for such art exceeds more the other, that merit major praise, and this such investigation, on the contrary wreath of such science, arise from the shadows, and light, or you want say light and dark. Therefore if you avert the shadows, you avert the glory of the art near them noble wits, and the purchases near ignorant people, whom nullity more desire that beauty of colors, not considerate the relief.

Which is more important in the painting, the shadow, or its features? CAP. CCLXXVIII. (278)

Of much greater investigation and speculation they are the shadows in the painting that them his features: and there proof of this itself insignia, that the features itself can trace with cover, or glass plans interposed below the eye and the things that must shine, but the shadow not they are comprise from that rule, for the insensibility of the their terms, whom the more of the times they are confused, just like one demonstrate in the book of the shadow and light.

Just Like one must give the light to the figure. CAP. CCLXXIX. (279)

The light must be used second that allocate the natural site whereas imagine be it your figure: namely whether it fantasize to the sun, ago the shadows obscure, and great squares of the light, and stencil the shadows of all them circumference bodies to earth. And if it figure is in wicked time, ago little difference from light to the shadows, and without become no shadow to the feet. And if it figure make into home, ago great difference from light to the shadows, and shadow for earth. And if there you figure window seal, and dwelling white, ago little difference between light and shadow: and one she is aluminate from the fire, ago the light reddish and potential, and the shadow obscure, and it dispersal of the shadows for them walls or for earth be terminated: and how much more itself distance from the body, so much more itself face ample. And if says figure trench illuminate part from the air, and part from the fire, ago that the light caused from the air, both more potential, and that of the fire both almost red, without similitude of the fire. And over all ago that the your figure painted match the light grand, and from high, namely that live which you depict, dominion the person that you see in the street, all have them light of above: and know how that none is thus your great concerns, which yield them light of below, you none durable fatigue to recognize.

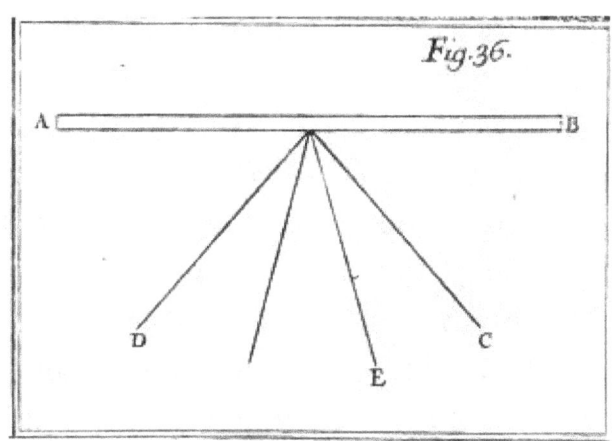

Fig. 36.

Whereas must star that which regarding the painting. CAP. CCLXXX. (280)

Establish that A. B. (Fig .36) both there painting view, and that D. both the light: I say that if there you place below C. & E. comprehending improperly the painting, and maximum if both nature to oil, or really varnished, because it luster, and both almost of nature of mirror, and for these causes, how much more you accordance to the point C. less see, because that place stand out the rays of the light mandate from the window to the painting. And if you establish below E. and D. that place both fine operated there your view, and maximum how much more you appreciate to the point D. because that place is less participant of dictate percussion of the rays reflection.

Just like one must place high the point. CAP. CCLXXXI. (281)

The point must be to the height of the eye of a man common, and the ultimate of the plain that borders with sky must be fact to the height of it term of the earth flat with sky, except that the mountains they are independent.

Which the figures petiole none to have for reason be finished. CAP. CCLXXXII. (282)

I say which the things that block of minute forms arise from be entrust with thing distant from the eye: exist thus, convene that below the eye and it thing both much air, and it much air impedes the evidence of the forms of it object, hence the minute particles of them bodies occur indiscernible and none experience. Therefore you, painter, do the petiole figure only accentuated, and do not finished, and if otherwise make, do against the effects of the nature your master. It thing rhyme petiole for distance grand that is between the eye and it thing, it distance grand close in inside without whether much air, it many air ago in whether big body, whom one impede and deduct to the eye the minute particles from the objective.

That field must use the painter in his figure. CAP. CCLXXXIII. (283) See above it CAP. 141

Then which the experience one sees that all the bodies they are surrounded from shadows and light, desire that you, painter accommodate those part which is aluminate, itself that finish without thing obscure, and thus it part of the body shaded finish into things clear. And this rule do great adjust without take over yours figure.

Precept of painting. CAP. CCLXXXIV. (284)

Where the shadow confines with light, have respect whereas it is more clear than obscure, and where it is more or less fallen through inverted the light. And above all you record that of it young you not face the shadows finished just like ago it stone, because it flesh holds a little the transparent, just like one see without overlook into one hand that both place below the eye and the sun, because it herself sees redden, and transpire luminous: and if there you want see which shadow itself requires to the your flesh, make yonder there a shadow with your finger, and second which there it you want more clear or dark, hold them finger more near or more far away from your painting, and that contrast.

Of imagine a site primitive. CAP. CCLXXXV. (285)

The tress and the herbs which they are more branched of thin branches must have minor subtlety of shadows, and those tree and herbs which is it major foliage exist cause of most shadows.

Just like must make advances seem natural an animal contrived. CAP. CCXXXVI. (286)

There both not be able do no animal whom not have his parts, and that each for whether without similitude not both with such as that one of the other animals. Therefore if you want make seem natural an animal contrived, given, affirm, which both a snake, grasp for it head one of a mastiff, or hound, and places them the eyes of cat, and the ears of porcupine and the nose of deer, and the eyelash brow of lion, and the temple of rooster old, and the neck of tortoise of water.

Of face that one must do, which combine relief with grace. CAP. CCLXXXVII. (287)

In the street time to westerly, owing to the sun at noon, the partition be into manner high, which that which is time to the sun none have to reverberate of it bodies shady: and good do the air without splendor, to the time that be see the side of the faces participate of the obscurity of the wall to those opposite: and thus the sides of the nose, and all it face time to the mouth of the way, do aluminate, for it which thing the eye that make in the middle of the mouth by such way to see such face with all the faces to him direct be aluminate, and those sides that they are faces to the partition of the walls be shady.

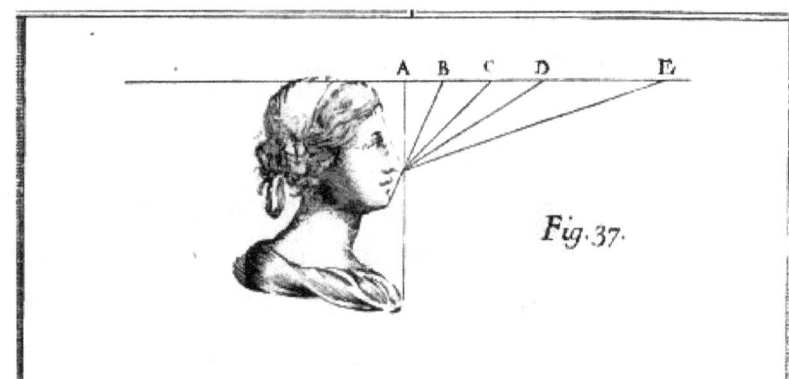

Fig. 37.

To this itself adjoin it grace of shadow with grateful damnation, private integrally from each end sent: and this arise for cause of the length of the light that passes below the covering of the homes, and penetrates below the partition, and ends over the floor of the path, and stands out for motion reflex neither places shady of the faces, and those rather brighten. And it length of the already called light of the sky printed from the terminate of the roofs with there his front, which be over it mouth of the way, illuminate almost inherent near to the birth of the shadows that remain under the object of the face: and thus hand in hand one it goes change into clarity, inherent which that ends over of the chin with obscurity insensitive for whatever direction. Just like if this light fuse **A. E.** (Fig. 37.) to see there line **F. E.** of the light that illuminate refined below the nose, and there line **C. F.** only illumine finally below the lip, and there line **A. H.** one extends refine below the chin, and here the nose remains robust luminous, because is to see from all the light **A. B. C. D. E.**

The divide and stand out the figure from their fields. CAP. CCLXXXVIII. (288)
To see over it CAP. 141. & 285.

There you have to put it your figure in field clear, whether make obscure; and if make albumen (egg white), place in field obscure; and if is white and dark, put it part obscure in the field clear, and it part white into field obscure.

Of the difference of the light places into different sites. CAP. CCLXXXIX. (289)

The light petiole ago grand and finished shadows over the body shady. The light grand do over it the body shady petiole shadows, and of confused end. When make included the petiole and potential light in the grand and less potential, same as is the sun in the air, to time the less potential linger in place of shadow over of the bodies from it illuminate.

Of the run-away the disproportionate of the circumstances. CAP CCXC. (290)

Grandness fault one demonstrate among of many painters, namely of make the dwelling of the men and other circumstances in such manner which the extend not give to the knees of the their inhabitant, once again that it be more close to the eye of the regarding that not is the men's which in that display be desire entrance. Contain have the arcade load up of men, and any of the columns of those ones supporters be in the fist to a man which to that one apologies to use of thin stick, and similar thing that they are from be with each study disgusted.

Of the terms the bodies said features, or rather contours. CAP. CCXI. (291)

They are the end of the bodies of so much minimum evidence, which into each petiole (small) interval that one interposes below it thing and the eye, it eye not comprehend the effigy of the friend, or relative, and none it concise, if none for the reside, and for the all over receives notice of the all together with the part.

Of the accident superficial that first one pardon in the move away of the body shady CAP CCXCII. (292)

The first things that one forgiveness in the move away of the bodies shady they are the finish them. Secondly into more distance one forgiveness the shadows that divide the parts the bodies which one touch. Third it size of the leg, and of the feet, and thus subsequently one forgiveness the part more minute, of manner that to long distance only remain one mass of confused figure.

Of the accident surface that before one forgiveness for the distance. CAP CCXCIII. (293)

It before thing which of the color one loses in the distance is the luster, their part minimum, and light of the enlightenment. Secondary is the light, because is minor of the shadow. Third they are the shadows principal, and remains in the last one mediocre obscure confused.

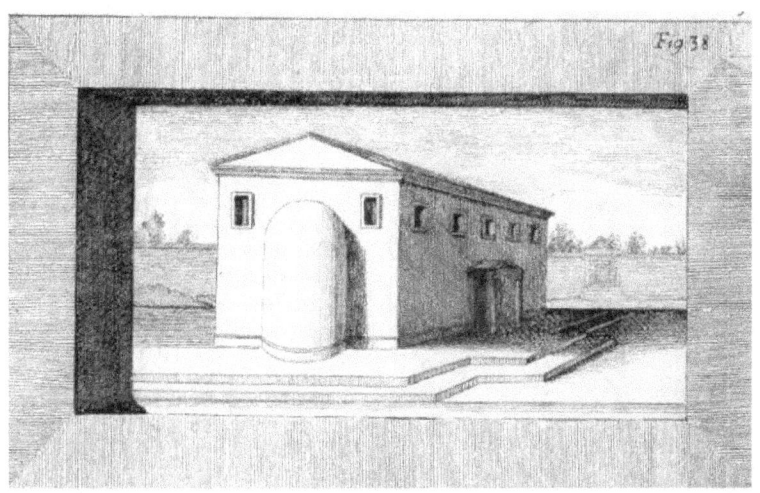

Of the nature of the terms of the bodies above the other bodies. CAP CCXCIV. (294)

When the bodies of convex surface ending above other bodies of equal complexion, the finish of the convex seem more obscure which that than with convex term will end. The term of the beam acquiescence seem in field off white of grand obscurity, and in field obscure seem more than other his part pale, ground the light which above the beam descend both above them beam of equal clarity. (Fig. 38.)

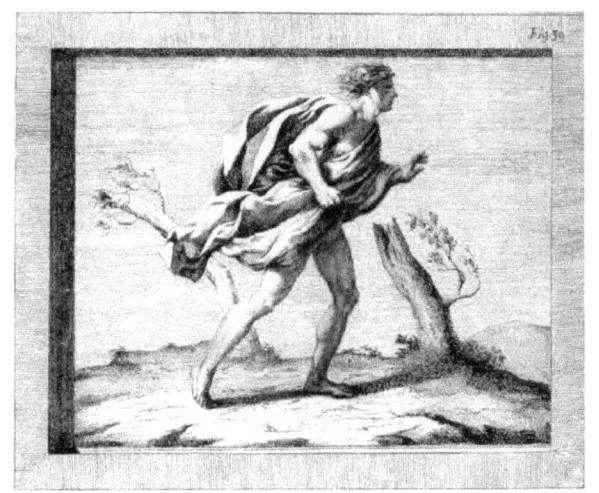

Of the figure that move against the wind. CAP CCXCV. (295)

Always there figure that one moves against the wind, for whatever line, not observes the center of his gravity with due disposition above the center of his support. (Fig. 39.)

Of the window whereas one portrays it figure. CAP. CCXCVI. (296)

Both the window of the room of the painter nature of the position without partition wall, and occupied of degree in degree inverse them his terms of grads colorful of black, in manner that the term of the light none both conjunct with term of the window.

Because measuring a face, and then daub into such greatness, he one demonstrate major of the natural. CAP. CCXCVII. (297)

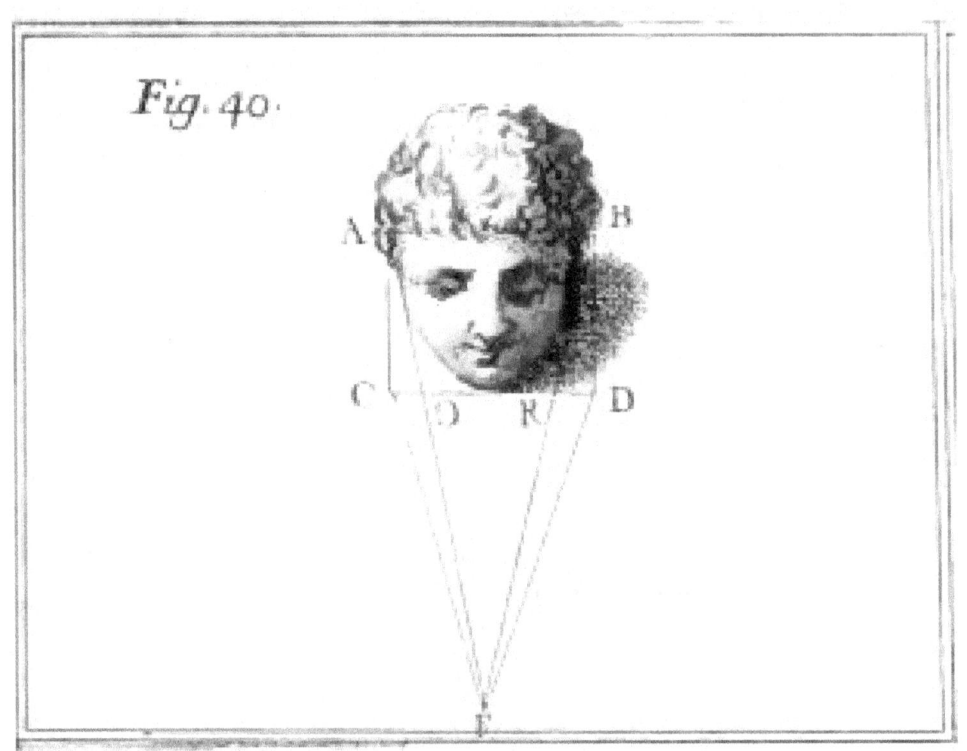

A. B. is it width of the situated, and is accounting item in the distance of the paper **C. F.** (Fig 40.) where are the cheek, and it contain without be into rear all **A. C.** and to the time the temples do deliver in the distance **O. R.** of the line. **A. F. B. F.** one which it is the difference **C. O.** and **R. D.** and one concludes that it line **C. F.** and it line **D. F.** for be more short has go without locate the paper whereas is designate the height all, namely the lines **F . A.** and **F . B.** whereas is it truth, is one ago it difference, just like I have adage, of **C. O** and of **R. D.**

If it surface of each body opaque participates of the color of his object. CAP. CCXCVIII. (298)

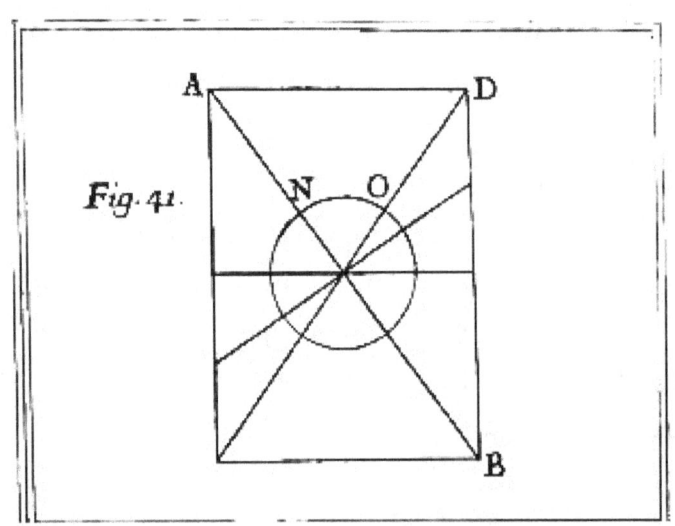

There you from intendment, whether make well-dressed an object off white below two partition, of which any both off white, and the other black, which you find such proportion below it part shady and it luminous of the called object, which departed that of the predicted partition: and if the object do of complexion blue, make the similar: hence having from paint do how follow. Remove the black for shadow the object azure that both similar to the black or rather shadow of the wall which you pretend that have without reverberate in the your object, and to want do with certain and well curd science, use make into this manner. When you both the your partition of which complexion one desire, catch an stalk elucidate, little major which that one use for cleanse the ear, major or minor second the grand or leafstalk works into which such operation itself has from exercise, and this elucidate have them his extremes of equal height, and with these measure the degree of the quantity of the color that you employ in the your mixtures: same as make when in said partition that you have fact the first shadows of three degree of obscurity, and of an degree of clarity, namely three elucidate secure, same as itself ago the measures of the grain, and this person three elucidate fuse of simple black, and an elucidate of white lead, there he remains fact any composition of quality certain without no doubt; time there you fact one wall white, and one obscure, and you have without put an object azure below them, whom object whether you want that have it real shadow and light that without such azure itself convince, conjecture from any part that azure, which there you want which remains without shadow, and suppose from canto (poem) the black furthermore deduct three elucidate of black, and compose, with an elucidate of azure luminous, and put with it there more obscure shadow. Fact this see if the object is spherical, columnar, or square, or same as itself both, and one he is spherical, cast the line from the extremes of the partition obscure to the center of it object spherical, and whereas they line itself cut in the surface of such object, there below much ending the major shadow, below equal angle, furthermore commence without brighten same as make into **N. O.** (Fig.41.) which leave much of the obscure how much it participates of the wall superior **A. D.** whom complexion mix up with the first shadow of **A. B.** with the same distinctions.

Of the motion of the animals. CAP. CCXCIX. (299) *You see above Cap 269*

Those figure itself demonstrate of major course whom remain more for ruin in front.

The body that for whether one moves make much more velocity, how much the center of his gravity is more distance from the center of his supporter. This is called for the motion of the bird, whom without clapping of wing or favor of wind from if itself movement: and this happens, when the center of his gravity is outside of the center of the his clapping, namely beyond of the middle of his residence between the two wing; because whether the means of wing both more behind that the means or rather center they called gravity of all over the bird, to the time it bird one moves forward and into low; but so much more or rather less in front, which into base, how much the center of the called gravity both more remote or closeness to the means of his wing, namely that the center of the gravity remote from the middle of the wing ago the descend of the bird much oblique, and whether it center make vicinity to the middle of the wing, the descend of such wing do of little obliquity.

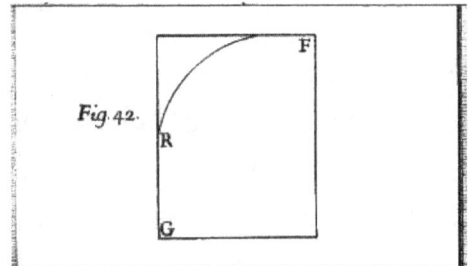

To make any figure that one demonstrates be high arm 40. into space of arm 20. and have limbs corresponding, and be tip into feet. CAP. CCC. (300)

Into this and into each other case none beauty offer boredom to the painter same as one be the wall whereas it paints, and maximum having the eye that regards this painting without to see from one window, or rather other spiracle: because the eye not has from await to the bridge, or rather curve of them parts, but only to the things which of the from this wall itself have to demonstrate for diverse places of the pretense campaign. But better itself do this figure in the curvetting F R G. (Fig 42.) because into it none they are angle.

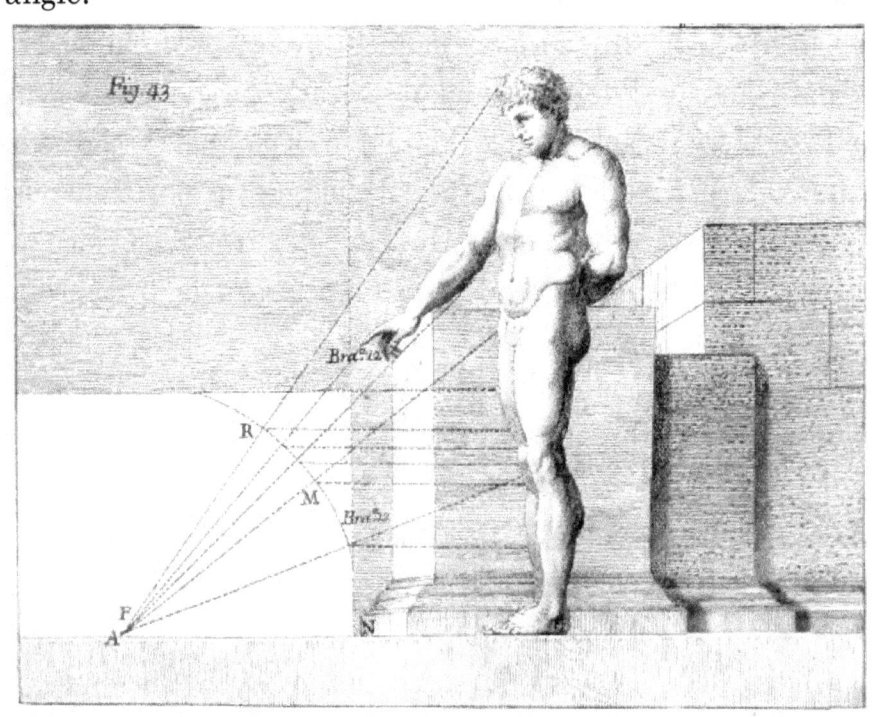

To make one figure in the wall of 12. arm that appear of the height of 24. CAP CCCI. (301)

If you want do figure or rather other thing that appear of height of 24 arm, make in this manner. Figure first it part **M. N.** (Fig. 43.) with the destination of man that you want make, of and then the other destination do in the time **M. R.** But ago before departed plain of one beacon the wall of the form which be the wall with the times whereas there you without do the your figure, of then do behind without they partition the figure designed into profile of which greatness you liking, and trace all the your line to the point **F.** and in the manner that it oneself cut departed the partition **N R.** thus the imagine late the wall that has similitude with the partition, and it all the heights and lead of the figure, and the widths, or rather thicknesses that one locate in the wall straight M. N. do it his precisely form, because in the escape of the wall it figure diminish for whether same. The figure which it goes in the time to you be essential decrease, same as if she fuse starboard side, whom diminution to you be necessary make into late one beacon well flat, and the make the figure, which lift from the wall **N. R.** with the his well curb thicknesses, and reduce into one partition of relief, and both good manner.

Regarding approximately the shadows and light CAP. CCCII. (302)

Adversely which always nor confines of shadow itself fracas light and shadow: and so much more derivation one fracas with the light, how much it is more distant from the body shady. However the complexion not one never simple: this one proof for the ninth, which says: The surface of each body participates of the complexion of his object, once again that she both surface of body transparent, just like air, water and similar; because the air grasp the light from the sun, and the darkness from the privation of it sun. Therefore one tinged into touch various colors how many are those between whom she itself interpose below the eye and them, because the air into whether none has complexion more which itself have the water, but the humidity which itself fracas with it from the middle region into down is that which the thickens, and develop, the rays solar that you pummel the illuminate, and the air which is from the middle region into on remains gloomy: and because light is darkness consists color azure, this is the azure into which itself tinge the air, with so much major or minor obscurity how much the air and mixed with major or minor humidity.

Painting, and light universal. CAP. CCCIII. (303)

Uses of do always in the multitude of men and of animals the parts of the them figure, or rather bodies, so much more obscure how much they are more base, and how much it they are more vicinity to the middle of the their multitude, fasten they be in

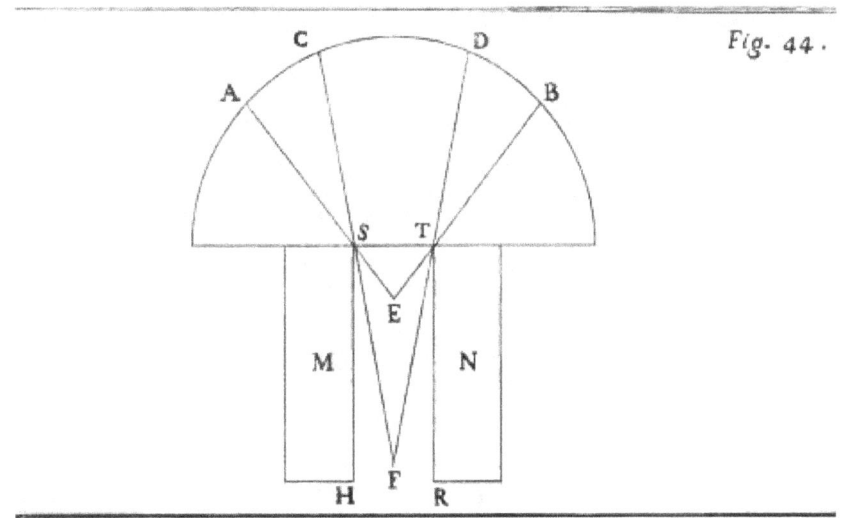

Fig. 44.

whether of uniform complexion: and this is necessary, because less quantity of sky, illuminate of the bodies, to sees neither low space interposed below them said animals which in the parts supreme about the same space.

Demonstrated for the

figure here parlay whereas **A. B. C. D.** (Fig 44.) is established for the arc of the sky universal illuminate of the bodies without him below. **N. M.** they are the bodies that ending the space **S. T. R. H.** below their interposed, in the which space itself to see manifestly which the situate **F.** (be only aluminate from the part of the sky **C. D.**) is aluminate from minor part of the sky, of that which both illuminated the situated **E.** whom is seen from the part of the sky **A. B.** which is greater than the sky **D. C.** therefore both more aluminate in **E.** which into **F.**

Of the fields proportionate for bodies that in they stand out, and before of the surface flat of uniform color. CAP. CCCIV. (304)

The fields of whatever surface flat of complexion and light uniforms, not seem separated from it surface, be of the same complexion and light. Therefore for the convers seem separated, whether do of complexion and light divers.

Painting of figure and body. CAP. CCCV. (305)

The bodies regular they are of two solid, the one of which is dress of surface curve, oval, or spherical, or the other is curcumin of surface lateral, regular or irregular. The bodies spherical, or rather ovals, appear always separated get their fields, although it body both of the color of his field, and similar happen of the bodies lateral: and this happens for be disposition to the generation of the shadows from some any of their sides, the which none it can happen in the surface flat.

In the painting be short before of notice the part of that body which make of minor quantity. CAP. CCCVI. (306)

Of the parts of those bodies that one remove from the eye, that be missing first of notice, which make of minor figure. From which of it proceed that there part of major quantity both the ultimate without be missing of her notice. Therefore you, painter, not finish them petioles components of those things that they are most remote, but follow the rule period in the sixth place.

How many they are those that in the figure the city and other things remote from the eye, do them terms perceive about the buildings, not otherwise that whether sufficing for vicinity propinquity: and this is impossible into nature, because none potential view is that which into one faraway distant can to see them predicted terms with real notice, because the terms of them bodies are terms of there are surface, and the terms of surface they are line, whom line not they are part no of the quantity of it surface, of it ethical of the air which like that surface. Therefore that which not is part of nothing is invisible, just like is proven in geometry. Therefore you, painter, if do they terms shipped and note, same as in custom, not make from there figurative itself remote distance, which for such defect not itself demonstrates vicinity. Once Again the angles of the building they are those that in the distance city not one must figurate, because from faraway is impossible to see, forasmuch they angles they are the competition of two line into a point and the point not has part, therefore is invisible.

Because one same campaign itself demonstrate no time major or minor than none is. CAP. CCCVII. (307)

Illustrate the campaign no time major, or minor than it none they are, for the interposition of the air more thick or thin of his ordinary, whom itself interposed below the horizon and the eye which him to sees.

Below the horizon of equal distance from the eye, that one itself demonstrate be more remote, whom both seen below the air more thick, and that one demonstrates more approach, which itself view into air more thin.

The things views unequal, in distance equal itself demonstrate equal, if there thickness of air interposed below the eye and them things make unequal, namely the air gross interposed below it thing minor: and this one itself proof through the prospective any colors, which ago that one great mountain point of view petiole to the measure, apparently major than any petiole vicinity to the eye, just like one to sees that a finger close to the eye covers any great mountain move away from the eye.

Observation different. CAP CCCVIII. (308)

Between the things of equal obscurity, magnitude, figure, and distance from the eye, that itself demonstrate minor, which both view in field of major splendor or whiteness. This ensign the sun seen behind at plants without leaves, which all the their ramifications that itself found to the meeting of the body solar they are so much diminished, than it remain invisible. The similar do a rod interposed between the eye and the body solar.

The bodies parallel places for the straight, be seen below it fog, itself have without demonstrate more big from head than from feet. Prof for the ninth, which says: There fog, or the air thick, penetrated from rays solar, itself display so much further white, how much she is further base.

The things views from faraway they are proportionately: is this born, which there part more clear sends to the eye his similarity with more vigorous radius than not ago it part more obscure. And I behold one woman dressed of black with cloth white by head, which itself display two concern major that the thickness of the hers back, whom be dressed of black.

Of city and other things views to the air gross. CAP. CCCIX. (309)

The buildings of the city seen below to the eye neither times of the obfuscation, and of the air swollen from the smoke of them fires, or other vapors, always do much less note, how much they are in minor height, and for the converse be much more send and note, how much itself look over in most height. Proof for the fourth of this, which says: The air be much more thick, how much is more low, and much more thin, how much is more high. And this one demonstrate for it fourth parlay without low: and affirm the tower **A. F.** (Fig. 45.) be view from the eye **N.** in the air gross, whom one divided into fourth degrees, how much more big, how much are more low.

How much minor amounts of air itself interposes between the eye and the thing view, how much less the color of it thing participate of the color of it air. Follow that how much major amounts both of air interposed below the eye and the thing view, how much more it thing participates of the color of the air interposed. Demonstrate. Be the eye **N.** to which contribute the five kind of the five parts of the tower **A. F.** namely **A. B. C. D. E.** I say that if the air fuse of uniform thickness, which such proportion area it

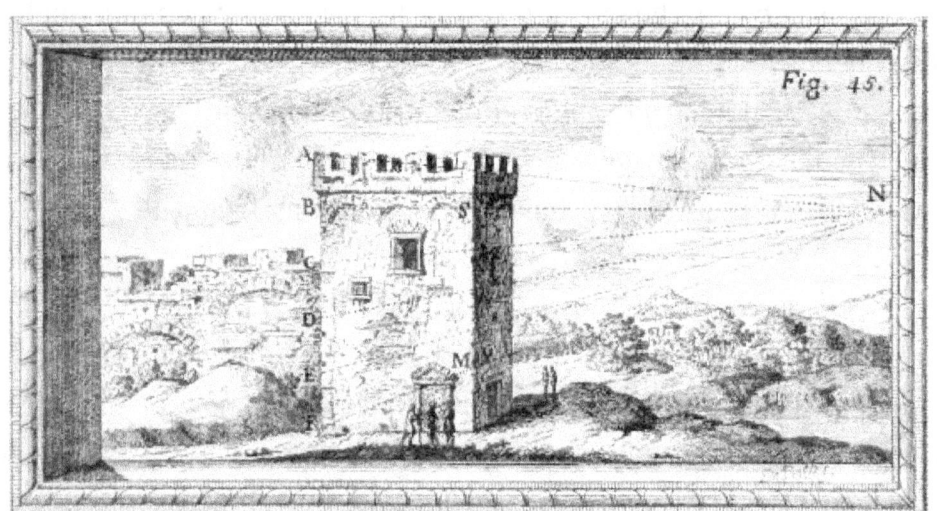

participate the color of the air which acquire the footer of the tower **F.** with it participate of the color of the air, which acquire the part of the tower **B.** which is the proportion that has the lengthiness of the line **M. F.** with the line **B. S.** But for it surface, which proof the air not be uniform in the its thickness, but how much more gross how much she is more low, he is necessary that the proportion of the colors into which the air tinge of whether the parts of the wall B. and F. be of major proportion which proportion above impose, acquaintance it line M. F. other the be more long than it line **S. B.** withered the air, than has thickness uniformly dissimilar.

About rays solar which penetrate the spiracles of the cloudy. CAP. CCCX. (310)

The rays' solar penetrator's of the spiracles interposed below the various density and globosity of the cloudy, illuminate everything the sites whereas is that itself trim, and illuminate even the darkness, and tinge of whether all of them places obscure, which they are beyond them, whom obscurity itself demonstrate below the intervals of them rays solar.

Of things that the eye sees below if mixed below fog and air thick. CAP CCCXI. (311)

How much the air both more vicinity to the water or to the earth, how much itself ago more gross. Proofs for 19.[a] of the second, which says: That thing less itself lever that area into whether most heaviness, followed which it most delicate more itself raises that it grave.

Of the buildings seen in the air thick. CAP CCCXII. (312)

Those part of the buildings do even evident, which itself see into air of major

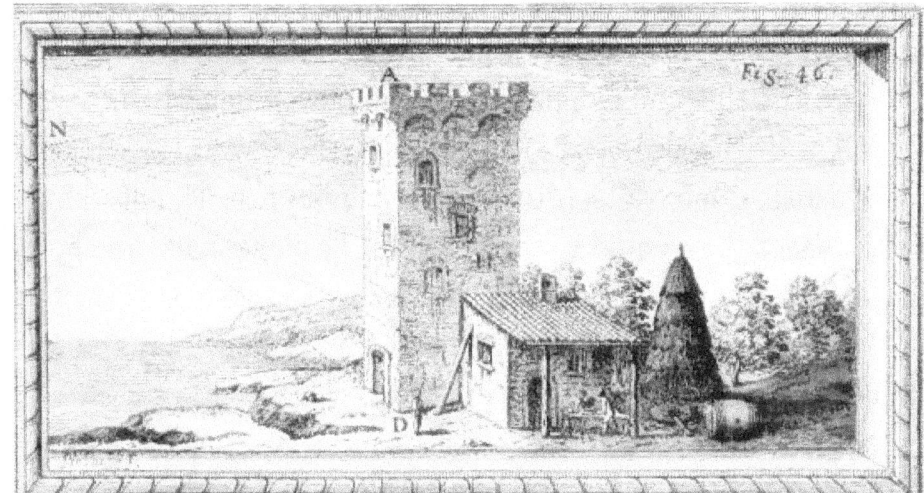

thickness: and thus and conversely make most note that which itself to see into air thin. Therefore the eye **N.** to see it tower **A.D.** (Fig. 46.) it of it to see into each grade of lowness part even note and more albumen, and into each grade of height part more note is less white.

Of the thing that itself display from faraway. Cap. CCCXIII. (313)

Those thing obscure itself demonstrate more albumen, whom do more remote from the eye. Follow for it converse which the thing obscure itself demonstrate of major obscurity, whom one rediscover more vicinity to the eye. Therefore the parts lower of whatever thing parlay in the air gross seem more remote from feet that the their summit, and for these it root bass of the mountain seem more faraway which it top of the same mountain, whom into whether is more remote.

Of view of any city in air gross. CAP. CCCXIX. (314)

The eye that below of if to see it city into air gross, to see the summit of the buildings more obscure and more note which theirs nascent, and to see the said summit into field clear, because the to see in the air bass and gross: and this happen for it surface coat.

The terms lower of the things remote. CAP. CCCXV. (315)

The terms lower of the things remote make less sensible that them their terms superior: and this very at mountains and collar, of the which theirs tops itself lure fields of the sides of the other mountains that they are beyond them, and without this itself sees the terms of over it more sent which theirs groundwork, because the terms of above is more swarthy, for be less occupied from the air gross, whom be neither places low: and this is those which confuses the said terms of the groundwork of the collar: and the same happens of it the trees and buildings, and other thing which itself rise below the air; and of here born which often the other towers views into long distance plan gross from head, and thin from the feet, because it part of over display the angle of the side which ending with the front, because the air thin not there the conceal, such it gross: and this happens for it 7.[a] of the first, which says that the air gross, which one interposes below the eye and the sun, is more lucent into low which into other; and where the air is more white, she occupies to the eye more the thing obscure, which whether such air fuse azure, same as itself to see in long distance: The blackbirds of the fortresses have the space their equal to the width of the blackbirds, and however seem very major the space which the blackbirds: and into distance more remote the space occupied and covers all the blackbirds, and this fortress its display the wall straight, and without blackbirds.

Of things views from faraway. CAP. CCCXVI. (316)

The terms of that object make even note, which without seen into major distance.

Of azure which itself exhibition be neither countries faraway. CAP CCCXVII. (317)

Of the things remote from the eye, whom be of that color one desire, those itself demonstrate of color more sky-blue, whom both of major obscurity, natural, or accidental. Natural is that which is obscure from whether; accidental is that which is obscure mediated the shadow which him is nature from other objective.

Which are those parts of the bodies of which for distance omit the notation. CAP CCCXVIII. (318) See above CAP 292. & 306.

Those parts of the bodies that make of minor quantity be the first of which for long distance one pertains it notion. These happens, because the species of the thing minors into equal distances come to the eye with minor angle which the major, and the knowledge of the things remote they are of so much minor notice how much it they are of minor quantity. Follow therefore, which when the quantity major in long distance come to the eye for angle minimum, and almost itself pertains of notice, the quantity minor to the all left hand of the his cognition.

Because the things how much more one remove from the eye not even itself consensus. CAP. CCCXIX. (319)

That thing do not even note, whom make more remote from the eye. These happens, because those parts first one forgiveness that they are more minute, and the second less minute are they are once again lose in the major distance, and thus subsequently continuing without little without little consumes the parts, one consume there notion of the thing remote, into way that to the end itself forgiveness all the parts together with everything: and left hand again the color for the cause of the thickness of the air that itself interposes below the eye and the thing view.

Why is that the faces of faraway obscure? CAP. CCCXX. (320)

We see clear that all the similarities of the things evident that it they are for objective, thus grand just like petiole, entrance to the sense for the petiole light of the eye. Whether for itself petiole entry passes the similitude of the greatness of the sky and of the earth, be the face of the men's between one grand similarities of things almost nothing, for the remoteness that the diminish, occupies itself little of it light, which remains incomprehensible: and contain from pass through from the surface to the impressively for a means obscure, namely the nerve grade, which seem obscure, those species not be of color potent, itself tinged into that obscurity of the way, and insert to the impressively point of view obscure. Other cause not itself more into none way teach depart that point, and nerve that be in the light: and because he and full of an mood transparent without guise of air, ago the ostium (small opening) that make one hole fact into one axis, which without regards for equivalence black, and the things views for the air clear and dark one confused in the obscurity.

Which are the parts that first one forgiveness of notice neither bodies that itself remove from the eye, and which more one retains. CAP. CCCXXI. (321)

These part of the body that one removes from the eye is that which less conserve it her evidence, and whom is of minor figure. This happens neither luster of the bodies spherical or column, and in the limbs more thin of the bodies, same as the deer, which first one remains of convey to the eye the species or rather similitude of the its legs and antler than of the his bust, whom for be more big, more itself conserve in the its

106

species. But the first thing that one pertains into distance they are the outlines that terminate the surface and figure.

Of the perspective lineal. CAP. CCCXXII. (322)

The perspective lineal itself extends in ostium (small opening) of lines visual without prove for measure how much it thing second is minor than it first, and it third than it second, and thus of grade in grade finally to the end of the things views. I find for experience, which if it thing second make much distance from the first how much it before is distance from the eye your, which although below them be of equal greatness, it second both the objective minor that it first: and if the third thing do of equal distance from the second ahead without it, both minor two third, and thus of grade in grade for equal distance produce always diminution proportionate, provided the interval not pass the number of 20. arms, and below said 20. arms the figure similar without you lose 2/4 of his greatness, and below 40. Lose ¾ and then 5/6 in 60. arms, and thus of hand in hand make his diminish, make it partition far from you two times it your grandness, which the make one single ago great difference from the first arm to the second.

Of the bodies seen in the fog. CAP. CCCXXIII. (323)

Those things whom be views in the fog itself demonstrate major very that it them real grandness: and this arise, because the perspective of the middle interposed below the eye and similar objective not accordance the color his with it magnitude of it object, because such fog is similar to the confused air interposed below the eye, and the horizon into time sunny, and the body vicinity to the eye seen afterwards it vicinity of the fog itself display be to the distance of the horizon, in which one grandness tower one demonstrate minor than the aforesaid men's according vicinity.

Of the height of the buildings seen in the fog. CAP. CCCXXIV. (324) You see *above Cap 313-315.,*

Those part of the vicinity buildings one display more confused, whom is more remote from earth; and this arise, because more fog is below the eye and it top of the buildings, which not is from the eye to the its base. And it wall parallel seen into long distance below it fog one dimension a lot of more thin, how much it both more vicinity to the his base. This arise for it surface treatment, which says: It fog one demonstrate much more white, and more often, how much it is more vicinity to the earth, and for the second of these, which says: it thing obscure seem of much minor figure how much she both view into field of potential whiteness. Therefore be more white it fog from feet that from head, is necessary which the obscurity of this tower itself demonstrates more embrace from feet which from chieftain.

Of the city and other building seen the evening or the morning in the mist. CAP CCCXXV. (325)

Of it the buildings seen into long distance from evening or from morning in the fog, or air gross, solo one demonstrate it clarity of their parts aluminate from the sun, which one found inverse the horizon, and the parts of the said buildings, which not they are views from the sun, remain almost of the complexion of mediocre obscurity of fog, (mist, haze).

Because the things more high place in the distance they are more obscure than the bass, once again the fog both uniform into thickness CAP. CCCXXXVI. (326)

Of the things posed in the fog, or other air gross, or into vapor, or smoke, or into distance, those both much more noted, which produce more high: and of the things of

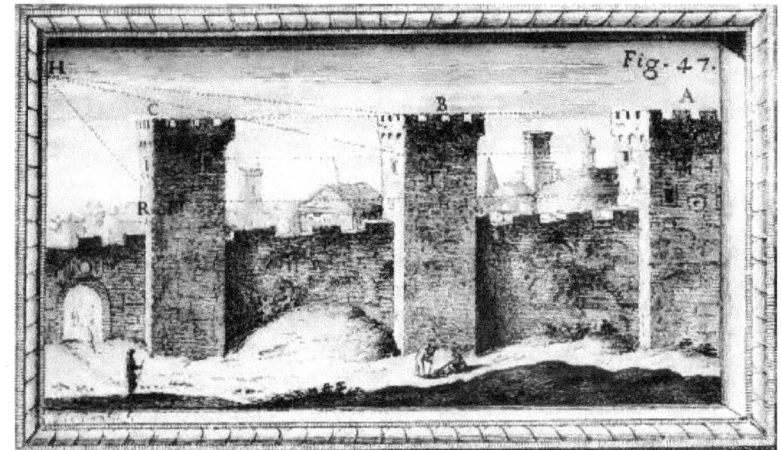

equal height that seem more obscure than camp into more obscure fog, same as happen to the eye **H.** (Fig. 47.) which seeing **A. B. C.** tower of equal height below them, sees **C.** summit of the first tower in **R.** lowness of two degree of profound into fog, and sees it summit of the wall of middle B.

into a only grade of fog, therefore C summit of demonstrate more obscure than it summit of the tower B.

Of the mark of the shadow that appear neither bodies from faraway CAP. CCCXXVII. (327)

Always the throat or other perpendicular rectitude that above of whether have no extruded produce more obscure that it face perpendicular of it jut. Follow, which that body itself demonstrate more aluminate that of major sum of a same light make seen. Look over into **A.** that not there aluminum part no of the sky. **F. K.** (Fig. 48.) and in **B.** there aluminum the sky **H. K.** and into **C.** the sky **G. K.** and into **D.** the sky **F. K.** entirely. Therefore the chest do of equal clarity of the front, nose, and chin. However those that I there have without record of the faces, is that there consider into those just like into different distance itself loses diverse quality of shadows, and solo remains that

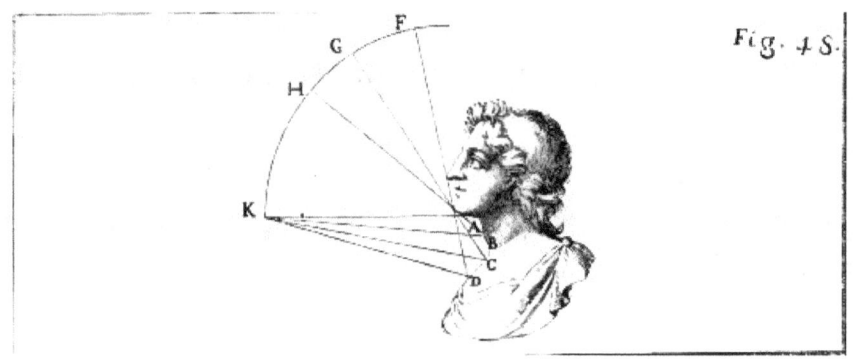

first mark, namely of the trounced of the eye, and other similar, and in the end the face remains obscure, because into those one consume the light, whom they are petiole thing without comparison of the shadow procuress: for whom thing without length move one consumes it quality and quantity of the light and shady principal, and one confounds each quality into shady procurer. And this is it cause which the trees, and each body, without certain distance one demonstrate produce into if more obscure than be those same vicinity to the eye. However then the air which one interposes below the eye and the thing, ago it thing itself enlightens, and hangs into azure: but more blue realm in the shadows, which in the parts bright, where one exhibition more it truth of the colors.

Because on the making of evening the shadows about bodies generated in off white partition they are blue. CAP. CCCXXVIII. (328)

The shadows of the bodies generated from the redness of the sun vicinity to the horizon always be azure: and this arise for the eleventh, whereas one says: The surface of each body opaque participates of the complexion of hers object. Therefore be the whiteness of the partition private to all of each complexion, one tinged of the complexion of its object, whom they are into this one case the sun, and the sky. And

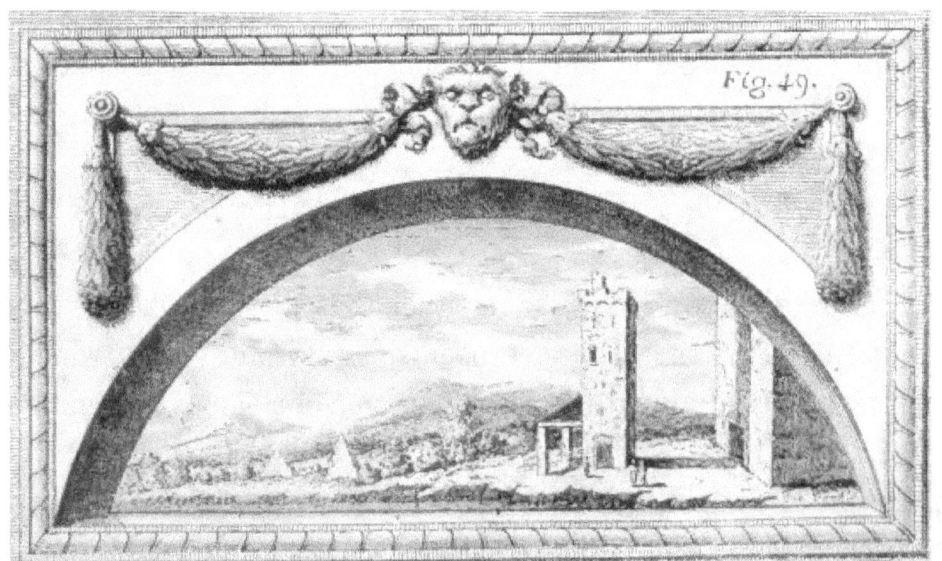

because the sun reddens towards it evening, and the sky itself exhibition azure, whereas the shadow not to sees the sun, for the octave of the shadow, which says: none luminous not see never the shadows of the body from him illuminated, that place do to see from the sky: therefore for it accordingly an tenth the shadow derivative is the percussion in the white partition of color azure, and the field of it shadow view from the redness of the sun participate of the color red. (Fig 49.)

Whereabouts is most bright the smoke. CAP CCCXXIX. (329)

The smoke seen below the sun and the eye make bright and lucid more than into no part of the country whereas arise. The same ago there dust, and there mist, whom, if thou do yet below the sun and them, thee will seem dark.

Of the dust. CAP. CCCXXX. (330)

It dust that itself lever for the course of no animal, how much more one lever, more is bright, and thus more obscure, how much less itself raise, standing it below the sun and the eye.

Of the smoke. CAP. CCCXXXI. (331)

The smoke is more transparent and obscure inverse the extremes of his globular than inverse his own means.

The smoke itself moves with so much most obliquity, how much the wind hers engine is more potent.

They are the smoke of many various colors, how many they are the variety of the thing that it generate.

It smoke not produce shadow terminate: and the his confines they are much less note, how much they are more distant from the their causes: and the things posed afterward them are much less evident, how much the lump of the smoke they are more dense, and much are more whites, how much they are more vicinity to the principle, and more azure towards the end.

The fire it seem much more obscure how much major sum of smoke itself interposes below the eye and it fire.

Whereas the smoke is most remote, the things they are from him less occupied.

Ago the country confused without guise (appearance) of often fog, in which one to see smoke into different places with the them flames neither principles illuminators of the more densely globular of be smoke, and the mountains more high most be evident than the their roots (all instances), same as one to see produce in the mists.

Various precepts of painting. CAP. CCCXXXII. (332)

The surface of each body opaque participates of the complexion of the means transparent interposed below the eye and it surface; and much more, how much it middle is most dense, and with most space one interposes below the eye and it accordance surface.

The terms of bodies opaque be less noted how much more distant from the eye that the see.

Those draw of the body opacity do more shaded or illuminated than both more vicinity to the shadow than the obscure, or to the luminous than the illuminate.

The surface of each body matt (opaque) participates of the complexion of its object, but with concern or major, or minor impression how much it object you know more vicinity or remote, or of major or of minor potency.

The thing view below the light and the shadow one demonstrate of major relief than those which are in the light or in the shadows.

When you do in the long distances the thing cognate, and send, they thing not distant but proximately one demonstrate. Therefore in your imitation ago that the things combine that part of the cognition which display the distance. And if the thing that to you be for objective produce of finish confused and doubtful, again you do the akin in your similarity.

The thing distance for two diverse causes one display of confused and doubtful end, the one of the which is that she come for much petiole angle to the eye, and one diminish much, which she ago the obstruct of things minimum, which, once again it be vicinity to the eye, he eye not more comprehend of that figure one both such body, same as they are the nails of the fingers, the ant, or similar things. The second is that below the eye and the thing distant one interposes much of air that she one ago dense and thick, and for the both whiteness tinged the shadows, and the sail of its whiteness, and them ago of obscure in a complexion whom is between black and white, which is blue.

Although for the long distance one lose the cognition of be of many things, regardless that which produce illuminate from the sun one rendering of more certain demonstration, and the other in the confused shadows seem bundle. And Because into each grade of lowness the air acquire part of thickness, the thing that produce more low one demonstrate more confused, and thus for the contrary.

When the sun ago reddening the cloudy of the horizon, the things that for it distance one dressed of blue be participants of such redness: hence one do one motion between the azure and the red, whom render the campaign much cheerful and light-hearted: and all the things that both illuminated from such redness, which be densely,

111

produce much evident, and redness: and the air for be transparent it into if for all infused such to red, hence one demonstrate of the color of the flower of lilies.

Always those air which be below the sun and the land, when itself lever or places, both more occupy of the thing which they are afterward she which none other part of air: this arise be she more to look white.

Not be facts terms of it profiles of a body that camping one over one other, but only it body for whether one stand out.

If the term of the things white itself collide above other things white, if it will curved, create term obscure for his nature, and make it more obscure part that contain the part luminous: and if camp in place obscure, it term seem it more clear part which have it part luminous.

Those thing seem more remote and stick out from the other which camp into field more varied from whether.

In the distances one forgiveness before the terms of the bodies that have colors similar, and that the term of the one both above of the other, same as the term of one oak above one other oak similar. Second into major distance one pertains the terms of bodies of colors procurer (panderer) terminated the one above the other, just like tress, ground worked, walls, or other ruins of mountains or of stones. Ultimate one pertains the terms about bodies terminated the clear in the obscure, and the obscure in the clear.

Below the thing of equal height which above the eye be situate, those that both more remote from the eye do more low: and if make situate under the eye, it more vicinity without it eye seem more low, and the lateral parallel compete into one point.

Even they are evident neither sites faraway the thing that they are of surrounding without the rivers which those that from such rivers and marshes they are remote.

Below the thing of equal suspension those that produce more vicinity to the eye seem more rare, and the more remote more dense.

The eye which make of major pupil behold the object of major figure. This one demonstrate in the look out a body celestial for a petiole spiracle fact with the needle in the paper, which for not be able operate of it light if not one stalk part, it body seem decrease much of the her greatness, how much it part of the light that it to see is failure from its greatness, how much there part of light that the behold is failure from her all.

The air which is enlarged, and one interposes below the eye and the thing, it render it thing of uncertain and confused ending, and ago it objective seem of major figure than none is. This arise because it perspective lineal not diminish the angle that port the its species to the eye, and the perspective if colors it push and remove into major distance than she not is, one that the one remove from the eye, and the other conserve the its magnitude.

When the sun is into occident (west) the mists which to be had again swell the air, and the things that not they are views from the sun remain obscure and confused, and those that from the sun be illuminate redden and yellows, second which the sun one demonstrate to the horizon. Once again the thing which from this they are destiny evidently, and maximum the buildings and homes of the city is town, because the them shadow they are obscure, and seem which such their certain demonstration born of confused and uncertain foundations, because each thing is of an complexion, whether not is view from it sun.

The thing illuminate from the sun is seem illuminate from the air, into manner which one create two shadow, of which that make more obscure than is the its line central straight to the center of the sun. Always it line central of the light primitive and derivative both with line central of shadows primitive or derivative.

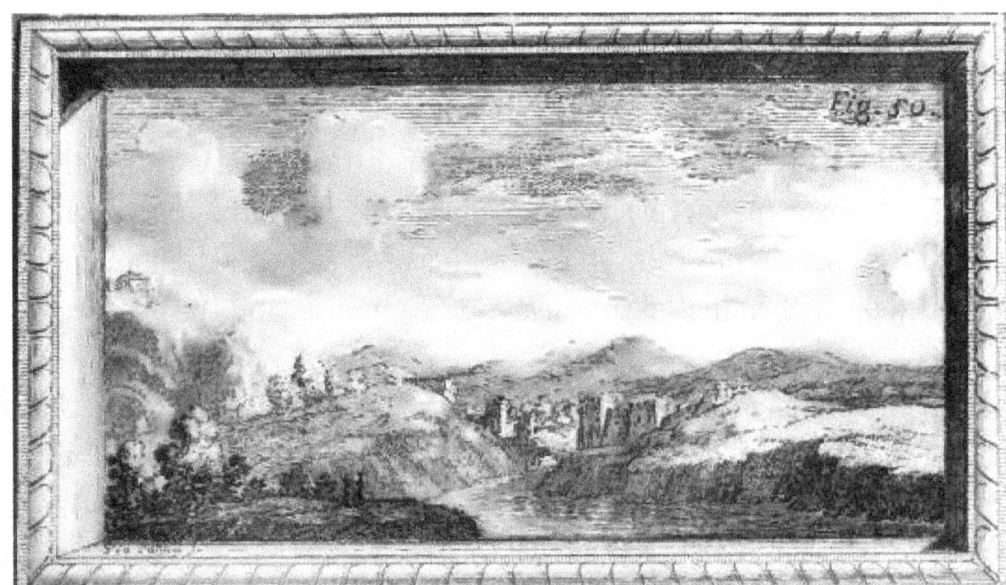

Beautiful exhibition ago the sun when is in west, whom illuminate all of them the other buildings of the city, and towns, and the tall trees of the campaigns, and the tinge of the hers complexion, and all the rest from that place into downward remains of little relief, because being solely illuminate from the air have little difference the shadow off one's chest light, and for this not stand out much, and the thing which between these more one increase they are toll from the rays solar, and same as one is called, itself tinged in the them complexion: hence there you've without tower of the complexion of which you both the sun, and that place of it you have without put into whatever color clear with whom there illuminate they bodies. (Fig. 50.)

Once again often times happens which an overcast seem obscure without have shadow from other overcast from him separate, and this happens second the site of the

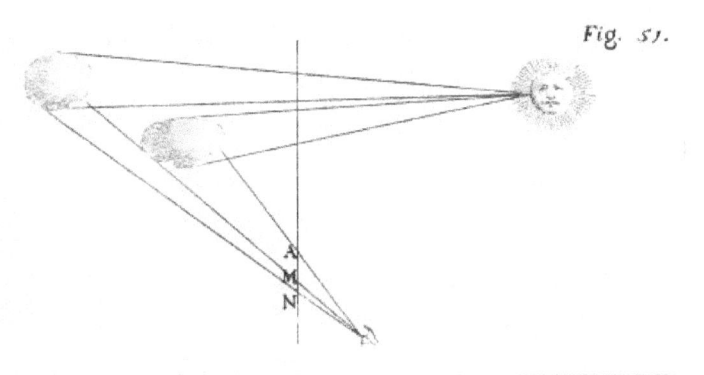

Fig. 51.

eye, because of the one vicinity itself to see only the part shady, and of the other one to see the shady and the luminous.

Below the thing of equal height that which make more distance from the eye seem most low. Viewed that the overcast first again that both more lower than the second, seem more high of him, same as it demonstrate in the lining the cut of the pyramid of the first overcast low into **M. A.** (fig 51.) of the second more high in **N. M.** This arise when there by seen an overcast obscure more high than an overcast light for the rays of the sun in east or into west.

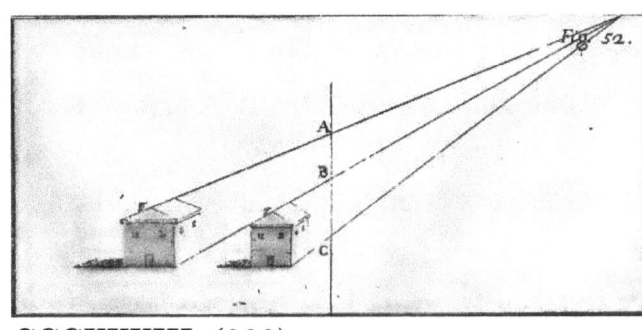

Because the thing painted, thus far she come to the eye for that same thickness of angle than that which is more remote from she, not seem much remote how much that of the remoteness natural. CAP.

CCCXXXIII. (333)

Say: The paint departed it part **B. C.** (Fig. 52.) one home which contain without seem distance of a mile, and of and then self about put elevation one which has it true distance of a mile, whom things they are into manner ordered that it partition **A. C.** size the pyramid with equal grandness; you do not say but with two eye seem of equal grandness, of it of equal distance.

Of the fields. CAP. CCCXXXIV. (334)

Principally part of the painting they are the fields of the thing painted, in the which field the finish of the things natural it have into them curve convex always one be familiar with, and the figure of such bodies into them fields, once again the colors of the bodies it of the same complexion of the aforesaid field. And this arise which the finish convex of the bodies not they are illuminates in the same manner than from the same light is illuminate the field, because such term many times make more light or more dark than it field. But if such term is of the color of this field, without doubt such part of painting prohibit it notice of the figure of such term, and this such elective of painting is from be disgust from the wits of the good painters, consistence the intention of the painter is of do seem the his bodies of here from fields: is in the above-named case happens the contrary, not only into painting, but in the thing of relief.

Of the judgment that one has from make above the work of a painter. CAP. CCCXXXV. (335)

First is that you consider the figure, itself have the relief that one requires to the situated: and the light that the illuminate, which the shadows not be those same in the extremes of the history that in the means, because other thing is be circumference from the shadow, and other have the shadow from an only side. Those they are circumstance from the shadow, which they are towards the means of history, because they are overshadowed from the figure interposed between them and the light: and those they are overshadowed from an single side, whom they are interposed below the light and the history, because whereas not to see the light, to see the history, and you one represents the obscurity of it history, and whereas not to see the history, to see the splendor of the light, and you one represents the its luminosity.

Second is that mine clearance, or rather comparison of the figure, both second the case of which there you provided both its history.

Third Party that the figure be with promptness intent to their particular.

Of the relief of the figures remote from the eye. CAP. CCCXXXVI. (336)

That body opaque (matt) itself demonstrate be of minor relief whom make more distant from the eye, and this one happens because the air interposed between the eye and it body opaque, for be it thing clear more which the shadow of this body, corrupts it shadow, and the enlightens, and the toggles the potential of the his obscurity, whom thing is cause of make lose the his relief.

Of the terms of limbs illuminates. CAP. CCCXXXVII. (337)

The terms of that components illuminates seem rather obscure than produce seen into field most bright, and thing seem most clear than both viewed into field moreover obscure. And if this term both plan, and seen into field fair similar to his clarity, the term both insensible.

Of the finishing. CAP. CCCXXXVIII. (338)

The terms of the things second not create never knowing just like the first. Therefore you, painter not finish immediately the things fourth with the fifth, same as the first with the second, because the term of one thing in another is of nature of line mathematics, but not line; because the end of a complexion is principle of a other complexion, and not has from be however in accordance with line, because none thing itself intermits below the ending of a complexion that both favor to at another complexion, if none is the finish, whom is things insensible of near, therefore you, painter, none the pronunciation in the things distant.

Of the incarnation, and things remote from the eye. CAP. CCCXXXIX. (339)

Be obliged to from the Painter put in figure, and things remote from the eye, solely the mark not finished, but of confused ends, and both fact the choice of such figure when is overcast, or into about it evening, and over all look out, same as I have called, from the light and the shadow finish, because content then tint when one to see from faraway, and turn out then works difficult and without grace. And you have without record, which the shadows never be of quality, which for the them obscurity you contain without squander the complexion in which one provoke, whether already the place whereas the bodies they are situated not fuse dark: and not produce profiles, not insulter spun on head countable (hair), not allocate light whites, if not in the thing white, and that they light match without demonstrate it first beauty of the complexion whereas one lay.

Various precepts of painting. CAP. CCCXL (340)

The terms and figure of whatever part of bodies shady breathe in one be acquaintance in the shadows and neither light theirs, but in the parts interposed below the light and the shadows of them bodies they are into first grade of notice.

The perspective whom one extends in the picture itself divides into three parts principal, of which it first is of the diminution that make the quantity of the bodies into diverse distances. There second part is that which section of the diminution of the colors of such bodies. The third is that which diminish it notion of the figure, and of the terms which have they bodies into various distances.

The blue of the air is of color compound of light and of darkness, it light I say for causes of the air illuminated in the particles of the humidity below it air infused. For darkness I say the air pure, whom not is uniform into atoms, namely particles of humidity, in which couple without preclusion the rays solar. And of this one to see the example in the air one interposes below the eye and the mountains shady for the shadows of the great facsimile of the tree which above it one found, or rather shady into that part which not is percussion from the rays solar, it what air one ago blue, and none not ago blue in the part its luminous, and much less in the part blanket of snow.

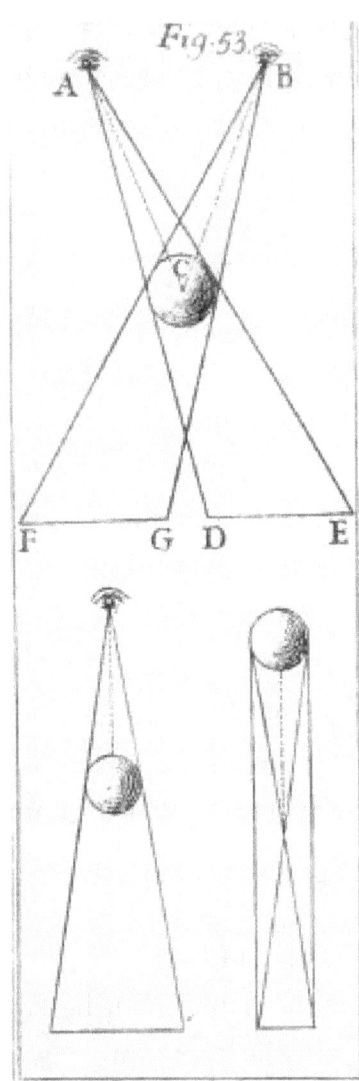

Fig. 53

Between the matters equally obscure, and of equal distance, those one demonstrate be more obscure than finished into further white field, and this for the contrary.

Those thing that both more painted of white and black appearance of best relief which no other. However records, painter, which clothes your figure of color more clear than you be able: which whether the make of color obscure (dark), be of little relief and of little evidence from faraway, and this because the shadows of all the things they are obscure, and if do one garment obscure, little diversity both from the light to the shadow; and neither colors clarify you both difference.

Because the things portrayed perfectly from the natural not content same relief what seem it natural. CAP. CCCXLI. (341) To see above chapter 53

Impossible is which there painting imitated with sum perfection of alimentation, shadows, light, and complexion, be able seem of the same relief what point of view it natural, whether already this natural into long distance not is seen from one only eye. Proof: Be the eyes **A. B.** (Fig.53) whom perceives the object **C.** with contest of the lines central of the eyes **A. C.** and **B. C.** I say that the lines lateral of it central to see behind without this object the space **G. D.** and the eye **A.** to see all over the space **F. D.** and the eye **B.** to see all over the space **G. E.** Therefore the two eyes to see of behind to the object **C.** awn transparent, second the definition of the transparent, behind whom nothing one conceal: which intervened not more without that which to see with an only eye an object major of it eye. And for that which one is called prune conclude the our question, because one thing painted occupies all the space which contain behind without if, and for none mean is possible to see part no of the field which it line its circumferential possess behind without whether.

Of do which the things plan specular from their fields, namely from the partition whereas they are painted. CAP. CCCXLII. (342)

Many more relief display the things in the field clear and illuminate that in the obscure. The reason is, which if there you make give relief to the your figure, you make that those part of the body that is more remote from the light not even participate of it light, hence come without remaining more obscure, and ending then into field dark, come without fall down into confused terms: for whom thing, if none happen reflected, the work awn without grace, and from faraway not appear if not the part luminous, hence convene that the obscure plan be of the field same, and thus the thing seem trim, and remove much less of the be obliged to, how much the field is obscure.

Precept. CAP. CCCXLIII. (343)

The figure have more grace place neither light universal which neither particular and petioles because the great light and potential embrace the reliefs of bodies, and the work make into such light eye-catching from faraway with grace, and those which they are portrayed without light petioles, blindside great sum of shadow, and similar work made with such shadows never appear from places faraway other than tints.

Of the figure the parts of the world. CAP. CCCXLIV. (344)

Be admonish, which neither places seafarers, or vicinity without those, direct at parts southerner, not face the real figurative of it the trees or meadows, same as in the parts remote from them seas and northerner do, except in the trees, whom every year throw leaves.

Of the figuratively the four of times of the year, or participants of those. CAP. CCCXLV. (345)

In the autumn do the things second the age of such tempo (timing), namely in the principle commences to turn pale the leaves of the trees neither more olden branches, more or less second that it plant is in place sterile or fertile: and none produce same as a lot of, which do all the strength of the trees, although from if be equally distant, of one same quality of green. Thus the complexion of the meadows, stones, and pedals of the aforementioned plants varies always, because it nature is variable into infinite.

Of the wind painting. CAP. CCCXLVI. (346)

In the figuration of the wind, other the bend of the branches, and overturn of the leaves reverse the incident of the wind, one must figurative the clouding over of the subtle dust mixed with the muddied air.

Of the principle of one rain. CAP CCCXLVII. (347)

It rain falls below the air, those obscuring with lucid (glossy) tincture, take from the one of lateral the light of the sun, and the shadow from the part opposites, such one to see produce at mist, and obscures it earth, which from such rain the is extracted the splendor of the sun: and the thing view of the from it they are of confused and not intelligible terms, and the thing which produce more vicinity to the eye be more noted: and more noted create the thing view in the rain shady, which that of the rain illuminates. And this one happens because the thing view in the shady rain, only pertains the light principal, but the thing that one carry in the luminous pertain the light and the shadow, because the parts luminous one mix with it brightness of illuminated air, and the parts shady they are brighter from the same clarity of the in accordance with air illuminated.

Of the shadows made from bridges over it theirs waters. CAP CCCXLVIII. (348)

The shadows of the bridges not produce never views above theirs water if before the water not loses the tenancy of the mirror for account of turbidity. And this one proof, because the water albumen is of surface luster and cleaning, and be reflected the bridge into all it places interposed below equal angle below the eye and the bridge, and mirrored the air below the bridge, whereas must be the shadow of such bridge, which not more make the water turbid, because not be reflected, but well receives the shadow, just like produce one street dusty.

Precepts of painting CAP. CCCXLIX. (349)

The perspective is bridle and helm of the painting.

The grandness of the figure painted be obliged to display without which distance it is view.

Whether you to see one figure grand to the natural, knowhow which one demonstrate be near to the eye.

Precepts. CAP CCCL. (350)

Always the precarious balance is in the line central of the chest which is from his bellybutton into above, and thus hold count the weight accidental of men's, just like of the his weight natural. This one demonstrate in the extend the arm, that the fist place in the his extreme ago the officiation which make one to see to the counterweight place in the extreme of lever scales; hence for necessity one pitch much weight of the from the belly button, how much is the weight accidental of the fist, and the heel convene which one raise.

Of the statue. CAP. CCCLI. (351)

If you want make one figure of marble, do first one of earth, whom then which make complete and shoal, place into trunk which both again capacious, afterwards it figure segment of it site, to receive the marble which you want sculpt of within without similitude of that earth. Then mass it figure of earth within to it trunk, have stick, which enter exactly for the his own punch hole, and incite in much for each hole, which each stick recto (printing) touch it figure into diverse places, and it part of them sticks that awn outside of the trunk tinge of black, and ago the contrary sign to the stick, and to the its hole, into manner that to your parlay one collide: and extract of the trunk the figure of earth, and lay the your piece of marble, and a lot lever from the marble which all the your sticks one hide-and-seek noble to the them gesture into said holes: and for be able do better these, ago that all to the trunk of can lever into high, and the deep end of it trunk remain always below to the marble, and without this manner of it be able remove with the irons with grand facility.

The do one painting of eternal paint. CAP CCCLII. (352)

Paint it your painting over of the paper stretch into loom well delicate and flat, and then from one good and gross imprimatur of pitch (tar) and brick (millstone) well black and blue: next from the imprimatur of white lead and yellow flax, then coloristic, and varnish of oil old clear and solid, and application to the pane (glass) well level. But is better do a painting of earth well glazed, and the imprimatur (ingrained) of white lead and yellow flax, and then coloristic, and varnish, then applicate the glass crystalline with it varnish well white without it glass: but ago first well dry out in heater obscure (darken) it vivid, and then paint (varnish) with the oil of walnut and amber, or rather oil of walnut firmed to the sun.

Manner of colors into canvas. CAP. CCCLIII. (353)

Place there your canvas into loom, and from the glue limp, and abandon dry out, and draws, and from the incarnation with brushes of bristles, and thus spontaneous make the shadow blend without your manner. The incarnation produce white lead, lacquer, and yellow flux: the shadow make black, and uppermost, and a little of lacquer, or you want solid. Soften that you have, abandon dry out, then retouch without desiccated with lacquer and gum, exist very times with the water rubberized together liquid, which is best, because ago the officiation hers without luster.

Once again for make the shadows more obscure, remove lacquer rubberized above-named, and ink, and with this shadow you can tarnish (semi-darkness) a lot of colors, because is transparent: and then semi-darkness the blue, lacquer, and different shadows, says why is that diverse light darkness of lacquer simple rubberized above the lacquer without tempera, or rather above the cinnabar tempered and dry.

Precept of the perspective into painting. CAP. CCCLIV. (354)

When you not considerate variety of luminosity or of obscurity below the air, at time the perspective of the shadows both shoo from your imitation, and solely you have without matter of the perspective of the diminution of bodies, and of diminution of colors, and of the diminish of the cognition of the thing to the eye opposing: and this ago seem one same thing more remote, namely it loss of the cognition of the figure of whatever objective.

The eye not have never for it perspective lineal, without his motion, cognition of the distance that is between the object and another things, if none by means of it perspective of colors.

Of the objective. CAP. CCCLV. (355)

That part of the objective produce more illumination then both more closeness to the luminous then the illuminate. It similitude of the things into each grade of distance loses the grade of potency, namely how much it thing create more remote from the eye, produce much less penetrable below the air with it her similitude.

Of the diminution of the colors and bodies. CAP. CCCLVI. (356)

Both observed it diminution of the quality of colors together with it diminution of bodies in which one affix.

Of interposition about bodies transparent below the eye the object. CAP. CCCLVII. (357)

How much major both the interposition transparent below the eye and the objective much more one transmutes the complexion of the objective in the complexion of the transparent interposed.

When the objective one interposed between the eye and the light, for it line central which one extends below the center of the light and the eye, to the time this objective both totally private of light.

Of cloths which dress the figure, and their folds. CCCLVIII. (358)

Them cloths which dress the figure must have the their folds accommodates without gird the limbs from their dressed, in manner which in the parts Illuminate not one place folds of shadow obscure, and in the parts shady not one face folds of too much clarity, and which the features of them folds it goes off into some part circumference the limbs from their cover, and not with features that cut the components, of it with shadow that break more inside then not is it surface of the body dress, and into effect the cloth both into manner adapted which not couple uninhabited, namely that not pair an grouping of cloth disrobe from the men's, same as one to see do make without many, whom one enchant much of various groupings of various folds, which of it employs all one figure, omit the effect because such cloth and fact, namely for dress and encircle the limbs with grace, whereas they one place, and not the clothing all of hint, or you puffball bulge over them take off illuminates of limbs. Not deny already that not one must do any nice layer, but both fact into part of the figure whereas the limbs below them and the body to shorten and reflect such cloth. And above all varies them cloths in the history, just like in the produce to any the folds with rift without facade, and this is neither cloths dense, and any cloths pair them folding weak, and the their times not laterite and other twist.

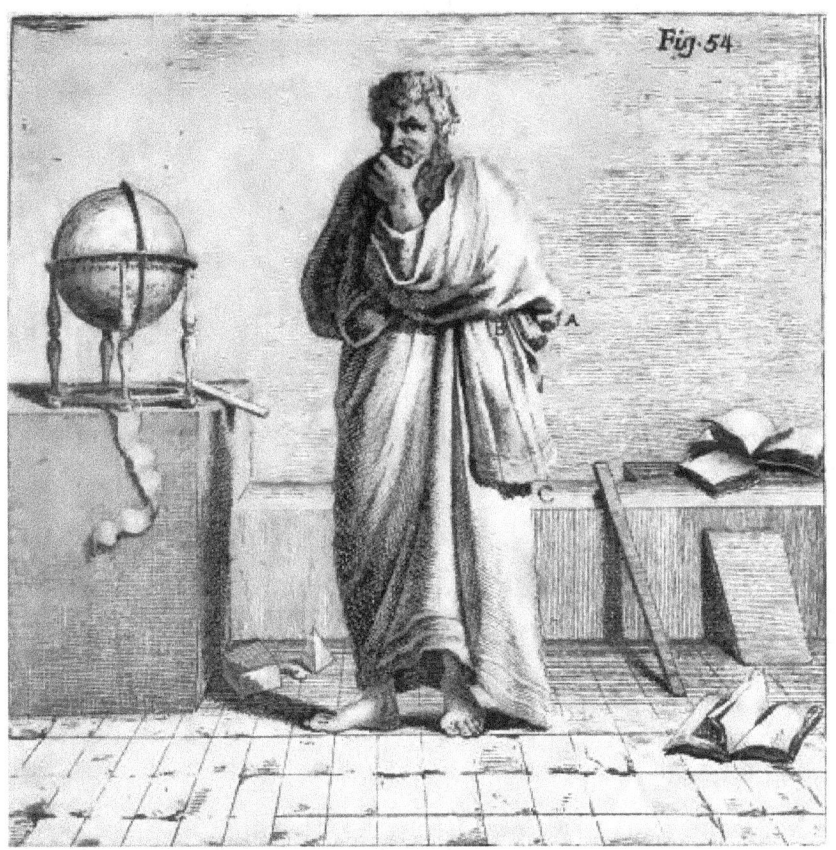

Fig. 54

Of the nature of the folds of cloths. CAP. CCCLIX. (359)

Many love the folding of the layer of cloths with them angles acute, crude, and briskly, other with angles almost insensible, other without any angles, but into put of those certain curvature.

Just like one must make them folds of cloths. CAP CCCLX.360

Those part of the folds that one locate more far away from his compelled extremes one reduce more into his before nature. Naturally each things desire maintain into his lie. The cloth, because and of equal density and weaving, one in the hers reverse same as in hers straight, desire of star plan: Hence when he is from some crease or layer constrained without leave she plantar, observes it nature of the strength into that part of whether whereas he is more constrained, and those part which is more faraway without them constringent find shrink more to the first its nature, namely of the star stretched out and ample. Example both **A. B. C.** (Fig. 54.) it crease of the cloth called of above. **A. B.** both the place whereas it cloth and bent and constrained. The to you proposed which that part of the cloth which time farther faraway to the compelled extremes one reduce more in her first nature: therefore **C.** locate more faraway, it crease **C.** both more wide which into nothing other hers site.

Same as one must the folds to the cloths. CAP. CCCLXI. (361)

Without an cloth not one must offer confusion of many folds, on the contrary make solely whereas with the hands or arms (limbs) they are consider, and the remainder let go fall from simply, and one must portray of natural, namely, whether to want do cloth wool, use the folds second those, and if make silk, or cloth fine, or from lout, it goes diversifying without each the its folds, and not do attire, just as many make, above the models covered of paper, or ropes thin, which you deceive talented.

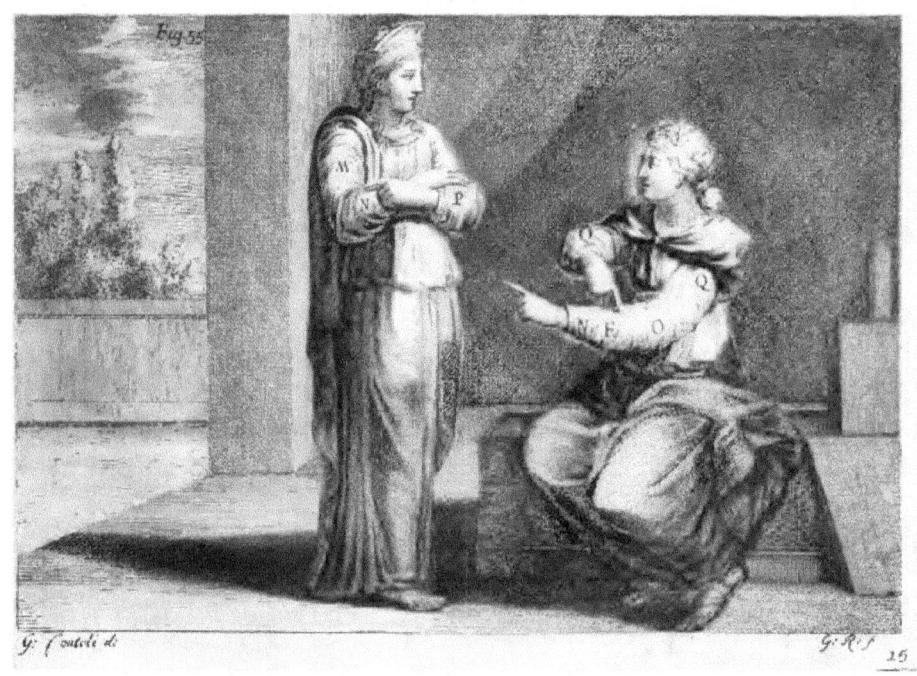

Of the folds about cloths into foreshortening. CAP. CCCLXII. (362)

Whereas it figure shorten faille (fabric) to see major number of folds which whereas it not shorten, and his limbs area circumference from folds dense and twist around to them limbs. And both whereas be the eye. **M. N.** (Fig. 55.) convey the means of each circles more far from the eye of their acute. **N. O.** the display straight, because one located without reencounter. **P. Q.** the give off for contrary.

Of the eye that to see the folds of cloths which circumference the men's. CAP. CCCLXIII. (363)

The shadows interposed below the folds of cloths encircle of bodies human, produce much more dark, how much it they are more reencounter to the eye with the concavity whereas such shadow are generate: and this interpret above mentioned, when the eye is situated below it part shady and it luminous of the predicted figure.

Of the folds of cloths. CAP. CCCLXIV. (364)

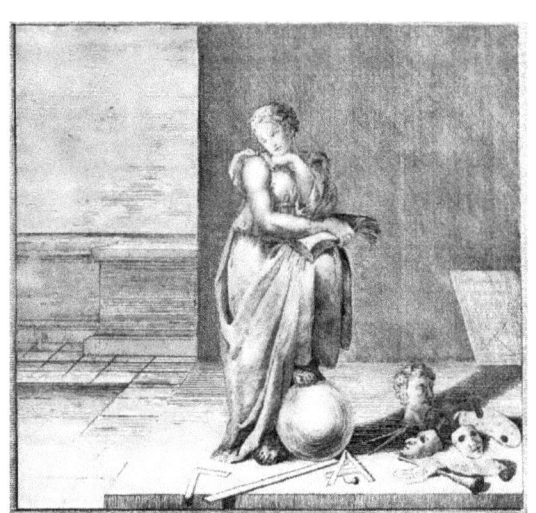

Always the folds of cloths situated into whatever act of the figures be obliged to with the his features display the action of such figure, into manner which not hand over ambiguity or confusion of the real attitude without who it consider: and which none crease with the shadow deduct no components, namely which pairs more without inside it profanity of the crease that it surface of the components dress. And that if you figure figures dressed of more cloths, which not pairs that the ultimate garment recluses behind without if the simplify bone of such figures, but the flesh together with those, and the cloth cloths of the flesh, with much thickness which one to the multiplication of his grade.

It folds of cloths which circumference the limbs must diminish of their thickness reverse the extremes of the things circumstance.

The length of the folds that they are narrower to the limbs must primp from that side which the limbs for his folds diminish, and cast from the opposites part of his bending. (Fig. 56.)

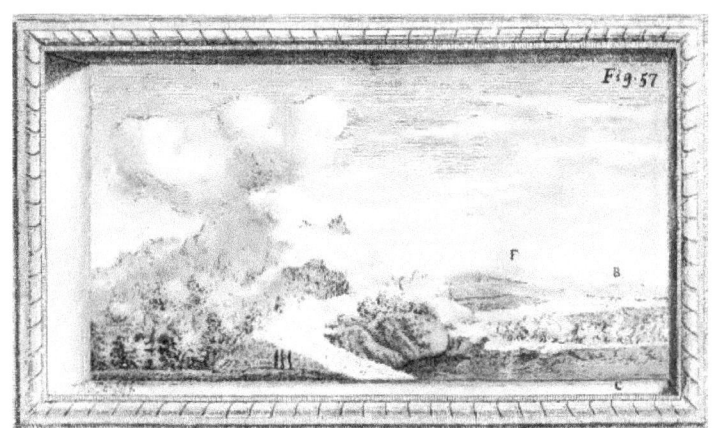

Of the horizon mirrored in the hence. CAP. CCCLXV. (365)

Spectator the horizon for it feast of these in the side seen from the horizon and from the eye, just like one demonstrates the horizon **F.** (Fig. 57.) seen from the side **B. C.** whom side is thus far seen from eye. Therefore you, painter, which have without figuration the invocation of the waters, recollect that from there not make seen the color of the water be highly bright or dark which one both the luminosity or rather obscurity of the site whereas you be, together mixed with complexion of the other things that they are beyond you.

IL FINE

Index
Of chapters this treaty

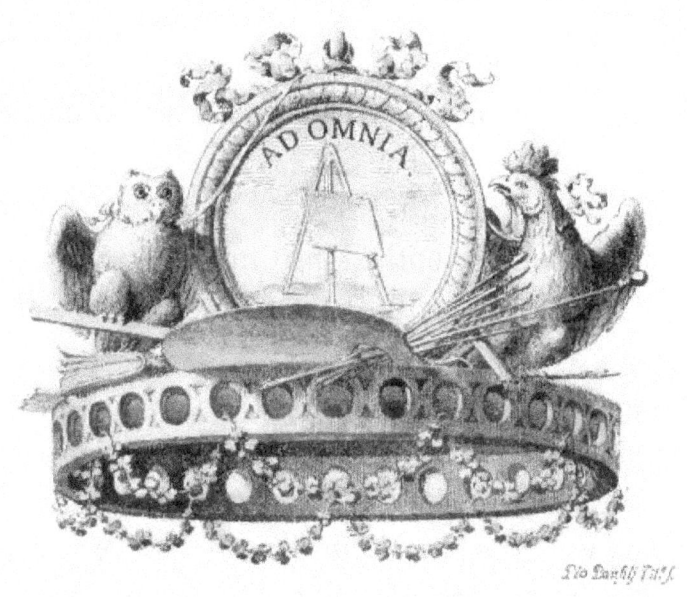

LEON

End

Leon Battista Alberti
Of painting
And
Of statue

To the many illustrious Sir my observant
The Sir
Carlo Errard
Painter of the king Christian
Much illustrious Sir

The dedication they are always conveniently employee, and converge principally without those that Professorship the same arts and science that neither books one teaches, because if esteem the proper virtues and reputation, strength is us combine also into merit the present which one ago without their: And be of strength be sufficient for resist at calumny of the envying, and at cavil of the ignorant, with the only characters of the their name preserve the works dedicated from each fascinating and venerate tongue. Motivated from this consideration, but many more from the desire that I have always possess of reveal with some action public the grand affection of the my servitude towards of V. S. the offer this person two treated from me revised, and almost resurrected, with additional the life of the their author Leon Batista Alberti, from she compelled worthy of accompany Lionardo da Vinci his villager even to the throne real of the virtuous Queen of Svetia (Sweden). Must rather the one and the other writer at care and exertion of V. S. which for make compare more pompous before without one great Princess, has desired with that number of rare ornaments that one seen embellish from head without feet. Await from she into other occasions things more hard and of major moment, because is for the profound and universal cognition of all the parts of the drawing, and for the abundance and wealth of the inventions, and for those his molts eloquence with whom one she expresses one perfectly the motions interior of the spirit, be able that to the his hand not you is object impossible. In the meantime the kiss one thousand times the hands.

Of V. S. many illustrious.

Affectional servantly
Rafaelle Trichet Du Fresne.

141

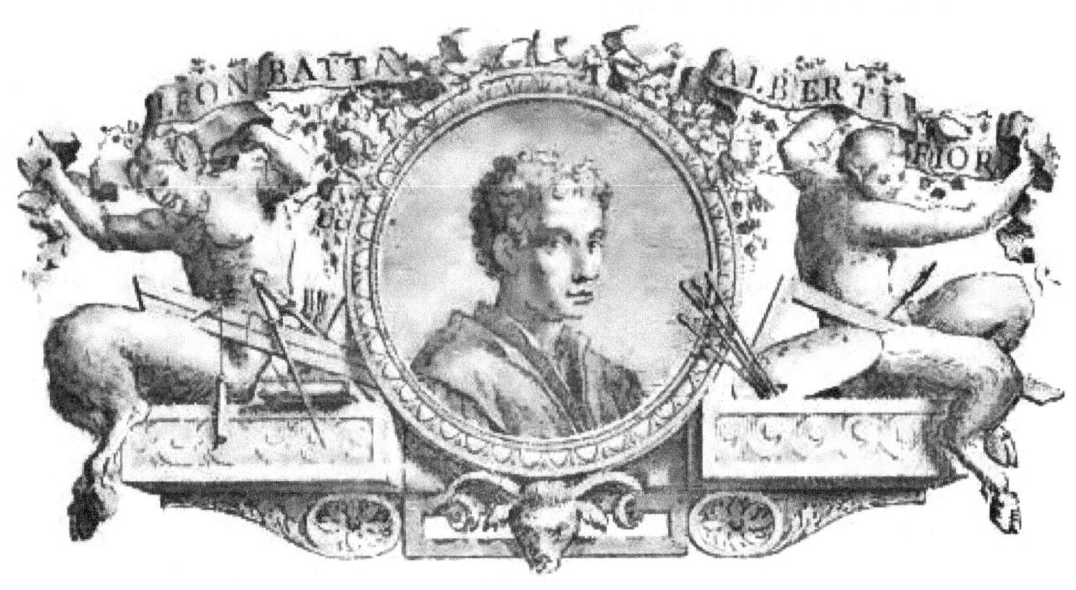

Life
Of Leon Battista Alberti
Described
From Rafaelle Du Fresne.

How much fuse ancient, noble and potential the family of the Alberti into Florence, of it make creed the history: and Scipione Ammirato, which for certain respects near remove the first name of Concini, not locate more nice and briskly invention, which of put into company with the Alberti, bestow one understanding origin to the one, and without the other dynasty. Without we suffice say that in the 1304. time by now of grand authorities into Florence, and that favored the faction of Bianchi, and the year 1384. in the sixth which one produce into Florence for the acquisition of Arezzo, the apparatus, and the fellatio of the Alberti take place of such magnificence, which seem more convenient without whatever great prince which without person private. Neither splendor of the republican one located that the Alberti they've own nine times the banner, which time the supreme grade into honor and into potential near which be able breathe the Florentine. However in the frequently abrupt, and motions of the things public not euphoric always the fortune favorable. The year 1387. Cipriano and Benedetto of him Alberti be intended shoo from homeland, and furthermore the year 1411. banish eventually for the child of that home. However in the 1428. departed raise the announcement, and given order which each one be able arrive, and be freely without Florence. The previously nominated Cipriano departed father of Alberto, of Lorenzo, and of Giovanni. Alberto Alberti late first canonical, and then the year 1437. Bishop of Camerino: and Eugenio father, which with much pump and demonstration of affection departed from Florence in the their city accept, having in the tempo which he you celebrate the council, fact proof of the virtues of that prelate, for sign of gratitude towards the his nationality, and for premium due to the his merits, the honor of the cardinalate. Lorenzo brother of Alberto leave more children, Bernardo, Carlo, and Leon Battista, them who rare quality extend ample matter of praise without this brief speech. With how much care, and with that discipline this person brethren fuse in the youth from the father raise, one regulation in the treaty which the same Leon Battista wrote of commodity, and inconvenience of the letters: whereas he recount that all the hours of they were into such manner without various them study distributed, which never remain idle. Be arrive at age more mature, beyond the study of the letters, Carlo embrace the care of negotiation domestics, but Leon Battista not keep account of other than of books, all over he gave to the culture of the intelligence, and make much profit in the sciences, which one leave ago how many with fame valiant men lived to the his time.

The first sage that he hand over of the vivaciousness, and acuteness of the his genius late in the deceive with one scholarly, and ingenious prank, and with more success that not make then the Sigonio, the judgment of scholar of the his times: because obtain in age of twenty age to the study of Bologna, composed of hidden one fable call *Philodoxios*, below first name of Lepido (witty) comic, whom then, almost arrive of new, and extract from old man manuscript, there public for ancient. And truly Alberti imitate into that with felicity prioress lettering of the comic Latin, which be attain in the hands of Aldo Manucci, whom departed from everybody compelled for comparison of the real and more pure Latin, he it do print into Lucca the year 1588. dedicating to Ascanio Persio, personality still he of profound erudition, just like if accommodate state work of writer ancient. Lepidam Lepidi (witty), *ancient poet, whoever that sum, tale to you myth, learnedly Past, who when at hand mine preempt, vanish unwilling: And antiquity reason babendam (chaos) be I consider. Multitude are there observation appropriate, here to you, together old age skilled inquiring, not displeased, to me certainly compose I appease,* However that the Alberti have composed these fairy tale in the twentieth years of the age, he same them has would desired in the prologue: *Not indeed desire, not make for into praise to draw, until thusly twentieth years my lifetime, this impetus writing story. Truth expect thenceforth have near you hither persuasion, not vacant me evidently, not exuding neglect mine arrive years.* Possess therefore Alberti into that age experiment the his strength, not you departed science which he with the study not one acquire, not abandon pass through no day without read or compose a few thing, same as he own affirm: and he had the intelligence thus easy, which seem equally born to each strong of disciplines: of it one ago if fuse better speaker or poet, if more excellent writer Latin or Tuscan, if more matter in the sciences practices or speculative, and if with more gravitates reason of things reveal, or with more loveliness and urbanity of the ordinary, and low.

Itself regulation that one moment Lorenzo of Medical, true Patron of his century, for pass through with even ailment the more great searing of summer, do in the forest of Camaldoli one assemble of characters illustrious into each strong of literature, between which Marsilio Ficino, Donato Acciaioli, Leon Battista Alberti, Alamanno Rinuccino, and Cristosoro Landiono be the principal. What fuse the conversation of himself scholarly person each one if it more imagine. However more of nothing other one do admire the Ablerti, whom with speeches reveal, and full of sublime doctrine do see without full which in the (Eneide) Aeneid below it peel of various, and vague appearance, one conceal the more other secrets of the philosophy, and which Virgilio era one true, and real philosopher, but dress fantastically and from poet. Thus facing reasoning make such impression in the soul of the listening, Cristosoro Landino (which into that occasion direct be the administrator of the assembly) the register all into a book, and of it form then those work that one see printed into language Latin below name of Questioni (Argue) Camaldolensi: in the which direction the end thus writes the Landino: *These are which of many that has a long life excellent basis, that person Leo Baptista Albertus memory, clarify and copiously, into size man sitting debate, remember desire.*

Abandon the Alberti many beautiful composition into Latin and into Tuscan, of which one to see here of below a copious index. Between the work Latin is worthy of eternal praise, and one it can compare with all the antiquities, that which is entitled the Momo (Motion), whom for his excellence, in the same year 1520. late print two times in Rome. And truly into that with extraordinary vagueness, and not ponder artifice, jest, laughter, mock, one explain in four book those things, which the other with manners serious, and stern wrote of the philosophy moral, be however he principally proposed of touch those that without form a perfect, and optimum principal one expect, and learn the customs of those proceed around. Bella still the operetta calling Trivia, or rather of the causes attention to the senators, and that which he entitle (*De iure*) Of drunk, namely of the administers the justness, of which not be able for what cause Cosimo Bartoli, which trope into language Italian, and do print into a volume a lot of booklet of Leon Battista Alberti, of them have fact the fifth and sixth books the Momo (Motion), or rather the Principal. Writes a booklet of fables, in which one says that in the oddness of the concepts have obsoleted (Esopo) Aesop. Compose so far a treaty of the life and customs of his dearest, and another over it there vice, potential with artificial manner goof off of things relevant, and serious, and philosophize of the beneath, and abject (despicable). In the language Italian has quit three of Economy, and any matter lovey into prose and into verses, and departed the first (such as writes Giorgio Vasari in his life) that tempt of reduce the versification vulgar to the measure of the Latin, such as one sees into that his epistle.

This in order to extreme miserable dimwit convey
Without you that disdain miserably we, etc.

But in the reflect of the singular genius of the Alberti in each general of polite letters, and of the place that he hold between men writers, me feel tight from people of other profession, namely from painters, and architects, which same as him pretend, and showing how much he has actions into painting and architecture, me call behind, and almost that him have without scribe the virtues of a other Alberti, to me conveyance of do passage from the sciences speculative to the arts practices, and mechanism. And truly departed concern the capacity and vastness of intelligence of the our Alberti, which cannot only with general information all the disciplines embrace, but descend once again to the particular of each, and applying without whatever thing, do believe without the human, which never to other not own the his nobility intellect employed, draw on the contrary advance those which into similar profession one esteem the improve. Exist in his tempo absolutely put out the study of the architecture, or if in order to some cognation if of it gain, being much corrupt, and distant from the politeness and nobility of the ancient century Roman, which in the operate productivity effect rough. Leon Battista Alberti departed the first that attempt of reduce those art to his before purity, and shoo the barbarity of centuries Gothic introduce into that the order, and the proportion, one which from all departed universally call the Vitruvius Florence. There fame of his name induced Nicolò V. Pontiff without mean of him in the order many manufacture into Rome, and without confide much more neither his counsel, how much that from Biondo Forlivese character of high merit, and his familiar departed particularly informed of his rare quality.

Do for Sigismondo Pandolso Malatsta Sir of Rimino the drawing of the Chiesa Church of Saint. Francesco, whom one principle the year 1447, and turn out one of the more superb, and sumptuous of Italy. Departed conduct to the term that today one sees, the year 1550. And because the Vasari, into occasions of minor moment very long-winded, in the description of this temple one is shown much scarce of words, although for stay which he make into Rimino (rhyme), whereas paint the S. Francesco that one see in the it greater of according factory, have be able observe minutely all the parts, we for substitute into part to the his negligence, and for honored much more the memory of architect, write those in the censor more direct it is seem worthy of be observed. And commence from the façade, affirm that one see a lovely plinth, all of marble of cloud, whom speed of surrounding without all the fabricate, and have for framer a beautiful ornament of foliage and weaponry Pandolfeschi, hinder together with vague invention. Over of it increase four columns stick of order composite, and of means relief. The three interspace they are occupied from three niches, of which that of means ago it port major, which it goes inside rather with a lovely foliage: follow then the architrave, the unrefined, and the cornice, above of the which, of impetus to the port you move with the same order two pillars with one niche into middle, whom if fuse state type, possess in receipt of for allocate light to the nave of means, and for position it statue of the Sir. In the flank of the temple of beyond, with proud and noble invention one to see seven arches grands, and below of them as much sepulchers, matters without parlay for serve of deposits of men illustrious Riminesi (Rimini). It part inner of it fabricate not surrender point to the exterior of it into grandness of drawing, of it into delicacy of ornament, whom, although coordinate one not sure that of Gothic, whether one consider it roughness of that century, not they are nevertheless without praise. The marbles of diverse strength, thus inside just like of outside, they are exist with profusion worshipped, and one jurisprudence in the life of Sigismondo, which he pass through with the his folks vicinity to Ravenna, of them spare with that occasion the churches ancient of Saint Severo, and of Clalsi, remove the incrustations, and conducting to Rimino all that which more the seemed without purpose for compare it his work, without such point which from Pio second late deserve blamed, and call profane. Into one of the hair (uncountable), which they are six, one see the sepulture very beautiful and rich of (Sigismondo) Sigismund, and of lsotta his wife, and above one (just like writes the Vasari) and the portrait of it Sir, and into other part of the same work that one of Leon Battista.

The year 1551. Lodovico Gonzaga marquis of Mantova, whom era devoutly affectingly to the Annunciata of Florence, for a vote influence from his consort, to cause of a birth fitting, make manufacture, with the drawing of Leon Battista, the chorale, or true tribune, which of present one see into that church, with the weaponry surrounding of the family Gonzaga: whom one just like ago faith of the magnificence of that sir, thus exhibition the value of the architect, which with manner whimsical, and much difficult order those building without guise of a temple round with nine chapel of surrounding. And because you they are certain thing that not respond to the eye with all that grace that one request again, seem for the outline of fabrication that the arches of the chapel, when one watch for profile, fall into behind, resend the reader without how much of it scribes the Vasari.

146

The same marquis want in the precisely city reconstruct from the foundation the church of Saint. Andrea, venerable for the blood of Christ, which you one conserve, the year 1472. name to if the Alberti, and significance the thought which he have of illustrate Mantova with a noble, and arbitrary temple, the make do the model of the new temple that these days one to see: Whom is all over of earth baked into form of Croce, with one time single which form it part lower of that, superimpose to the body major of the church, long arms 104. , and wide arms 40. , without chain any of iron, or wood that the support, and is all of work composite, with three chapel grands for part, and as many stalk. In the arms of the cross you they are two chapel for each opposite the one additive another. The means then of the square, whereas one must manufactured it dome, is wide arms near without forty. Other the square of the dome you is the chorale of form oval, long arm 52. , and wide how much is the body of the church, whom with the aforesaid square ago the year of the Savior 1600. supplied until to the ultimate consciously, conformity to the model ancient of the Alberti. The façade is compatriot into three port, there major of what which is in the means, is ornamented of marbles whites, with foliage beautiful diligently carved, and the doors from the sides they are of marble ashen, work also them. He who want to see each thing more particularly described read Donesmondi in the book sixth of the history ecclesiastical of Mantova, from which contain extract how much one is mentioned of above. Mario Equicola in the history Mantovana there insignia that the same Alberti in the same city offer principle to the church of Saint. Sebastiano. He had for assistant, and faithful executor of his drawings without Mantova a Luca Florence, whom produce already work for him to Florence in the fabricant of the chorale of the Annunciata.

However if Roma, Rimino, and Mantova be obliged to much to the industry of Leon Battista, not less one sense obligated him his homeland to his virtues, possess he extremely contributed without it her beauty. Departed ordination into Florence with his drawing the façade of the church of Saint. Maria short story, and with vague blending of marbles blacks, and whites artificially ornamented, and corresponding to the grandness of all the body of the building. Without Cosimo Rucellai he gave the drawing of the place which he make do in the street that one called La vigna (The vineyard), and in the church of Saint. Brancacio himself to see one (uncountable) hair of his invention. Produce he a lot of other things, which for brevity one neglect. Abandon few works of painting Paolo Giovio, which composed his praise, and the hand out place between the illustrious writers, praise the portrait which he made of whether same: Whom in time that Vasari scribed, one locate into home of Palla Rucellai, with other Paintings of the same Alberti.

One to see therefore from how much obtain written of above, which for the study about the letter, and for the cognition of the drawing, Leon Batista Alberti himself more with optimum reason register between the men famous of one, and other profession. On the contrary for marry further strictly together, direct that the speeches of the one serve at illustrator the operation of the other, be converse those arts that for the past tense they were remain almost silent, abandon the precepts with lovely style scribing into Latin. The sculpture departed it first of which one he undertake of debate, writing into language Latin a booklet entitled of the Statue. Scribing latter in the same language three books of the Painting, from all the intentions supremely extol, one for the lettering noble, and unequivocal, as though also for the importance of precepts. In the first one explain the principles of the arts, traits from it geometry. The second contains the true rules, from whom not must never depart the painter, so much in the composition, how much in drawing, and coloration, which they are the three things at which one reduce all the consideration, which do one be able in the Painting. In the third book one reasons of officiate of the painting, and of the end which he must proponent in the paint.

The ultimate work of Leon Batista Alberti, and it more deem of all, be state with more study, and diligence worked, is the book which he scribes of the architecture, in which with exquisite order, and facilitates grand, one unearth all the secreted of those art, which before in the obscure writings of Vitruvius they were withdraw from others: of it one public if not afterwards the his death from Bernardo his brother, which it dedicate to Lorenzo of Medici (doctors), same as have destined of do the same author. Departed turn into language Italian, and illustrated of drawings from Cosimo Bartoli gent man Florentine, which the present without Cosimo about Doctors the year 1550. The same Bartoli translate still the book of the Painting, and Sculpturing, and the do prints the year 1568. with the other booklet of Alberti. One locate already another version of the treaty of the Painting, sort of the Domenichi, and printed the year 1547.

Afterwards contain for the accompanying of these volume with langue without we foreigner reasonable of the virtue of Leon Batista, and delighted the fruits of his fertile intelligence, other not it remains without say, if not which desire for the merit of one great men, and thus far more for the useful public, and for the glory of the letters, which one recount a of all the his works together: and these of it put at this point of below the list. Pass away Alberti into Florence his homeland, and departed buried in the church of holy Cross.

LIFE
INDEX
Of the work of Leon Battista Alberti
Work printed.

LEonis Baptiste Alberti Florence Momus. Rome former shrine Iacobi Mazochii
1520. 4. , & into folio (large book of large size paper) the agreement year with this title:
Leo Baptista of Albertis Florence of Prince. Rome among Stephanum Guileretum.

Leonis Baptiste Alberti Florence Trivia, or of causes senator, into Ciceronis place
book. 2 about workshop, short and accurate interpretation, to Laurence Medicem. Basel
1538. 4. with Petri Ioannis Olivarii scholar into fantasy Ciceronis.

About picture provide & never enough praised arts book three absolute Leonis
Baptiste about Akbertis, Basileae 1540. 8. , & ultimate the year 1649. into Leida with
Vitruvius.

Leonis Baptista Alberti man expert about horse animating to Leonellum
Ferrariensem formost leaflet, Michaelis Martini Stelle care and study discovered, &
now finally into light edits. Basileae 1556. 8.

Leonis Baptista Alberti Florence man clarify book about ruler edificatory. Paris
1512, & into other places.

Lepidi comic old Philodoxios fable, from antiquity cast to Aldo Manucio. Lucae
1588. 8.

Baptist about Albertis poet crowned about love free best. Begin. Among officiate of
pity, and of humanity 1471. 4.

Baptist about Albertis poet crowned work preclarum (pre-clear) into love remedy
happily begin. Legitimately lover & recognizing. 1471. 4.

Dialogue of Messer Leonbatista Aberti Florence, about republic, of life civil, about
life rustic, about fortune. Begin. To see I Microtiro (small trick) my, run for to grasp, or
part of spirit my. *In Vinegia* 1543. 8.

Work of the Alberti not my printed

About drunk tract. Begin. Although without attire unquestionable writings.
Translate Dal Bartoli with the title. Of administer it reason.

About comities, & inconvenient handwriting to Carolum brother. Begins.
Laurentius Albertus parent. One regulation however in the library of Gesnero, which
this treaty both state printed in Italian, but when and whereas, not him declares.

Life Sancti Potiti martyis.

Transaction Cisera inscribed

Transaction Mathematics addressed.

Leaflet statue epithet.

About Musca (fly)

Oration funeral for brute his. Begin. Sum into arrears amongst.

Libel Apology. All of them translated, and printed from Bartoli.

Chorographical city Rome antique. Of it since mention Pocciantio in the catalog about writers Florence, same as also of the following.

People Ship inscribed. The mentions the Gesnero.

Three Books of economic. Scribes Filippo Valoni (Philip Valoni) which one conservation manuscripts inyo house his. The Pocciantio of it ago mention.

Varies works of Leon Basttista Alberti translated into language Italian.

The architecture of Leon Battista Alberti translated into languge Florance from Cosimo Bartoli gentlemen & academic, with it addition about drawings. Into (Firenze) Florence 1550. fol. & into Venetia 1565. 4, . and the same year in the mountain Royal. fol. with it painting of the same Alberti translated for M. Ludovico Domenichi.

The painting of Leon Battista Alberti translated to M Ludovico Domenichi. IN Vinegia 1547. 8.

Booklet Morals of Leon Battista Alberti gentlemen Florence, translated and part correct from M. Cosimo Bartoli. Into Venetia 1568. 4.

Follow it list of said booklets.

Motion (Momo) or rather the principal.

About speeches from Senators, otherwise Trivia.

Of administer it reason.

Of commodities, and the inconvenience of letters to Carlo his brother.

The life of Saint. Potito.

The Cisra.

The pleasantness Mathematics.

Of republic, of live civil and rustic, and of fortune. Believe which this treaty both state Tuscan written from Alberti, and have noticed above.

Of statue.

Of painting.

Of fly (inquisitive people).

The brute (dog).

Hundred Apologia

Hecatopbila. (Computations.)

Deiphira. (Economic.)

These two ultimate works not they are state translated from Bartoli, however the same that those of above one they are imply below the title: about love, & remedy love, written into language Tuscany from Alberti.

Of
Painting
By
Leon Batista Alberti
Books III.

Painting

By

Leon Batista Alberti

Book I.

Having self to scribe of the Paint into this person briefest commentaries, accommodate the speck mine both more clearly, take first place from Mathematicians those things that to me seem without say to proposition. Whom interpret that one do, declare (for how much to me serve the intelligence) from them principles of the nature, which object be the Painting. However into all my reasoning desire that one assembly, which ego speak of these things not as much as Mathematical, but as though Painter. Concise that the Mathematicians with the intelligence only consider the spices and the forms of the object, separate from what one desire material. But because ego desire that there object it originate parlay before to the eye, I serve writing, just like one uses say, of one most abundant treasure trove: and truly I seem have fact to suffice, if the Painters in the decipher, understand into some manner this material effectively difficult, and of whom for how much self-have seen, not is state not any that for still of it have written. Ogle therefore of grace that this person my writings is it interpreted, not same as from pure Mathematical, but from Painter. Pertinent be necessary first place be able that the point is a sign (for mode of say) which not one it can divide into parts. Point; Sign name him into this place, what one desire object that both so much into one surface, which she one can comprehend from the eye. However which those object that not they are comperes from the eye, not is no that not confess that you not have nothing that do with Painter. Concise with the painter one weary of imitate only those things, which by means of it light one pass through to see. This person points whether continuously for the order one lay the one near to of the remaining, elongate one line. And the line near than we make a gesture, the length of the which one be able divide into parts, but do so much thin that never not one can send: and certainly the example. ---- Of the lines no is direct, no is pie: the line straight is a sign tight without rectitude for the long from a point to another; the bend without rectitude for it place from a point to a other; the bend is that which do drag not without rectitude from a point to a other, but make arc ⌣. Many line, same as wire into canvas, if adapted one conjoin together, make one surface. Concise what the surface is that extreme part of the body that itself considers not inasmuch without profoundness no, but only inasmuch to the width and to the length, which they are the precisely quality its. Of the quality of it they are any so much intrinsic in the surface, which if it not come of the all altered, not can into mode not any of it move of it separate from she. And any other quality are so make, which maintain the same face about the surface, fall so much below the view, which the surface seem without those who that the regards, altered. The quality never-ending of the surface are two. One is certainly that which it come into cognition through those extreme circuit from what is sluice the surface: whom circuit any call Horizon: We, if it is lawful, for via of one certain similitude the call with vocabulary Latin *mouths*, or if more it liking, the about around. And do this about around terminate or from one single, or from more lines. From one single; just like is the circular: from more; just like from one bend and from one straight, or true thus far from more lines straight, or from more twisted. The linear circular is that which embraces, and contains in whether all the sweep of the circle. And the circle is one form of the surface, which is surround from one line without guise (appearance) of crown. Into Middle of whom if you do a point, all of them the rays that for length one originate from this point, and end up to the crown or circumference to straight, do between their equal Table. 1. Fig. 1. And this same point one calls the center of the circle. The line straight that incise two times the circumference, and become for the

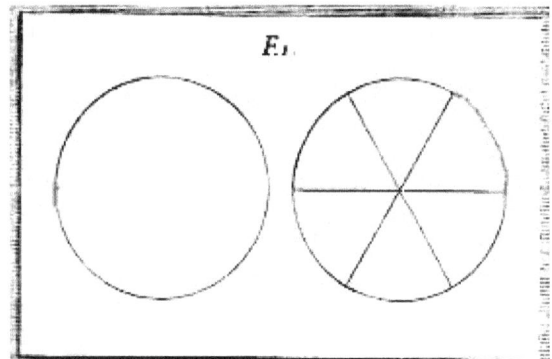

center, one call near to the Mathematical the diameter of the circle. We dub this same centrist. And false into this place persuaded that which say the Mathematical, which none line that cuts the circumference, not more, into she circumference, make angles equal, if none that which touches the center. However return at surface. Arduous from those things that I have saying of above, one it can interpret easily, just like mutated the pull of the final lines, or rather of about roundabout of one surface, she surface lose it fact the name and the face his premier, and which that maybe one dud triangular, one call time quadrangular, or maybe of more angles. Convene mutated the about round each time that the line, or the angle one make not only more, but more obtuse or more long, or more acute or more brief. This place of it advise that one tell me something of the angles. And really the angle that which one ago from two lines which one intersection together, above the extremities of one surface. Three they are the strength of the angle, without square ruler, below square ruler, and above square ruler Fig. 2. The angle to

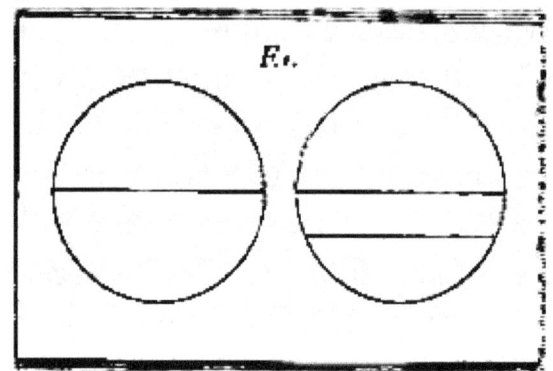

square ruler, or to want say rectum, is one of those four angle, which one ago from two lines straight which reciprocally one intersection together insomuch that he both equal to whatever one both of the other three that remain: And from this happen that him say, which all the angles right they are between them equal. Angles above square ruler is those, which is major of the without square ruler. Acute, or below square ruler is those, which is minor of the without square ruler. Return of new to the surface. We said into that mode, mediate an about around, one imprinted in the surface one quality. Remain without speak of other quality of the surface, whom one is (for say thus) almost same as one pelt expanse above all the face of the surface. And this one divide into three. Inasmuch no they are plain and uniform, other they are spherical and inflated, other they are sunken and concave. Adjoin without these for the fourth those surface, which of the said one compose. Of these negotiate of afterwards: express time of the first. The surface plain is those, above whom stake a rule, touches equally for all each part of them. Much akin without this do the surface of one finest water which be conscription. The surface spherical mimics the about around of one sphere. The sphere say that is a body round, unstable for each direction, in the means of which is a point, from which all the last parts of it body they are equally distant. The surface concave is that which

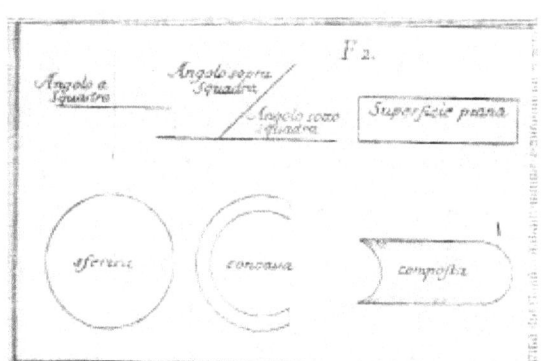

from the side of inside has it his extremity, which is below, for say thus, to the skin of the sphere, same as they are the intimate surface of inside of it shell of it you want. However the surface compose is that, which has one part of whether same plain, and the other or concave, or around, same as they are the surface of inside of the reed, or the surface of outside of the columns, or of the pyramids (Table. 1. Fig 2.). For so much, the quality which one locate be or in circuit, or in the make of the surface, have imposed diverse names, just like one affirm, to the surface. But the quality, whom without alters the surface, variants them linger, they are on average two. Inasmuch mutated the place or the light, eye-catching varied to those who that the look out. Indicate of the place before, and then of light. And be essential certainly first consider into what mode, mutated the place, they quality of which are in the surface, no pairs which it mutation. These object truly one expect to the strength and virtues about the eyes. Inasmuch he is of necessity

155

that the about around or for move away or rather change of place, there no pairs or minor or major or dissimilar to the all of that which before here appear. Or same that the surface there no pairs or rather accurate, or defrauded of complexion. Whom things all are that which we will measure or discourse with the square ruler: and same as this square ruler or view one face, move time investigate. And commence from the sentence of Philosophers, which say that the surface one examine through certain rays ministers of the view, which therefore the convene visual, namely that for them one imprint the imagery about the object in the sense. Inasmuch these same rays between the eyes and the surface view, intent for their own nature, and for one certain admirable thinness their contribute splendidly penetrating the air, and other similar bodies rare or diaphanous, and having for steering the light refined without much that one compare into some body dense, and not of the all obscure; in what place fair of point, right away one stop. But not late near to of the ancient small dispute, if these rays be drawn from the eye, or from the surface. It which dispute into true many difficulties, and how

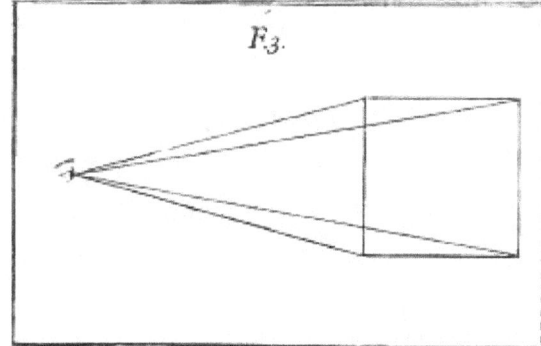

much to we not necessary, the abandon from part. And fatigue licit imagine that these rays is it about that thinness line fasten from a head vertical, just like factor a bundle, and that you is it received for entrance the eye it whereas one form or creates the view; and there grasp not otherwise that a truncated of rays: and from which place be drawn without

of long the weary rays, just like vertical direction, flow to the surface that is there to reencounter: But below this person rays is no difference, whom is well that one can, inasmuch us are different and of strength and of officiate: Consider what any of their touching the about around of the surface, comprehend all the quantity of the surface. And these, because us proceed fly and to penalty touch upon the extreme parts about the surface, the call rays extremes or last. Aversely that this surface one display into face because one position view the four rays last that function to point, from which she

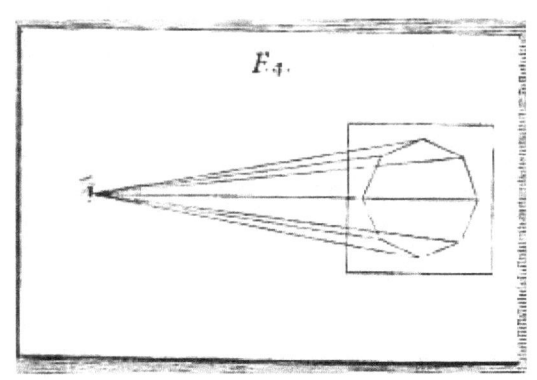

is terminate. (Table. I Fig. 3.) Other rays or be drawn from all the face of the surface, make even they the obligation them, entree for that pyramid, of whom to his place speak little of below. Inasmuch he one fill in about same colors and light; of which glimmer it surface. And yet call these, rays of means, or procurer (panderer) (Table. I. Fig. 4.) All the picture is one single

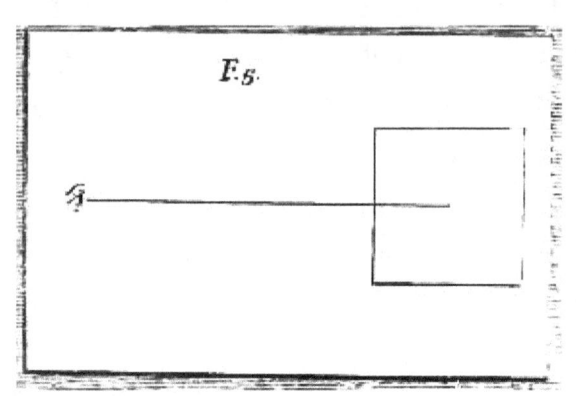

F.5.

surface; but obtain to paint inside one octagon, one display the rays which one call pimps (procurer), which go from the eye to points of the compartment of the octagon. About rays yet whether of it locate one so do which to similitude of that line centric which we enunciate, one she can call out radius centric or the of center, therefore that he be of manner in the surface that cause from each band around to if angles equal (Table I. Fig. 5.) One that we contain find the rays be of three strength, the last, the pimps and centric: function time investigate that which, certain both the one of these robust of rays, bestow to the view: And the first object speak about the last, of furthermore talk about pimps, and lastly about centric. With the last rays one comprehends the quantity, and the quantity is really that space which is below duet points disjoint of the about around, which passes for it surface, whom space and included from the eye with these ones last rays, almost same as for manner of say with the sixth: and they are many quantity into one surface, how many they are the points separated into a about around which one concern it one the other. Inasmuch we with it panorama our acknowledgement it length through it her height or lowness: the width through from right, or from left: the thickness through from near or from faraway: or genuine all the other measures still, whatever she one is it, comprehend solely with this person rays last. The hence one as they say affirm that it view one ago through a triangle, it base of which one is it quantity viewed, and the side of which they are those same rays that exit from the points of it quantity and come

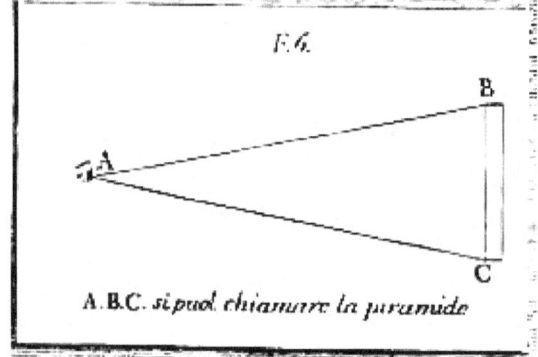

F.6.

A.B.C. si puol chiamare la piramide

refine to the eye. And is this certain that not one sees quantity any, if not through this one triangle. The side therefore of the triangle visual they are manifest. However the angles into this one same triangle are duo, namely modify those heads from it quantity. However the third, and principle angle, is that which to reencounter about it base one ago neither the eye. (Table. I. Fig 6.) Of it into this place one has to dispute if it view one stillness, just like him say, into it splice of the nerve interior, or if too one appear the images into it surface of the eye almost same as into one mirror animated. But not one must into this place recount all him officiate about the eye how much to the see. Concise what make to sufficient put into these commentaries briefly those object that us will seem necessary. Consisting therefore the principal angle visual in the eye him whether of it is glean this rule, namely that how much the angle make in the eye, more acute, so much us seem minor it quantity view. The hence one sees manifest, for why cause take place that from a long interval, seem that it quantity view one wear thin, almost which it arrive at a point. But thus far that the object is it into this manner, future nevertheless into any surface, which amounts more one approach their the eye of who the regards, so much the pairs minor: And quantity more the eye one move away from them, so much more by major that part of the surface: the which one see manifest in the surface spherical. The quantity therefore through the interval no pairs any time or major or minor to who them regards. Of whom thing who can okay the reason, not doubt point, which the ray's pimps any time become the last, and the last, mutated the interval, become pimps. And therefore is it from be able that when the rays go-between (pimps) do become last, right away the quantity him seem minor: And for the contrary when the rays last one reconcile entrance to the about around; how much more him do far from the about around, so much appear it quantity major. At this point therefore sheet self to my well-disposed home entrust with one rule, which how many more rays we occupy with the view, so much have to ponder that both major the quantity view, and how many of it engage needless, so much minor. Ultimate this person rays last embracing by part to part universally all about around of one surface, turn to around by around almost same as one pit, all it surface. The hence us say that the view one ago through one pyramid of rays. Be essential therefore say that thing both it pyramid. The pyramid is one figure of body long, from the base about whom all the lines straight draw to into departed ending into one point. The base of the pyramid is the surface viewed, the sides about the pyramid they are them rays visual, which we dub the last. The point of the pyramid one conscription that place entre to the eye, wherein the angles of the quantity one conjoin together. And this be sufficient of rays last, of which one ago the pyramid, through whom one see for each reason, which he import greatly which and hundred intervals ever between the eye and the surface. Reflex to treat of rays pimps. They are the rays pimps that multitude of rays, whom to surround from rays last one located be inside to the pyramid. And these rays do that, which one says ago the Chameleon, and similar fair dismayed for fright, which sole take hold the colors of the object more vicinity to their, for not be found from Cacciatori. This is that which do the rays pimps. Inasmuch from the truncation their about the surface even to the point of the pyramid, expedient for all this segment the variety of colors and of light, whether of it stain so much, which into whatever place that you the cut, protrude of their into that same place that light same, and that same complexion;, of that one they are immerse. And these rays' pimps for the fact same stand out one is seen that for long interval be missing, and provoke the sight more weary; lastly then one is locate the reason why this happen. Concise which this person remain, and all the other rays visual, be lined and weigh on of light and of colors, pierce for the air, and the air be thus far she lined of some thickness, happen that for the much part of the mass, while that they flow for the air, is it draw same as to tire out to the into downward. And however say okay, which how much the distance is major, so much the surface seem more darken and more obfuscate. Remain to debate of the ray centric. We call ray centric those, which only injure the quantity of manner, which the angle equal from fine the part respond to the angle that are theirs to chant: and really for how much one be part of to this ray centric, is thing direction that this of all the rays is the more proud, and of all lively. Of it one it can deny that none quantity appear never to the view major, if none when the ray centric do into it. Potrebbonsi recount more thing of the power and of officiate of the ray centric.

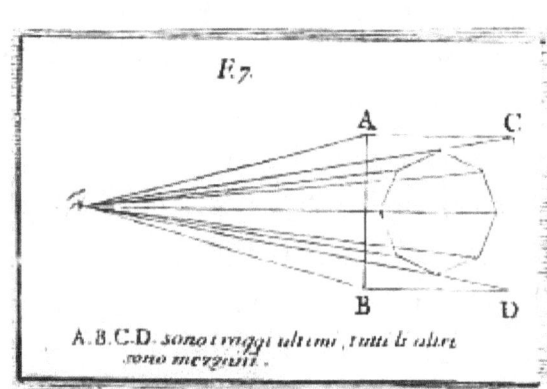

A.B.C.D. sono i maggi ultimi, tutti li altri sono mezzani.

However this single thing not one leave behind, which this ray only is agitator from all the other rays that if it they've placed into middle, almost that coordinate sort one certain united congregation for facilitate, so much that one he can without reason call the chief and the principle of rays. Leaves into behind the other thing that seem more pragmatic apparent to the display of the intelligence, which appropriate without those thing that we will we have orderly of say: many object still one indicate of rays more comfortably to places them. The ray's pimps of the octagon one can call one pyramid of eight faces inside to one pyramid of four faces. (Table I. Fig. 7.) And suffice into this one place have recount those thing for how much entail the brief of commentaries, for the which not is not any that doubt, which the object be into this mode; the which self-creed one both display to substance, namely that mutation of interval and mutated the positions of the ray centric, forthwith appears that the surface one both altered. Inasmuch it appear that is minor, or major, or mutated second the order contain below of theirs the lines, or the angles. Therefore posture of the ray centric, and the distance bestow greatly to the real certainty of the view. Here thus far one other certain third thing, through whom the surface appear without who the flyleaf (blank page inside a book cover), distorted and various. And this is the recipient of light. Inasmuch him one it can see in the surface spherical and in the concave, which if him you make a light solely, the surface from one part appear rather obscure, and from the other part more clear. And from the same interval first, and remain conscription the positive of the ray centric first, pure that it surface come exposed to a light diverse from the first, you see

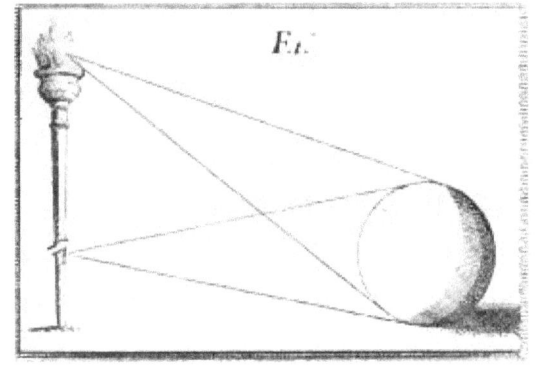

which that parts of the surface that to the first light appearance clear, time mutation the light appear drastic cut, and the obscure appear clear. And beyond to this if you do more light nearby, appear into thus make surface diverse obscurity, and diverse clarities, and various second the quantity and the strength of light. This thing one proof with the experience. (Table II. Fig I. and 2.) However this place of it warned, which one be obliged say no things of light, and of colors. Which the colors one various, through the light, is thing manifests; concise that what one desire complexion not appears in the shadow to the aspect ours, like that which one he appears when he is place to rays of light. Inasmuch the shadow exhibition

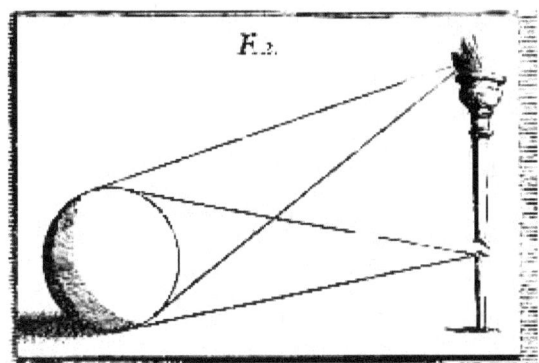

the complexion obscured, and the light the ago clear and open. Indicate the Philosophers, which not one he can see thing not any, if she not is dressed of light, and of complexion, and however is one grand relationship below the colors and the light, to do the view; whom how much both grand one to see from these, which be missing the light, they colors thus far deviant of little by little obscure be missing still them, and revert the span or the lamp, revert thus far together with those the colors to the view ours through the virtue of light. Whom thing be thus, make good the first object debate of colors, and afterwards go investigating into which manner the said colors one varies through the light. Abandon from part that dispute Philosophical, through whom one proceed investigating the birth and the first origin about colors. Inasmuch that important to the Painter the have smarty, into which mode the complexion one generate from the mixing of the rare and of the dense, or from that of the hot, and of the dry, or from that of the cold and of the wet? Of it disregard ego however those who which philosophizing dispute of colors into such manner, which they affirmation that the species of colors they are seven, namely, which the white and the black they are the duet extremes below the what you neither is one in the means, and that below each of this person duet extremes, and that of the means, from each part you of it they are duet other: and why the one of these duet one combine more to the limit than the other, the position into mode that seem which there doubt of the place whereas lay. To the Depicted (Painted) is to be sufficiently the know how such as altar the colors, and into that mode us one combine to serve of them in the Painting. The not desire be recoup from those that more do, whom whereas continue the Philosophers, say that in the nature of the thing not one locate if not duet real colors namely the white and the black, and which all the other mask from the mixing of these. The truly just like Depicters her intend into this manner how much to colors that for the blend of colors mask other colors, almost infinite. But nearby to Painters four they are the real generate of colors, just like are four thus far the elements, from whom one extract many and many species. Therefore which he is that because parity of fire, for say so, namely the red: and then that from the air that one calls blue (azure): that from it water is the green: and that from it ground has the (grey/ish) = cener/ognolo. All the other colors we see that are matters of combine, not otherwise that us believe that both the Diaspora and the Porphyry. They are therefore the cause of colors four, from whom through the mixing of the white and of the black one generate countless species. Concise that we see the leafy branch green lose so much of it their greenness of little into little fine to that it become white. The same see thus far in the air very own, whom sometimes clinch it quality of some vapor white towards the horizon, revert in pluck by little upon little the its own complexion. Other of this see even now this same in the rose, any of whom this time are light up of complexion, which imitate the crimson, other seem of the color about the cheeks of the young girl, and other seem white same as ivory. The color of the ground thus far through the mixture of the white and of the black has them its species. Not therefore the mixing of the white change the cause of colors, but generate, and create them species. And the same strength similar has thus far the color black. Inasmuch for the mixing of the black one generate many spices. The when remain much conveniently; therefore that it complexion through the shadow one alters, whereas first one see manifest: therefore swell the shadow, the clarity, and whiteness of the complexion left hand, and surge the light become more clear and more bright. And however one he can to sufficiently persuade to the Painter that the white and the black not they are real colors, but the alternator, for affirm thus, of colors. Concise which the Painter not has expedient object no more than the white, through whom he can express that one last candor of the light, of it object any with whom us can represent the obscurity of the darkness more which with the black. Increase to these things, which you not find never into no place the white or the black, which he same not fall below some generate of colors. Negotiate time of it strength about light. The light they are or of constellation, namely that is of the Sun, or of the Moon, and about the Star of Venus, or true of enlightenment materials and of fire: and below these is one grand difference. Inasmuch the light of the Sky (Heaven) render the shadows almost that equal to bodies; but the fire the render major that not they are the bodies, and the shadows one cause from the be intercepts the rays of light. The rays intercept, or him they are folded into other part, or he one redouble into them remain. Bend, just like when the rays of the Sun strike in the surface of the water, and afterward then climb into of it platforms, and each bending of rays one ago, just like affirm the Mathematicians, with angles between them equal. But these thing one belong to one other part of Painting. The rays which one fold, one immerse into some part of that color, which him locate into that surface from whom he they are folded or reverberated. And this watch we which originate, when the make of those who that hearth for the meadows, it one represent green. Art have treaty therefore of the surface: Art have treaty of rays: Art have treaty into that mode in the see one face of triangles the pyramid. Art I have proven how much greatly important that the interval, the positions of the ray centric, and the reception of light both determined and certain. But then that with a solely look we see not even if one surface single, however more surface to a section: and then that one is agreement and not indifferently of each surface from for if, time us remain to investigate, into that mode more surface conjoin together us one apprehension to the eye. Each surface certainly thrive particularly stuffed of his light and of his colors, one just like one is called, of it her own pyramid. And being the bodies covered from the surface, all the quantity of bodies that we will see, and all the surface, cause one pyramid single, full (for mode of say) of many pyramid minor, how many they are the surface that through that view are comprehended from flare of as says view. And being the thing so make, tell maybe someone, that has longing the Painter of so much consideration? Or that usefulness the will to the paint? This certainly one ago oblige that him know how that he is for having become one optimum master, each time that he know excellently the differences of the surface, and advise the them proportions, the which is state well-known from very little. Inasmuch whether him do request, which both that thing that he attempt that succeed them in the tinge that surface, be able respond very much better to each other thing, which be able say it reason of that which he one fatigue of make. For which self-pray that the scholars Painters me grasp to listen. Inasmuch art learn those thing that be of use, not departed ever incorrectly, from whatever both longing master. And acquire really while that us circumscribe with the lines one surface, and whereas that us chaperon of colors the designed and terminated places, which none thing one search more how much is that into this one solely surface us one represent more forms of surface. Not otherwise that if this surface that him chaperon of colors, fuse almost that of glass or of other object similar transparent, such that for it pass all the pyramid visual for see the real bodies, with interval determined and draft, and with conscription posture of the rays centric, and of light places into air faraway to them

162

places: and that this one both thus, the demonstrate the Painters, when he one recall into behind from it object what him paint to consider from faraway, that guided from the nature go looking for into this manner of the point of this very own pyramid. The hence one notice, which from that place consider and judge better all the object. However being this one solely surface or of table, or of wall, in the which the Painter one weary to want paint more and diverse surface and pyramid consist of from one pyramid solely, make of necessity that into not any of his places one cuts this pyramid visual, oblige into this place the Depicted and with the lines and with the painter can express the surroundings and the colors that the will the blending. Whom thing being thus, those who that regarding the surface painted, see a certain cutting of the pyramid. Will be therefore it painting the cutting of the pyramid visual second a determined space or interval, with it her center and with determine light, represented with lines and colors above one proposition surface. Time from that contain called that the Painting is a cutting of the pyramid, we congregate obtain to go investigating all those object, through whom you become well-known all the part of thus completed blending. Obtain therefore of new to talk of the surface, from whom one is display that come the pyramid that one have to incise with the Painting. Of the surface any of it they are without recline into ground, same as they are pavement (floors), the spaces of the building: and any other of it they are, which are equally far away from the space. Any surface are upright, same as they are the wall and the other surface that have the same strength of line that the wall: uphold those surface stay equally faraway between them, when it distance that is between of them, and equally from to all the same. The surface that have the same strength of line, are those that from each part they are touch from one continuous line straight, same as they are the surface of the columns square, which one place to filaments into one lodge. These are those thing that one have to adjoin to the thing that above one discord of the surface. However to those thing that we will said of rays, so of the last just like of those of inside, and of the centric, and to the things that one are recount of above of the pyramid sight, be essential adjoin that sentence of mathematical, with whom one proof, which if one line straight cut the duo side of some triangle, and do this line cutting, such that face ultimately one other triangle, and equally far away from the other line that is base of the first triangle, make then certainly that triangle major proportional of side to this minor. This say the Mathematical. But we oblige the talk ours both more open to Painters, explicate more clearly the object. And be essential that we be able such as both that thing that we into this place desire call proportional: we say that those they are triangles proportional, the sides and the angle of which have below of them it same agreement: Which if one of side of the triangle both more long of the base for two times and means, or another for three, all the so facts triangles is it they either major or minor of those, even if that he combine it same correspondence of side to the base, for say thus, make between them proportional. Inasmuch that respect that has the part to the part her in the triangle major, the have so far it part to the part in the minor. All the triangles therefore that do so fact, near to of we one call proportional: and because this both understood more openly, of it give one similitude. Will one man small proportional to a grand through the cubit: provided that one servants the same proportion of the palm, and of the foot, for measure the other parts of the body into this person, for manner of say, namely into Euandro, that one observe into he who namely into Hercules, of which Gellio affirm that era of stature grandest more of all the other men. Of it late still other proportion of it limbs of Ercole (Hercules), that one fuse that of the body of Anteo (Antaeus) Giagante. Inasmuch so just like the hand corresponded into each into proportion of the cubit (ulna), and ulna into proportion to the capo (head) and to the other components with equal measure below of them, the same intervene of it our triangles, which he do some robust of measure below the triangles, through whom the minor corresponded to major into the other things, except that in the grandness. And if these things one intend so much that suffice, deliberate, through the sentence of Mathematicians so much how much ago to our purpose, which each reduction of whatever triangle likewise far away from it base, generates and ago a triangle similar one same as they say to that their triangle major, and same as the say we proportional. And because all those things that they are between them proportional, the parts so far them are into of it corresponding, and into those things, in which the parts they are diverse and not corresponding, not they are proportional; the part of triangle visual they are other at line, even them rays, whom do certainly review the quantity proportionality of the Painting, equal how much to the number to the true, and into those which not make proportional, not do equal. Inasmuch one of these quantity not proportionality, occupy either more rays, or even. Thou you've noted therefore into which mode one which one desire minor triangle, one call the proportional to the major, and to you memories that it pyramid visual itself ago of triangles. Therefore reciprocate all our reasoning which obtain have of triangles, to the pyramid. And persuade, which none of the quantity views of it surface, which likewise hay far away from the reduction, make in the Painting alteration any. Inasmuch they are really quantity equally far away, proportionality in each equally distance reduction from them their corresponding: whom thing being thus, of it followed this, which not of it succeed in the Picture alteration any of distortion, and which none they are altercate the quantity, from the such as the field or the space one impious, and from whom they are measured or including the surroundings. And is manifest that each reduction of the pyramid visual, which both equally distant from the view surface, is likewise proportional to it view surface. Have spoken of the surface proportional to the reduction, namely of the equally distance to the surface painted. However because we hermitage without paint more diverse surface that not do equally distance, must of these do more diligent investigation, oblige one explicate which one desire reason the reduction. And because make thing long and much difficult and obscurely into this reduce of triangles and of the pyramid narrate each object second the rules of Mathematicians; however speak second the costume our same as Painter, proceed. Recount briefly any things of the quantity that not they are equally distant, be able whom us make simple interpret each consideration of the surface not equal distance. Of the quantity therefore not equally distance of it they are any of lines similar to rays visual, and any, which they are equally distance from any rays visual: the quantity similar into all without rays visual, because it not make triangle and not occupant the numbers of ray, not one gain therefore place not any in the reducing. However in the quantity equal distance from rays visual, how much that angle major that is to the base of the triangle, make more obtuse, so much even of rays receive that quantity, and however it not even of space for the cutting. We have call that the surface one cover of quantity, and because in the surface often happens, which you do one some quantity, which make equally distant from the reduction, and the other quality of the same surface not do equally distant; for this take place that those sun quantity that they are equally distance in surface, not be sensitive to in the Painting alteration any. But those quantity that not make equally distance, how much is it angle more obtuse than do the major in the triangle to the base, so much more receive of alteration. Finally to all these thing be essential adjoin that opinion of Philosophers, through whom they affirm, which if the sky, the stars, the seas, the mountains and they animals, and furthermore all the bodies, become for will of God, the destination minor that he not they are, us own that all these things not us seem profit into part no decreased from that which it season they are, though it grandness, the smallness, the length, the shortness, the height, the lowness, the tightness, is the width, the darkness, the clarity, and all the other thus make thing one be able locate, and not find in the thing, the Philosophers the call accident: and they are of such strength which the whole cognition of them one ago through there comparison. Said Virgilio that Aeneas (Enea) advancing of all the shoulder all the other men. However if one make comparison this person to Polyphemus, us seem a Pygmy (Pigmeo). Assert that Eurialo departed lovely, whom if one compare to Ganymede (Ganimede) ravish from Goive, seem brute. In Spain any young girl are compelled for candid, whom into Germany create compelled for olive trees and black. The ivory and the silver are whites of complexion, and nevertheless if breast do comparison with the swan, or with the whites clothes linens, seem somewhat further pale. For this respect us appear the surface in the Painting beautiful and glimmer, when into of it one sees those proportion from the white to the black, which is in the things same from the light to the shadows. One that all these things one learn, through the do comparison. Concise that in the do comparison of the thing, is one certain force, for whom one acquainted with that than you both of more, or of less, or of equal. For which we will call grand those thing which is major of one minor; grandness those as is major of the grand; luminous those than is more clear than the obscure; brightly those than both more clear of the luminous. And one ago really the comparison of the thing to the thing that first us is it manifestly. However being the man more of all the other thing to the men well known, say be Protagoras that the men era the model and the measure of all the thing, and intended for this that the accident of all the thing one be able and well experience, and make comparisons with the accident of the man. These things us subdue to this, which we interpret that whatever strength of bodies we daub into Painting, us seem grand and small second the measure of the man that there make paintings. And this strength of the comparison my partiality to see that much excellently more than not any of the ancient there intend Timante, whom Depicted, portraying above one small table the Cyclops that sleeping, to you the painted near the Satyr (part-man, part-goat), which embrace the finger big of the sleeper, oblige through the measure about Satyr, he who that sleeping appeared infinitely major. Obtain infinitive here said, almost all those things that one expect to the strength of the see, and know the reduction. But because assist to the chance ours cannot only that which both, and of that thing the incision, but just like even he one face, us awn to say of this reduction, with such as art in the paint he one expresses. Of this therefore, let go the other object from part, recount self that which face, while that self-depiction. There first what in the paint one surface, self-there drawing a quadrangle of angles righteous grand how much to I like, whom I serving for one open window from whom one obtain without to see the history, and that place determine the grandness of the men which self you want make into painting, and divide it length of this person man into three parts, whom to I they are proportionally, with that measure which the common people call the arm. Inasmuch it is the three arm's length, just like one to see clear from the proportions of limbs of the man, because such is the common length for the more of the body human. With this measure therefore divide the lines from low that be to says of the designed quadrangle, and see how many of thus do parts entirely into it: and this same line adjacent of the quadrangle is to I proportional to the more vicinity to transverse equally far view quantity in the space. Afterwards this self-mold a point

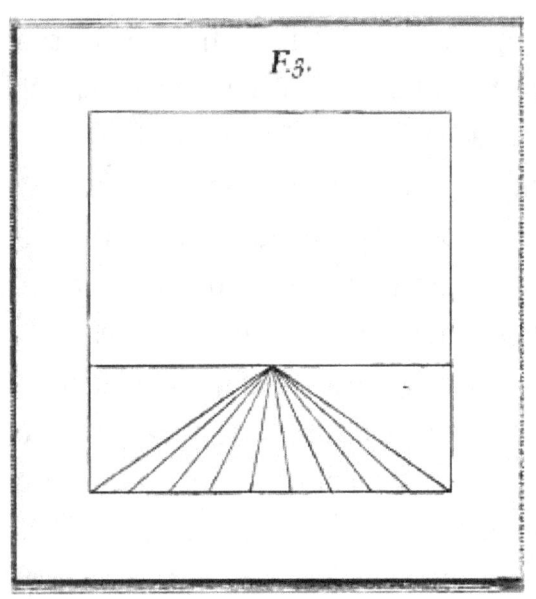

only whereas obtain to course the view, inside to the quadrangle, whom point preoccupied that place to the which have to arrive the ray centric, and however the call the point of the center: establish this point conveniently, not more high from the lines that says, which for how much is the height of the man that you one has to paint however into this mode and those who that regards, and the object painted seem that is it to a plan equal. Position the point of the center, pull lines straight from it point to each of the divisions of the line straight that says: whom lines really I demonstrate, into that mode having self to proceed fine to the infinite and ultimate distance, and one take in the quantity from transverse to the appearance and view my. (Table. II Fig. 3.) Here air any that draw enter to the quadrangle one line equally distant from the already uniform line, and divide into three parts the space that make do between the said two lines. Of then with this rule would pull another line likewise distant from this second line, likewise distant, so that the space that below the first participate line, and this second line to you parallel, or equally distant, divides into three parts, exceed of one part of if same that space which is between the second and third line, and of then adjoin the other lines, so much that always that space which continue ahead of below the lines, fuse for the half more, for talk same as the Mathematical. One that into this manner proceed these people, whom if well say of follow one excellent via in the paint, self nevertheless ponder that they err not little. Because having place to case the first line parallel to the principle, if well the other parallel are put with rule and with order, not they've however thing for whom they pair certain and determined place of the point of the pyramid from be able well to see the object; from that of it succeed easily in the Painting not small errors. Attach without this, which the rule these people air very much false, the whereas the point of the center fuse position or more high, or more low of the statue of the man depict: consist that all those that make, say that none of the things painted, conform to the true, if it not do parlay with certain rule distant from the eye, not one watch, neither discern. Of whom thing express the reason, whether mine us write of these demonstration of the Painting, whom already made from we, the friends our while the watched with marvel, the called the miracles of the Painting. Inasmuch all these things that self-have said principally one expect to that part: return therefore to purpose. Being these things thus make, self therefore I have found this optimum mode. Into all the other things self-vision original back to the same line, and to the point of the center, and to the division of the line that gather, and to the draw from the point the lines to each of the division of the line that gather. However in the quantity from transverse self-engage this order. Art I have one space small, in which self-pull one line straight: this divide into those parts that is uniform it line, which gather one quadrangle. Of then modeling departed high a point over this line so much high, how much is the height of the point of the center in the quadrangle, from the line adjacent uniform, and pull from this point to each division of she line them their lines. Of then determine how much distance self-want that both, below the eye of who regards and the Painting, and there ordered the place of the cutting, with one line upright to lead, be able the reduction of all the lines that it locate. Line to lead is that which fall above another line straight, cause from each band the angle to square ruler. (Table II. Fig. 4.) This line to lead I allocate with the her intersecting therefore all the terminate of the distant that is it to be below the lines to transverse parallel of the floor, in what mode self is drawn in the floor all the parallel; of whom how much you it is pull to reason, here of it offer indication, if one same continuous line straight do in the painting floor, diameter of quadrangle conjoin together: And is near to without Mathematicians the diameter of a quadrangle, that line straight which originated from one of the angles it goes to the other without him opposite, whom divides the quadrangle into two parts, so that countenance of called quadrangle dual triangles. Given therefore diligently end to these things, self-pull of new of above another line to transverse, equally far from the other of below, whom intersecting the duce side right of the quadrangle grand, and entry pass for the point of the center. And this line I serving for term, and space, through whom none quantity exceeds the height of the eye of the regarding. And

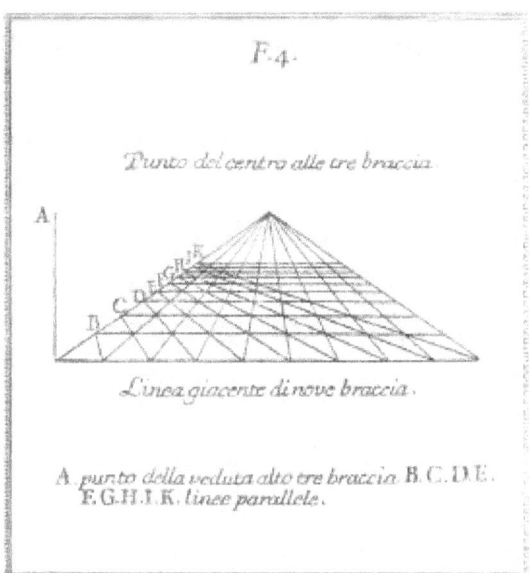

F. 4.

Punto del centro alle tre braccia.

A

Linea giacente di nove braccia.

A punto della veduta alto tre braccia. B. C. D. E.
F. G. H. I. K. linee parallele.

because it passes the point of the center, therefore is called centric. From that happen that those men that make paintings below the two more beyond lines parallel, do the same many minor that those that do between the anterior lines parallel: of it is for this that us altar minor of the other, but because they are more distant, appear minor, whom thing into true it demonstrate manifestly the nature that so both. Periodic we see for the Chief the heads of the men that strolling, almost go always to one same height equal, but the feet of complexion that they are very far, it seem that correspond to the knees of complexion that there are in front. All this rule of the divide the floor principally one expected to that part of the Painting, whom we to her place call complement. And is similar, that self-doubt that for be object new, and for brief of these mine commentary, she have to be little agreement from who law: inasmuch one same as easily know, through the works ancient, which it near to of our major for be obscure and difficult not late known: Concise that near to of the ancient last one great exertion to find history any that both well compote, well painted, well formed, or conveniently carved. For whom thing ego I have said these things with briefness and same as self-think, not also obscurely. But self-know chance, and what it they are, which of it for them be able acquire any praise of eloquence, and those who which not them interpret to the first view, duration grandness exertion without can never ever comprehend. They are things very easy and beautiful to the wits thin and inclined to the Painting, into whatever mode one declare, but without the men rough and little proceedings, or inclined from nature to these noble arts, although of them one speak eloquent minded, serene little giving, and perhaps that these same things recited from we mindlessly without no eloquence, do read not without bothersome. However I would like that me fuse pardon, whether while that principally ego I have desired be understood, self I have awaited to do what the my writing both clear, more pragmatic that composed and adorned, and those things that follow, cause for how much self-hope, not even tedium to those that read. We have therefore treaty of triangles, of the pyramid, of the cutting, and of those things that it seem from say. Of whom things even ego was customary reason with the friends my very much more long with one certain rules of geometry, and exhibit them the causes, because thus future, the when ego I have ponder of let go behind for briefness into this person my commentaries. Because self into this place I have recount solely the first principles of the Painting, and them I have to want call the first principles, periodic him they are the first foundations of the art for the Painters that not know how. However he are such, that those who which the intended well, considerate that the benefit from not little, how much to the intelligence, and how much without concern the definition of the Painting, and how much still to those things that we have to say. And not both not any that doubt, which he who not become never ever good Painter, which not intends excellently that which in the depiction he search for of make. Inasmuch into space one draws the arc, if first not you've designate the place whereas you want direct the arrow. And I would like certainly that we here persuade, this person only be for become optimum Painter, whom time has learn to arrange excellently all of around, and all the quality of the surface. And for the contrary ego affirm that not succeed never good Painter this person, which not know how precisely, and diligently the things that we have allocate. And however is state necessary all that which one is called of the surface, and of the reduction (cutting). Remains time that one teach the Painter, of the mode that he is to hold in the mimic with the hand, the thing that he one do imagined first in the mind.

Of

Painting

By

Leon Batista Alberti

Book Second. II

However because this study of the gain have reason perhaps seem too much laborious to young blood, therefore I part from display into this one place how much the Painting both not unworthy from be able place each our study and each our diligence. Conceive that it has into if one certain strength divine this that not only it ago that which say, which ago the friendship, which it represents into be the person that they are distant, but it here place in front of to the eyes thus far complexion, which the many and a lot of ages old they are I am dead, that so one see with great marvel of the Painter, and dilettante of who the regards. Recounts Plutarch (Plutarco) that Cassander (Cassandro) one of Captains of Alessandro (Alexander), in see the effigy of the dead Alessandro, be familiar with into it that majesty royal commence with all the bodies without tremble. I say thus far Agesilao Lacedemoiese be able of be ugly, not to want that it his effigy fuse view from descendants, and therefore not the pleasure never be of it painting, of it sculpted from none. One that the direct of dead live into a certain mode one long life, through the Painting. And that the Painting it have expressed the Gods, which they are revere from the gents, is from ponder that this both state a grandness gift conceded to deadly. Conceive that the Painting has benefit from too much greatly to the religion, through whom we are principally conjoin to the Gods, and to persevere the animate with one certain complete religion. Assert that Fidia made into IIia (Elide) a Jupiter (Giove), the beauty of the certain adjoin very to the conception religion. However how much the Painting be of use honorary choice of the spirit, and how much ornament it cause to the things, one she can of somewhere else and from this one principally to see, which you not locate almost for the more thing no although preciosity, which for the accompanying of the Painting not become very much more dear, and very much more precious. The ivory, the gems, and the so made object exquisite, become, mediated the hand of the Painter, more precious. The gold same anchored adorned from the Painting, is highly valued very much more than the gold. On the contrary not that other the lead more of all the other metals vile, if Fidia or Prassitele of it possess with the their hand fact one statue, be for adventure endurance more into merit, that not do as much silver coarse and not worked. Zeuxis Painter have start off to donate his things, because such as he assert, it not one can pay with what one desire price. Conceive that he judged that not one be able find price not any, which located gratify to he who that in the paint, or sculpt the animals, fuse almost that one other God below the deadly. Has these praise therefore the Painting, which those who that of it they are masters, not only one marvelous of the work them, but one according be similar to the Gods. Which tell self that the Painting is either the masters of all the arts, or almanac the principal ornament? Inasmuch the Architect, whether ego not me deceit, has taken from the Painter solely the molding, the capital, the base, the columns, the frames, and all the other thus make laud from the edifices. Inasmuch the painter through the rules and the art his has instruct, and given mode to the gouge, to the sculptors, and to all the workshops of smithy, of woodcutter, and of all those who that working of factories manuals, such that not one rediscover finally art any, although abject, which not have regards to the Painting, hence ego intrepid of affirm which all that which is of ornament in the object, both obtain from the Painting. However principally ago from the ancient honored the Painting of these honor, which be state call almost the major part of the other author, Craftsman following of Latin, the Painter only not late include below the Locksmiths. Whom things be thus, ego are usual of say below the friends me that the inventor of the Painting departed, second the sentence of the Poets, that Narcissus that one convert into flower. For that which be the Painting the flower of all the arts, well seem that all the fable of Narcissus both benefit accommodated to she thing. Inasmuch, that other object is the depicted, which embrace and seize with the art that surface of the source? Ponder Quintilian that the Painter ancient fussing usual without draw the shadow, second which the Sun them extend, and then the art both of hand in hand with achievement increase. They are no that recount that a certain Philocles (Filocle) Egypt, and a Cleanthes (Cleante), of it be able self which, fussing the first inventors of this art. The Egyptians assert that near of them era stand into use the Painting six thousand years first that it fuse transported into Greece, and our say that it come of Greece into Italy afterward that Marcello he had the victories of Sicily. However not important much know the first Painters, or the inventors of the Painting. Conceive that we not desire recount the history of the Painting same as Pliny (Plinio), but again deal of the art. Of whom fine without age not us of it is memory no let go that self-have view from the writing ancient: Even that him say that Euphranor (Eufranore) Hischimio wrote not certain that of the measure and

173

of colors: And which Antigonus (Antigono) and Xenocrate compose any things about the Paintings, and that Apelles (Apelle) thus far mass of the Painting any things together, and the convey to Perseus. Recount Laertius Diogenes that Demetrius Philosopher so far wrote no comments of the Painting. Beyond of this self-esteem still that be from our pass through state mass into written all the good arts, which the Painting still not fuse be let go into behind from our writers Italian. Inasmuch they were into Italy ancient the Etruscans, valorous more of all the other of it the art the Painting Deem Trimegisto ancient writer that the Painting and the Sculpture were born together with the religion, inasmuch he affirm thus to Asclepius (Asclepio): The humanity recollection of the nature and of the origin her, figured the Gods from the similitude of the face hers. And who both that reject, which the Painting not one both attributed to if same into all the object, thus public, just like private, so secular, same as religious, all the more honors parts? Such that not locate artifice no near to of deadly which from each of it both fact account major. Recounts merit almost incredible of the board painted. Aristide Thebano trade one Painting single, hundred talent, namely, sixty thousand florins. Recount that the table of Protogene late cause that Rhode not fuse embraced from the King Demetrio, because not to want that says table be aflame. Be able therefore affirm, which Rhodes (Rodi) departed redeem from them sign for one single Painting. Sonsi mass together, beyond to these, many other thing similar, for whom can you comfortably interpret, which the good Painter they are be always greatly laud, and own into merit from each, such that the noble, and portly Citizens, and the Philosophers, and the King one I am delighted not only of the things painted, however of the paint again. Lucio Manilio Citizen Roman, and Fabio into Rome man noble they were Painters. Turpilio Knight (Cavaliere) Roman painted in Verona. Sitedio Praetor, and Proconsule one purchase with the depiction. Pacuvio Poet Tragic, grandson of Ennio Poet, born of the daughter, painted in the square, Hercules, Socrates, Plato, Metrodoro, and Pyrrhus Philosophers, be excellent in the Painting. Nero (Nerone), Valentiniano, and Alessandro Severo Emperors, they were studious of the paint. Will item long recount how many Principles, and how many King they are status inclined to this noble art. And not is again reasonable stay without recount all the infinite multitude of Painters ancient, whom how much both status grand, one it can see from these; which into not even of four hundred days they were of the all cease to Demetrio Valerio son of Fanostrate, three hundred sixty statues, part over the their horses, part above the wagons, and part above the eyes. And if in that City departed so much the great number of the Sculptors, remain we in doubt that not us fussing Painters infinite? They are really the Painting and the Sculpture arts conjoin together of relatives, and nourished from a same intelligence. However ego put

174

before always the intelligence of the Painter, same as that which one affects into what many more difficult. However return without proposition. Infinite departed the multitude of painters and of the Sculptors into those times, conceive that the Principles, and the plebeian, (historical Rome), the scholarly, and the ignorant one delighted of the Painting. And custom below the first plunder that they accompany about the provinces, to put into public in the Theater the boards, and the statues, the thing end up so much earlier, which Paul Emilio, and no other not many Citizens Romans, section teach to the children for surely, and blissfully live together with the good arts, the Painting. Whom optimum custom near of Greeks one observed exceedingly, which the youths noble and liberal well bred, learned together with the letters the geometry, and the music, and the art thus far of the depiction. On the contrary the faculty of the painter late thus far objective honored to the women: And celebrated from the Writers Martian daughter of Varrone, because she know how depiction. And departed certainly into so much merit, and worthy of so much praise the Painter near to of Greeks, which he forbid for public deliberation, which not fuse licit to servants learn the Painting; of it this really without reason, inasmuch the art of the depiction is really deserving of the animate liberal and noble: and how much to I is meagre always one evidence of optimum and excellent intelligence that of he who ego I have known-it-all that one beloved greatly of the Painting. And is this art single that which likewise delights greatly and to erudite and to the ignorant, whom thing not occur never into no other art, which that thing which delights to those that make, provoke thus far the ignorant. And not find nothing that easily not demand greatly of own fact profit in the Painting. And is manifest that it nature one delights in the depiction. Conceive which we to see that the nature figure of it seas, the centaurs, and the faces of King with the beards. On the contrary I say that into one joy of Pyrrhus (Pirro), you pellucid daub from the nature same the nine Muse (poetical inspiration) with their insignia. Addition to these things that him not is almost art none, in which the men that do and those that not do, in the uneven and in the exercise one affection with so much delight all the tempo of the life them, more that into this. We are licit of say that which intervenes to I: If never happen that for my pleasure and for my delight ego me put to paint, which self-know certain much often, when I advances tempo from the other affair, self this fixed with so much I liking without make that work that to great penalty laying believe that self you both state so much than it is already past three or four hours: one that this art generate with him delight, whereas that you the honorary and praises and riches, and fame perpetuate whereas that you the produce excellent mind. Whom thing be thus, furthermore that the Painting is an optimum and ancient ornament of the things, deem of men liberty, grateful without erudite and without the generated, console how much majorly can the studies youngster, which for how much he pass through, give greatly works to the Painting. Afterwards contain those who which they are studious of the Painter, which function behind to learn it perfect art of the depiction, not pardon of it without effort, of it to diligence any. Divert without care, you that looking for be excellent in the painting, it first thing, the considerate which names and which fame one procure the ancient. And you benefit from of remind that always it avarice is remain antagonize to the praise and to the virtue. Conceive that the mind intent to the gain, rare times obtain the fruit of it posterity. The I have seen no nearly into departed the considerable of the learn, right away be information to the gain, and therefore not they've furthermore procure of it riches of it fame no, whom if own with the study wean the intelligence, make easily become famous, it hence of it enclosure glean riches and delight: for so much both of their lowest without here called to be sufficient. Time return to proposal. We divide it Painting into three parts, whom division contain extract from she nature. Inasmuch ingenuity the Painting of representative the object to see, consider into which mode they object approach to the view ours. Principally when we scrutinize certain object, we watch those thing be a certain than, which occupies place. And the Painter circumscribe the space of this place; and this mode of the design the surrounding with words convenient call circumscription. Afterwards this in the watch we considerate into that mode one conjectural together the divers surface, of view body, below of them, and drawing the Painter these conjoining of the surface to them places, be able and good call the composition. Ultimately in the watch we discern more distinctly the colors of the surface, and because the representation of these thing in the Painting, receives almost always entirely his own differences from the light, commentate we be able that call out the receipt of light. The surroundings therefore, the composition, and the receipting of light make perfect it Painting. Remain therefore to deal of those things shortest minded, and first of surroundings, either true of the circumscription, whom is that draw which one ago with the lines to back to back of surroundings, from modern called design. In this say that Parrasio Painter, that which Senofonte introduces to talk with Socrates, late worshipful: therefore that he say that he consider wafer-thin the lines. And in this drawing ponder that principality one has to procure, which he one face with lines thin, and that to all not one discern from the eye, one same as I say that used to do what Apelles Painter in the exercise, and combat to who more thin the make, with Protogene. Inasmuch the design not is other, which sketch of surroundings, the which if one make with lines that appear too much, not seem margins of the surface into she Painting, but will seem no fissure. Afterwards ego desire that in the drawing not one head to other that to the circuit of surroundings. In what design self-affirm that it material needs exercise vehemently. Conceive that none composition, none receipt of light never do praise if not you make design. On the contrary the design only, the more of the times, is gratitude. Mean therefore work to the drawing, and to impart very well this not creed that one can find object no more accommodated, which that veil than self below the friends sheet call the cutting, the mode of the use whom they are state self the first which art have found, and is thus fact. The deduct a veil of line thin, textile rare, and both of which one desire complexion, this divide self of then with row somewhat more gross, doing four how many me liking above a loom all equal, and art put into between the eye and the object from to see, oblige that the pyramid visual penetrating entry pass for the rarity of the veil. Has really this cutting of the veil into if not modest comfort: the first thing, he you represent always the same surface motionless, conceive that positives one time the terms, chance upon forthwith the primary point of the pyramid, with whom you begin; whom without this reduce of the veil is thing really difficultly. And both how much both impossible in the depiction, mutate righteously anything, because not maintain perpetually to who painted the same appearance and view: and from this come that more easily one resemble those thing which one depict from the thing painted, which those that one portray from the sculptures. You know any beyond of this, how much it thing view, pairs altered, through the mutation of the interval, either of the position of the center. For so much the veil or it net you cause this not small utility that the thing always you one present to the view the same. The other utility, is that you can arrange easily in the paint it your table, into places most certain, the sites of place vicinity, and the ends of the surface. Inasmuch to see you into that knitting of the net it front, and into that which them is to singing, the nose, and in the more vicinity then the cheeks, into that underneath the chin, and all there other things so make, arranged to them places: be able the very one arrange perfect departed it your table or in the wall compartment even they with one goal equal to that. Ultimately this goal or veil extend great comfort and help to give perfection to the Painting; therefore that you to see it object reviled and inflated designed, and painted in that plain of it net. Through the which things, we can easily and for the judgment and for the experience consider, how much utility of it provide it mesh, to good and perfectly depiction. Of it me liking those who that say that us not is good than the Painters one habit without these things, whom if good arcane grandness help to the painting, they are nevertheless such, which without they, a Painter without great penalty can never do from if same thing any. Conceive though we not study on condition that the Painter, whether I not me deceit, have without last one fatigue infinite; however praise that Painting which has great relief, and which it pairs many akin to bodies that she has to represent. Whom thing certainly not be able

177

self to see in that manner can leave again to any even if poorly without the help about it net. Be necessary therefore of this removal, namely of this net those who which one fatigue of do profit. Which if too do any that without net one delight of experiment the intelligence, procure with the view this same rule about the knitting, such that always there one imagine be cut one line to transverse, from one other make without lead, the whereas they statuesque the term watched in the Painting. However because the more of the times to Painters not practice appearance doubtful and uncertain the surroundings of the surface, just like intervenes of it faces, of it what not discern this time into which place principality is it finished the temples from the front, therefore be essential teach them, into which mode and proceed acquire to know this thing. The nature really there the ensign perfect. Inasmuch, one same as we visualize in the surface plain, which are beautiful when it have the them precisely light, and the their exactly shadows, thus in the surface spherical and concave it seem that it detain well when that it almost divide into more surface have diverse mark of shadow and of light. All the parts therefore each from for if that have different light and different shadow, one have to consider same as likewise surface, which if one view surface continues from the its shadow be missing by little by little fine to the her major light, one be obliged to in that moment mark with one line the means that is below the one space and the other, oblige that one have even dubious of the rule that you is it without hold in the embellish the space. Remain to deal thus far something of design, the provided one expected not little really to the composition: however is well know how, which object both the composition in the Painting. And really the composition that mode or rule in the depiction, through whom all the parts one compound together in the work of the Painting. Greatly works of the Painter is the history: the parts of the history they are the bodies: the parts of the body they are the limbs: the parts of the limbs, they are the surface. And be the design, that rule or mode of the depiction, through whom design the surroundings to each of the surface, and of the surface be not any tiny, just like those about the animals, and any grandly same as those of giants and of the building; of the design the surface small, suffice those subdue that one are said fine to here. Conceive that he one is demonstrate same as it one design well with the net. But in the design the surface major it be essential find other rule. For the which here be necessary reduce to the memory all those thing that one they are educate of above of the surface, of flare, of the pyramid, of the reduce. Finally you to you recollection of that which ego say of the lines parallel, of the space or floor, and of the point centric, and of the line. Above of the floor therefore designed with the lines parallel, one have to raise the averse of walls, and what other things similar one to want, that we name surface erect. Assert therefore briefly that which self be able how in the raise these things. The first thing ego myself begin from them foundations, and design in the floor the width and the length of the wall; in the designate the what thing self I have learned from the nature, which from one view single not one can see more than two surface conjoin together upright from the plan of what one desire body square fact to angle to square. In the design therefore the foundations of the wall, self-observe this one of draw singly those faces or sides, which me one represent to the view. And the first thing self-communicate begin from the surface that me they are more vicinity, and from those maximum that they are likewise distant from the reduction. For so much self design these before at other, and deliberate through they lines parallel designate in

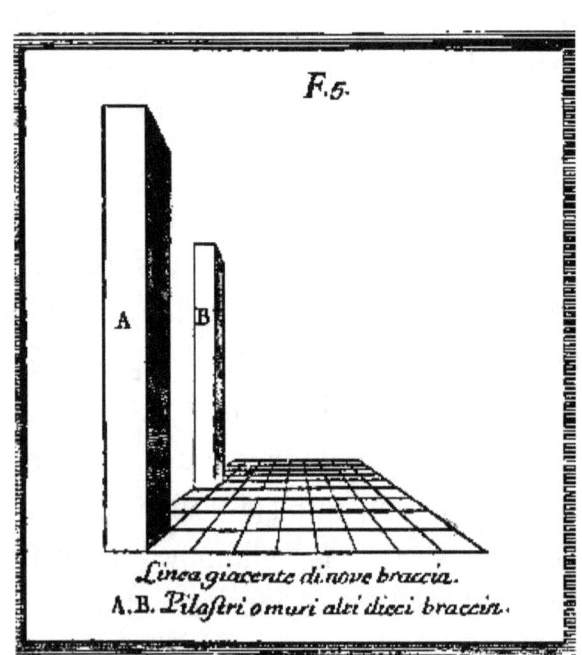

F.5.

A   B

Linea giacente di nove braccia.
A.B. *Pilaftri o muri alti dieci braccia.*

the floor, how much I want to that they wall is it long and wide. Inasmuch ego countenance touch parallel how many self-desire that it be arms (limbs), and expression the half of the parallel from there reciprocal intersection of each diameter of them parallel. One which for this measure of the parallel, self design perfect the width and the length of them wall that one reveals of on the plan. Afterwards confer from this not difficulty thus far it height of the surface. Inasmuch that measure that is below the line centric and that place of the floor whence begins to note the quantity of the building, all that quantity will observe the same measure. And if you want that whetstone be quantity that is from floor to the summit, both for four so many how much the length of the man depiction, and the line centric do parlay to the height of the man, make really at that time from the more low part of the quantity finally to the line centric three arms. However you that you want which this quantity grow fine to the twelve arms, trace to the by departed for three times that quantity that is from the used for low fine to the line centric. Be able therefore through the rules adduced for the depiction, draw well all the surface angular (Table II. Fig. 5.). Stay to deal of the design with theirs of the surroundings the surface circular. The surface into circle really one extract from the angular, which self be able into this one mode. The drawing inside to a quadrangle of sides equal, and of angles to square a circle, and divide the sides of this quadrangle into as much parts, into how much departed divide the line of below of the quadrangle into the Painting, and despot the lines of the divisions from each point of they to the other to him opposite, fill that space of small quadrangles, and above you drawing a circle how much self the want grand, of manner that it circle and the parallel reciprocally one intersecting together, and known the places of all the points of the intersection, the what places gesture thus far into them parallel of the floor

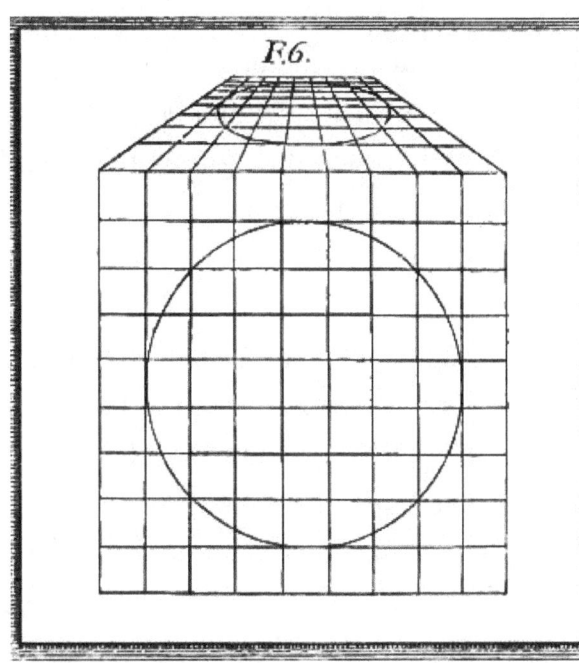

F.6.

designed for Painting, or Perspective. But because would be one fatigue extreme intersect with dense, and almost infinite parallel all the circle, fine to a lot of, that with a numerous teaching of points one continuous the of surrounding of the circle: And however self-known only with eight, or with how many more me be agreeable intersectional, and in retrospect pull through the intelligence the circumference or sphere of the circle to the already marked terms. Maybe belong way more short, designate this of the surroundings to the shadow of oil lamp, even if which the body, which cause the shadow, receive the light with rule certain, and fuse place to her place. (Table. II Fig. 6.) One which we have call, same as through the assist of the parallel one design the surface major angular, and circular. Finished of debate therefore of each fate of drawing, it remains to debate of the composition. And really the composition that rule of the depiction, through whom the parts one compose together in the work of the Painting. There major works that face the Painter, not is one statue grand how much a colossus; but is one history. Conceive that one located major praise of the surroundings for one history, which by a Colossus. The parts of the history they are the bodies, the part of bodies they are the limbs, and the parts of the limbs they the surface, because of these one make the components, of the components the bodies, of bodies it history, of whom one ago that accomplish, really and perfectly finished works of the Painter. From the composition of the surface, of it born that loveliness and that grace, which these people call beauty. Conceive, which that face which is it no surface great and any small, which into a place wretched too much apart from, and in the other one hide-and-seek too much well-versed , same as one to see of it face of the old lady, do this to see certainly thing ugly. But into those face, in which the surface do of manner conjoin together, which the sweets light one converted to little by little into shadow agreeable, and not us do any harshness of angle, this call we to reason face nice, and which has arrival. Therefore into this composition of the surface be necessary go investigating greatly the grace and it beauty. But into which mode we be able obtain these, ego not I have inspiration via more certain, which go to considerate the nature very same, and however look diligently and for long tempo, in

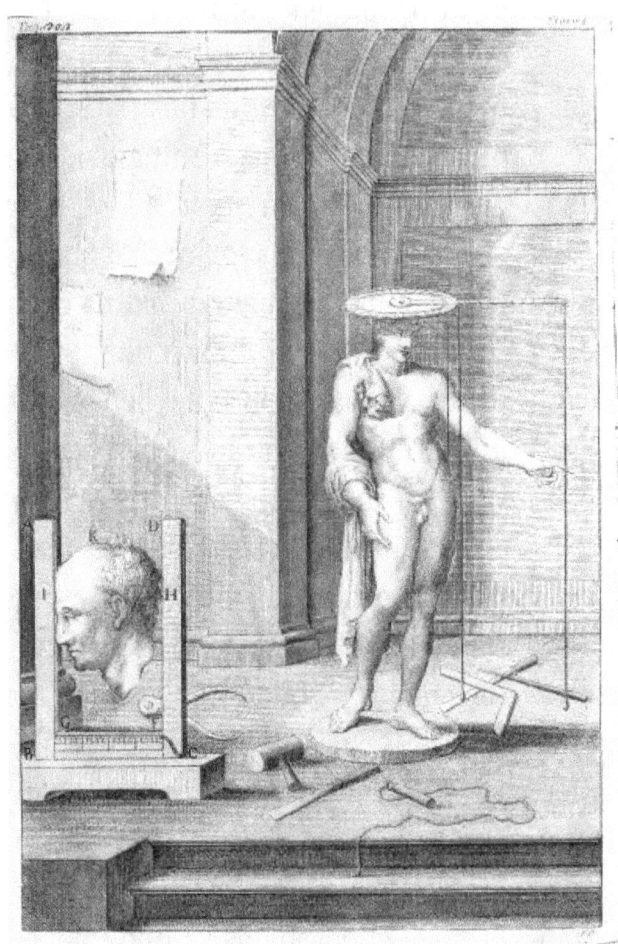

which mode the nature marvelous author of the things, have composed the surface in the beautiful components. Of it art imitate whom poverty exercise with all the thoughts and diligent ours, and expand greatly, same as we said of the net. And when we harem then quarried the surface from beautiful bodies, and the harem to put on into works, deliberate always the first thing the terms, through whom we can pull the lines to places their designation. Basti have call inherent to at this point of the composition of the surface. *(Table. II. Fig. 7.)* Remains that we say of the composition of limbs. In the composition of components the first object be necessary procure which all the components between them is it proportionately. Uphold that it they are well proportionate, when they correspond and how much to the grandness, and how much to the officiate, and how much to the species, and how much to the colors, and to the other things similar, if no more there us of it they are, to the beauty and to the majesty. That whether into no figure do a head grand, one chest small, any hand very much grand, a footer swollen, a body inflated, this composition for true do bad for concern. Be essential therefore, how much to the greatness, hold one certain rule in the measure, whom benefit from much in the paint the animals: go the first thing examining with the intelligence, which is it the bones, which they have, in as much these, since it not one bend, occupy always one seat and place certain: Afterwards be necessary put to places exactly the nerve and the muscular them: and ultimate dress of meat, and of skin the bones, and the muscles. However into this place it create maybe of those that I recoup, because ego I have called of above, which to the Painter not one expected any of those thing, which not one to see. Indicate really these people well; however just like in the dress be essential envisage first below the naked, whom then we desire involve to carvings of garment, thus in the paint one naked, be necessary before dispose and arrange to places them the bones and the muscle, which you have afterward for order to cover of meat and of skin to such an extent, which not difficulty one have to consider into what place is it situation they muscles: However why is that having it nature explained all these measures and express post in front of to the eye, the scholar Painter locate not small utility into recognize those same with the fatigue his from it nature. And however the scholars attitude this fatigue, oblige all that which of study and of work them is it position into recognize the proportion of the components, he be acquainted with have benefit from to hold conscription in the memory those thing that them is it acquire. Achieve slowly nevertheless the first thing of these, which in the measure the animal he one grasp someone of membership of it same animal, for whom one measure all the other components. Vitruvius Architect measure it length of the man with the feet. However self-think that both thing more judge, whether there other limbs one correlate to the quantity of the head. Even that ego I have considered that for the more is almost common of it the men, which so much is it measure of the feet, how much is from chin to all it head: One that occupied one of these limbs, all the other one have to accommodate to these; so much so that not both member any into all the animal, which for length, or width not corresponds to the other. Beyond of this one has to have concern, which all the limbs fascination them officiate yours, for that which it are made. And convenient to a provided speed, range the hands not less than the feet, but a Philosopher that expression one oration, I would like self that into each hers member fuse more modest, which a gambler of arms. *Demon Painter*, expressed Hoplicite into a fight so much so which you assert which he perspire, and one other that pose so much so the weaponry, which you assert, us to take again without penalty the breath. Departed once again who paint *Ulisse* of manner, which you recognize into he not it well curb, but the feint, and simulated madness. *Lodasi*, nearby of *Romans*, it history in which *Meleagro* is result via dead, and complexion which him generate, appear that one hurt, and with all it limbs one fatiguing, and into he who which is death, not there is member any, which not appear more than dead, namely each object falls down, the hands, the fingers, the head, each thing lethargic sway. Finally all the object converge together to express the death of the body; whom is it more difficult of all the things. Inasmuch the resemble it limbs idle into each part into a body, is thing of worshipful master, one just like is the do that all it limbs lives create something. Therefore into each Painting one be obliged watch these, which whatever one is it limbs fascination of manner him officiate for provided that them are made, which none artery, well that minimum, omit of the officiate his, so much so that the limbs of death pair to hair everyone death, & those of live everyone lives. Therefore one says that a body lives, when from his parlay him face a few motion. And dead affirm that is when the limbs not be able more exercise it officiate of the life, namely the motion and the sense. Therefore those imagery of bodies that the Painter want to which apparition lives, make that into these all the limbs lay into action their motions, however into each motion be essential end up behind to the beauty and to the grace. And they are greatly lively and gratefully those motions of bodies, which raise go towards the air. Beyond of this affirm which in compose the limbs be essential have regard to the species. Inasmuch provide thing much unseemly, if the hands of Elena (Helen) = (daughter of Zeus) or of Ifigenia (Iphigenia) appearance hands of old women or of peasant. Either if to Nestor (Nestore) one do a chest from young, or one head dainty. Or if to Ganimede one create one front masses of creased, or the legs from a driver of arms, or if to Milone robust more of all the other one produce the hips slender and thin. Beyond of this thus far into that imagine that is it the face prime and plump same as one says, create thing ugly do that if them to vague the arms and the hands structures and consumed from it desire. And for the contrary who depiction Achaemenid (Achemenide) into that mode and with that face that Virgilio says be state found from Aeneas (Enea) in the Island (Isola), if the other limbs not corresponded to that thinness, produce certain such Painter ridiculous and crazy. Beyond of this I wish that one corresponded between them thus far of complexion. Inasmuch those imagery that have the faces to guise of roses, beautiful, and dewy, not is convenient that coordinate the chest and the other limbs drastic and horrible. Therefore in the composition of components we have called to room that which one must observe how much to the grandness, to officiate, to the species, and to colors. Conceive that us be essential that each thing correspond, second the truth of the thing. And not is convenient do one Venus (Lucifer), or one Minerva (Roman goddess of wisdom) clothing of Pitoccho; of it create a Jupiter (Roman god), or a Mars (Marte) clothes of one garment from woman, airs' convenient. The Painters ancient in the depiction Castor (Castore) and Pollux (Polluce) warned that over to that is point of view born to a body, into one nevertheless one sight one nature more robust, in the other one more agile. Beyond of this to want that Vulcuno below his clothes appeared lame. So much era the study that they posed in the expression the things second art officiate, the spices, and the dignity them. Ensue the composition of bodies in which consists all the intelligence and all the praise of the Painter; of the any composition one are said anything abide by to the composition of components. Inasmuch it be essential that how much to officiate and to the grandness all the bodies one agree together in the history. Conceive that if you paint into a feast the centaurs that turbulent together, would be affair from crazy, into so much unrestrained and beastly riot that us fusses any that sleeping, through the wine daily allowance. Beyond of such occur thus far defect if the man into equal distance appeared major these because those, just like that if into painting one make the dogs great how much the horses. And not produce again little from vituperate, that ego vague the most of the times paintings into one building the men same as that withdraw from others into a coffer, in which one noose to great penalty to be seated, or confined into a circle. All the bodies therefore be obliged to suitable, through it grandness and through it officiate, to that thing for whom are facts. But the history that reasonably both from praise and watch with marvels, be essential that both such that with no allurements one demonstrates be so much delightful and ornamented which entertain long the eye of those who that produce, and of those that not make, with pleasure, and with delectation of the mind. The first thing that of it the history cause, and you offer pleasure, is it copy and variety of the things. Inasmuch one same as of it nourishment, and of it the music always it new and unusual abundance, one doubt for the other things, one thus far delights not without marvel for those cause that is diverse, and different from the things ancient and usual: Thus into each variety of things, and into each abundance the mind one welcomes, and delights. And therefore of it the Painting it variety of bodies, and of colors is Mona Lisa. The tell which that history is copious in which to their places make mixed together old human men, young, little angel, matrons, maidens, children, animals domestics, pooch, bird, horses, sheep, building, and province; and praise what one desire abundance, just to that it one conforms to the what matter that there one he wants represent. Conceive that he come that regarding, in consider it things, consumption yonder more times, and the abundance and riches of the Painter acquire grace. However ego would like that this abundance fuse adorns, and provide of if one certain variety, serious, and moderate, through the dignity, and the reverence. The not praise those Painters whom for think copious, and because not to want that of it the things them there remains point of vote, therefore not go behind to composition any, however sow each what foolishly and confusedly, for the that not part that the history represents that which she wants make, however that turmoil, and perhaps that which the first matter demand of it the his history, it dignity. Inasmuch one same as into a Principle the reveal little causes majesty, just to that one connoisseur the senses of the words, and the commandments, thus into one history a reasonably number of bodies causes worthiness, and the variety causes gratitude. Ego I have into hatred of it the history it solitude actually not laud it abundance that renounce to the dignity. On the contrary in the history only greatly that which ego vague be state observed from Poet tragic from Comedians, him represent with needless number of person it fable them: And really second the judgment my not be essential refill one history of so much variety of affair, which it not can worthily be composed of nine or ten men. One just like self-judge that to this one apparent that called of Varrone, whom to want be disgusted in the excited the term oil, not invited my more which nine. However being into whatever history, Mona Lisa it variety, that Painting nevertheless is gratitude to all, in which her postures and her attitudes of bodies they are between them many different. Struggle therefore no from be impolite all into face, with the hands high, and with the fingers resplendent, steady above one of them feet, other struggle with the face into profile, and with the arms to low and with feet of the equal, and each contain from for if the his bending and the his attitudes. Others effort to sit down or kneeling, or almost adjacent: is it any naked if this is convenient, no other for the mixing of one and of other art there ever part naked and part clothed, however possess always care to the honesty and to the reverence. Conceive that the parts shameful of the body, and the other similar that have little of the gratitude, cover yourself either with cloths, or with frond (leafy branch) or with the hands. By instinct daub only that part of the face of Antigono, from whom not appeared the defect of the eye. And Homero (Homer) when arouses Ulysses in shipwreck from the slumber, for not do which he proceed naked for the forest behind to the voice of the women, one law, which it gave to that man one of the fronds of the tree, to that which one cover the shame. Recount that Pericles have a head long and ugly, and however from Painters, and from the Sculptors not departed fact my without head uncovered, same as the other, but always with it conceal into head. Beyond of this Plutarco (Plutarch) recounts that the Painters ancient used to the depiction the King, if he have defect any how much to the form them, not to want that he believe that they the burden left into behind, but save the similarity the amend how much more be able. This modesty and this reverence, desire self that into all the history one observe, to that which the things obscene or one laxity from part, or one amend. Finely same as self-express ponder that both from fatigue that into none imagine one to see the same gesture, or the same attitude. Create beyond of this the history stay the spectator with the attitude attention, when those man that there make quiet, represent exceedingly the motions from animate them. Inasmuch him happens from nature, of whom not one located what no that both more rapacious, of it that it throws more of the things similar, which we mourn with who weeps, laugh with who laughs, and it condolences with who one regrets. But these motion of the mind one consist, through the motions of the body. Inasmuch we to see, same as the melancholic, because there they are affiants from the worries and weary from the infirmity, same as it they are for manner of say grandiosity of all the senses and strength them, and such as there one stand slowness with the limbs pale and which almost fall down them. Inasmuch those who which one regret, they've real the front low, the head languid, and all there other limbs finally

185

same as to tire out, and abandoned him fall down. However him irritable because the animation whether him inflame for the vexation, and the face and the eye him swell, and it turn red, and the motions of all the components, through the fury of the anger, they are fast and feudist. However when we so far so good happy and cheerful, in that moment have the motions loose and grateful through no attitudes. And praise Euphranor, which into Alessandro he painted so much the face of Paride, and the face, in which you easily could recognize and Judge about the Goddess, and fell in love of Helen, and together charmer of Achilles. Marvelous praise is still that of Daemone Painter, which in his boards be able recognize be the irascible, the unjust, the unstablc, and together thus far the execrable and the clement and the merciful and the glorious and the humble, and the fierce. However below the other recount that Aristide Thebano equal to Apelles, expressed greatly these motions of the attitude: whom is thing certain that we thus far be able many well do when we establish into this thing those study and that diligence that there one convince. Be essential therefore that the Painter know excellently the attitudes and the motions of the body, whom self-judge that one combine to draw from the natural with infinite diligence. Inasmuch there thing is difficult through the infinite motions of the attitude, for whom one variants still yet the motions from the body. Over of such whoever consider, if not whoever of it has fact the experience, which he is difficult whenever you to want paint one face that return, disgust those for whom he seem more promptly weep than laugh? Beyond of this who make that which can without great study and diligence express the faces, of them which and the mouth, and the chin, and the eyes and the cheeks and the front side and the cilia (eye lashes), one confrontation and unison together and to the pain and to the laughter? And therefore be essential diligently proceed find oneself from the natural, and reproduce always the things more inclined. And principality one be obliged to paint those things whom leave to the animate most from to ponder, which those that one vigor from his eye. However recount we no things, which we have fabricate with our intelligence how much to the attitudes, and part thus far learn from it nature. The first thing I creed that he be essential that all the bodies below of them one move, with one certain grace and convenience, direction that object of whom one section. Beyond of these I be valued that in the history both somebody which advise the spectator call with the hand without to see those things that there one they do make, otherwise same as that it desire which that negotiation both secretive, menace with face cruel and with eyes frightful that you not you pull close it, or you demonstrate there be some great nuisance, or certain thing marvelous. Either that with his gestures you invitations or to laugh with him, or perhaps to cry. Finally he is of necessity that all those thing which they do below of them, and with those who still which the look, contribute to make and to demonstrate the history. And praise Thimante of Cyprus into that table, in which he won Colloteico, because having fact Calcante melancholic, produce more melancholic Ulisse: and because in the paint Menelao distressed he there possess place all the intelligence and consumed all the art his, having worn out all the affections, not finding mode from be able to paint the face of the sorrowful father, involve the head of those into a fabric for leave into he more of that if him be able discern in the face, of the pain that possess of it the mood. Lodasi her ship into Rome, in which Giotto our, Painter Toscano (shearing), expressed to such an extent the eleven frightened, and amazed disciples, through the companion that stroll above the hence of the sea, which each from for if gave particular clue of the disturbed spirit his, and with the attitudes of the body still such that each represent variously the fright which the they've. However is convenient perforate via briefly all this place of motions. Inasmuch of the motion of it they are any of the spirit, whom from the scholarly are called passions, same as is the anger, the pain, the joyfulness, the fear, the desire and similar: of it they are still of the other which they are of bodies. Inasmuch him one says which the bodies one move into many modes, namely when he increase, or when he wane, or true when being principled into infirmity, or when from the infirmity return to the failure; when haunch one mutation of place, and for similar other cases one it says that one move the bodies. However we Painters that through the motions of limbs to want express the affections of the animate, let go all the other disputes from part, negotiate only of that motion, which we affirm that one both fact when one produce mutated the place. All the thing that one move of place, they've seven from move toward; inasmuch or it one advance to into departed, or to into downward, or towards the right, or towards the left, or departing or approaching to we, and the seventh trip is when it one move circumvent to around. All these motions therefore desire self which is it in the Painting. Consist in any bodies that vaguely into towards of it, any other if of it move away, any move towards the right and other towards the left. Beyond of this exhibit no parts of them bodies to reencounter of who them regards, any return back, no one raise to in departed, no one lower. However because in the draw these motions one passes no times it rules and the order, me to will into this place recount nothing of the situated and of motions of limbs, which ego I have extract from the natural, acuminated one vigil manifest with that modesty there contain to serve of them motions. The certainly I have seen in the man, which into each his attitude he submit all the body to the head, member more of all the other serious. Beyond of this if one so hold up with all the body above of a foot only, always he foot just like if fusses base of the column, come to lead below to the head, and almost always the face of he who that remain above a foot, front into that part toward whom is to right the foot. However the movements of the head I have self-advise that never they are to great penalty such towards one of the parts, which he not have always below of if any part of the rest of the body, from whom both rectum the great weight, or rather that him not distend towards the other part certain other member to guise of one part of the scale that the counterweights. Inasmuch we see the same when someone expanse the hand support some weight, which with the other foot just like one both firm the fused of the scale, one conscription to the encounter with all the other part of the body for counterbalance the weight. Art I have apprised that the head of one which be straight in foot, not one time never more departed, than for how much he watch with him eye the means of the sky, of it one turn towards thigh never into no of the side more that a lot of how much which the chin him beat above the bone of the shoulder; and into those part of the body which we there band, to great penalty there direct never so much that the shoulder come for straight line above the bellybutton. The motion of the leg and of the arms they are rather more liberal, provided not obstructed the other honestly part of the body, and into these I have considered in the nature that the hands for him more not one raise above the head, of it the elbow above the shoulder, of it one raise the foot above the knee, of it the foot one separate never from the foot, if not for the space of a foot. I have seen beyond of such, provided, if we increase into height no of the hands, all the other parts of that side in the end to the foot proceed continue that motion, this which fine to the heel of that foot one reveals from the floor, through the motion of it arms. They are infinitely thing similar to these, whom inform the diligent master, and perhaps those that ego I have account all in all to now, they are thus manifest all in all to time, which can seem superfluous. However not them I have abandon behind because ego I have visas many make mistakes into this thing greatly. The attitudes and the motions too much striven express and display into one same image, which chest and the loins one to see into one only view, the though being impossible to do, is still inconvenience to see. However because these such sense that those imagery seem majority more live, how much more do force attitudes of limbs, however divvy up each dignity of the Painting, suit imitating into that those motion of ejaculatory. The hence not only the works them they are naked, and without grace, either loveliness any, but express still the too much burning intelligence of the Painter. I have the Painting have motions sweet and grace, and covenant to that which he desire representing. Eye-catching in the maidens the motion and the predilection venerable, the adornment elegant and simple concede to the age, the positions his obtain more tough of the gentle, and of the quiet, which of the act to the agitation. Still that to Homer backside to which one end up Zeuxis, pleasure still in the sowing one beauty sturdiness. Furnish of it the young women the motions more graceful, and more light-hearted, which idol, signal of spirt and of force valorous. Furnish of it the man the motion moreover detain and predisposition beautiful, act to one velocity deliver of arms. Of it old people furnish all the motions late, and be them attitudes to tire out, this than not solo one royal above amenders the foot, but one lean to something with the hand: and finally recount second the dignity of each all the motions of the body to those affections of the enliven, which you to want representation. Afterwards finally he is of necessity that the signification of the grandness passion of him enliven apparently and one express paramount into them bodies. And this rule of the motions, and of the attitudes, is many common into what one desire strong of animals. Conceive that not remain good, which an ox that serving to plow, face the same attitudes, which the generous horse of Alessandro (Alexander), Bucephalus. However that so much celebrated daughter of Inaco (Inachus), which late converted into Vacca (whore), depiction perhaps we comfortably, just like that she elapse with that head high, with the feet raise, and with the tail spoils. Suffice have catch sight of these things briefly of motions of the animals. However because self-think, which all these motions, of which have spoken, is it still necessary how much to the things inanimate, in Paining, self-think that both good debate into that mode them one move. Inasmuch the motions and of hair, and of the crowns (head of hair), and of branches, and of the foliage, and of the clothes expressed in the Painting revel still them. The certainly desire, which them hair represent all to seven those motions that ego I have recount. Inasmuch wind up into outline doing a node, scattering into air imitating the flames, *launch* moment snaking below other hair, moment one relief into direction such and that other part: Consist in still the bending of branches and the them concave with arc towards the other; part revert into within, part one envelop to guise of rope. And this same degustation in the folds of cloths, which one same as a stump of one tree spring up into divers part many branches, thus from one crease small pocket many folds, just like from the stub the branches: and into these selfsame one to see the many, such which not there both no fold of cloth in which not one summon up almost all the said motions. However is it all the motion, the provided ego perceive dense, moderate and sweets, and display more pragmatic of them grace which marvel of the fatigue. However afterward which we want which the cloths is it proceedings to motions, and being the cloths of them nature serious, and which continuously swoop to ground, and therefore escape each bending; good therefore one pose in the Painting the face of zephyr or of austere, which bury below the swarms to one point of the history, from whom all the cloths to see incite direction the contrary part: from whom object of it come still that gratitude which those sides of bodies, whom produce beaten from the wind, because the cloths one pull close for the wind to bodies, they bodies appearance almost naked underneath the covert of the cloth: and from the other parts the cloths agitated from the wind make folds, inundate in the air, beautiful. However into this clapping of the wind must beware, which none motion of no cloth originate contra to the wind, and which the folds not alter too much sharply, of it too much routes. These things therefore which one are said of motions of the animals, and of the things inanimate, one must greatly observe from Painters, and dedicate all the other things still diligently to execution, which one are said of above of the composition of the surface of components and of bodies. One that we have determine two parts of the Painting, the design, and the composition. Remain to negation of receptions of light. Of it first principal one demonstrate to presentences which strength have the light into various the colors. Therefore spin fermium the genres of colors, we teach into which mode they seemed time more clear, and time more darken, second the application of light, or of the shadows, and which the white and the black they were those colors, through the which we in the Painting express the light and the shadows: and which the other colors they are from be estimated for the material, with whom one adjoin the alteration of light, and of the shadow. Therefore leave the other things to backside be supposed to declare into which manner the Painter one has from serve of the white, and of the black. Marvelous the Picture ancient that Polignoto (Polygnotus) and Thimante (Thimante) one servants only of four colors, and which Aglaofone (Aglaophon) one delight of single color, just like that if into much number that he ponder be of the colors, fusses little that those excellent Painter of it have mass one few into use, whereas judge that to a copious master one belongs to put into work what one desire multitude of colors. The really affirm, which variety and the abundance of colors cause many gratitude, and many loveliness to the Painting. However ego I would like that the valiant Painters evaluate that one it had put each industry and each art in the dispose and position well the white and the black, and which into place this person conveniently, and well accommodate, one have to pore all the intelligence, and what one desire extreme diligence. Inasmuch one same as the event of light and of the shadows ago that him one to see in what place the surface one relief, and into which you break, and how much each of the parts declines, or one fold; thus the mend good of the white and of the black ago those that era attributed to praise to Nitia Painter Athenian, and that which the first thing has from desire the master, which the his Picture appear of great relief. Affirm that Zeusi (Zeuxis) noble and ancient Painter, departed almost the first which know how grasp this rule of light and of the shadows. However to the other not is attributed this praise. The certainly not think that none both, not that other Painter poor, which not be able many good which strength have every shadow and each light into all the surface. The praise those faces depiction, with good grace of scholarly and

190

of the ignorant, whom same as which of relief pairs which Aeschylus out of them boards, and for the contrary disapprove of those of it which not one view maybe point of art, if not of it of the surroundings. Art I would like which the composition fusses well designed and excellently vivid. Therefore because he not is it vituperate, and because he deserve of be laud, there first thing must mark diligently the light and the shadows, and must to consider which into that surface above whom injure the plunder of light, it color both how much more one it can clear and luminous, and which beyond of these be missing without little without little the strength of light there one put by little by little complexion somewhat more dark. Finally be necessary advice into which manner correspond the shadows into part contrary to light, which not do never surface of no body that both for light albumen, which in the same body you not recover the surface to that contrary which not both cooperate, and charge of shadows. However for how much appertain imitate the light with the white, and the shadow with the black, self to you advise that you place the principle study into consider those surface which are touch either from light, or from the shadows. These learn you good from the nature and from the things very own: And how many finally you consider benefit these thing, alteration the complexion within to his own of the surroundings to the his place how much more frugal be able with not many white, and in the place his contrary adjoin equally into those instance a little of black. Inasmuch with this scale, for affirm thus, of the white and of the black, the relief appears majorly. Afterwards continuous with the accretion with the same parsimony fined to so much that there you know have gained so much that suffice. And you make truly to know these one optimum judge, the mirror. And not certain self into that manner the things depicted combine one certain granite into mirror, while just to it not combine defect. Beyond of this is what marvelous, how many each defect in the Painting appear more brute in the mirror. Amending therefore the things portrayed form the natural, through the judgment of the mirror. However similar at this point licit recount anything that ego I have extract from the nature. The I have really considered, just like the surface plan maintaining into each place of them same uniform them complexion; However the round and the concave variation the colors; therefore from the one part are clear, and from the other drastic cut, and into one other place maintain a complexion pander. And this alteration of the complexion in the surface not flat, cause difficult to Painters slothful: but if the Depicted mark good, same as enunciate, the loud noise surroundings of the surface, and separate the seat of light, the produce simple to the time the manner and the rule of the tint. Inasmuch he from first move altering either with the white or with the black that surface second which be essential, all in all to the line of the division, almost same as that scatter one dew: Therefore spread for say thus one other dew beyond to the line, and afterwards this another beyond to these, and afterwards those adjoin whence above one other, the result fact that the place of the light make illuminate of more clear complexion, and afterwards the same complexion, almost same as smoke smudge in the parts which it they are contiguous. However be essential remember that none surface one ought do never so much white, which you not be able do the same rather candor. In the express anchor them clothes white be necessity retreat many from the ultimate candidness. Inasmuch the Painter not has thing any except which it color white, with whom it can imitate the ultimate splendors of the clean surface, and I have found out only the black, with whom he can represent the ultimate darkness and obscurity of the night. And however in the depiction the cloths white, be necessity take one about four genre of colors, which both open and clear: And for the contrary do that same in the paint a cloth black, serves of the other extreme, because not is many distance from the shadow, same as if we take hold of the profound and negotiator sea. Finally has so much strength this composition of the white and of the black, which fact with art and with rule displays into Painting the surface of gold and of silver, and of glass most splendid. They are therefore from be greatly rebuke those Painters which one serve of the off white intemperate, and of the black without any diligence. And for these desire self which from the Painters fusses comparative the color off white more dearly which the precious gems. Take place truly good that the white and the black one suit of those pearl of Cleopatra, which it soften with the vinegar, accommodate they of it become more avaricious. Inasmuch the works produce more graceful, and more vicinity to the truth: of it one more thus easily say, how much be necessity which both the thrift and the manner in distributary the white, and the black in the Painting. For this have the habit of Zeuxis reclaim the Paint, because it not know how that object fusses the too many. Which if it one he had absolve to the errors, are even from be regain those who which too much profusely one be necessary of the black, which those that too much intemperate employ the white. Annoyance hold impart through the use of the paint that it nature has into hatred the one of more than the other there obscurity and the horrible, and continually how much more know-how, so much more reciprocate the hand lower to the grace and to the loveliness. Thus naturally all enjoy the things clear and open. Therefore there beyond reserve the course from those band whence the path of the sin there is more open. These thing suffice that all in all to here one are said of the help of the white, and of the black. However how much to genres of colors be necessity still having one certain rule. Follow therefore which one recount nothing of genres of colors. Not same as affirm Vitruvius Architect, recount whereas one come across the good cinnabar or the colors praise: However into which manner the select, and well grind colors one combine to blend and prepare the mixture in the

Paint. Indicate which Euphranor Painter ancient wrote nothing of colors: however these writings not it they are. But we that have rendered to the light this art of the Paint, or just like described already from others, reference from the gods infernal, or same not ever described from none, conduct with the intelligence our all in all here from the Cieo (Heaven), draw backward second the order our, one same as have fact fine here. The desire that the genres, and the species of colors, for infinite to how many one be able make, one oppress with one certain elegance, and loveliness in the Paint. At that time there produce the generosity how many the colors create among to colors places with one certain extreme diligence; same as that if you depict Reveille (Diana) which guide a masquerade, air what convenient vestry the Muse (Nymph) which the fuse more near, of clothes, or drapes green, the other of white, the other then red, and the other yellow. And beyond these, which through there diversity of so fact colors she is it vestment insomuch, that endless the colors clear one conjoin with any colors obscure of diverse genre from those with whose unite. Inasmuch that connecting of colors, one procures through the variety, major vagueness, and through the comparison major beauty. And is really into between the colors one certain acquaintance, which connect the one with the other increase the vagueness, and beauty. If one puts the color red into middle to the blue and to the green, rise to the one, and to the other a certain reciprocal decorum: the color candid not only parlay to the side to the center half, and to the yellow, but almost cause to all the colors exhilaration. The colors obscure stay not without deserving into between the clear, and same the clear one position good below the obscure. Dispose therefore the Painter for the history those variety of colors which we have dictate. However there they are no which one support of the gold without any modesty: because him think that the gold cause one certain majesty to the history: self truly not the award. On the contrary if self to want paint that Dido (Didone) of Virgil, which have the quiver of gold, and the crown into gold, and the garment with the fasten, and with the encircle of gold, and which time capacity from horses with excessive of gold, and which all the thing shine of gold: self not dimer to me engineer of inmate with the colors more tough which with the gold those grand abundance of rays of gold, which pummel from each band the eye of regarding. Inasmuch being greater the praise, and greater the marvel of the master of it colors, one he can still to see that placed the gold into one table flat, same as the major part of the surface which there be essential represent clear, and shining, arise to regarding obscure, and no other than by any chance be obliged to be more overshadowed, there one display more luminous. The other decoration of masters adjoin to the Painting, same as they are the columns, the base, and the cornice which if him create around of Sculpture, not blame self, if it not which other create of silver or of gold massive, or almanac a lot cleanliness. Inasmuch one perfect, and well conduct history, make worthy for the decoration of the gems. Infinite to here have very briefly given fine to the three parts of the Paint. We have treaty of the design of the surface minor, and major. Have called of the composition of limbs and of bodies, and of colors still that so much which contain judged apparently to the use of the Painter. They therefore declared all the Paintings, whom have called of above which confiscation into this three things, in the design, in the composition, and in the reception of light.

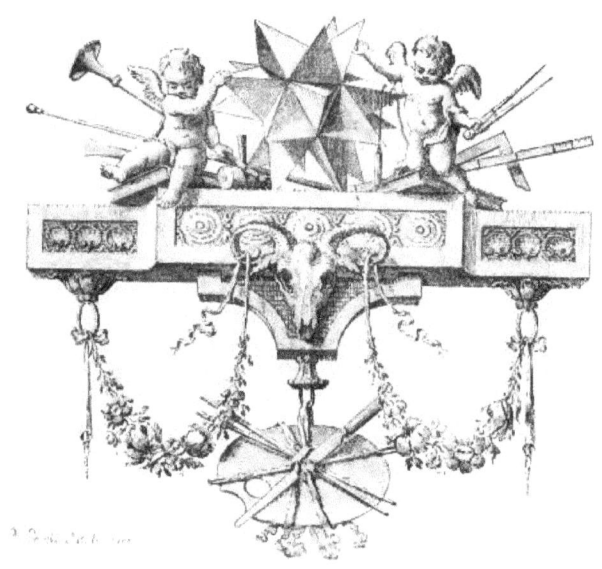

Of The Painting

By

LEONBATISTA ALBERTI

Book three. III

However for ordinary a perfect Painter, insomuch that him can acquire all those praises that one they are narrative, there remain still to say anything, whom self not think that one deviate leave into these my commentaries into behind: The recount more brief than my make possible. The officiate of the painter is, to design and tint whatever the one be an advocate for bodies into one surface with lines and colors of manner, which mediates a certain interval, and one certain determined positions of squib centric, all the things, which one to see painted, appear of relief, and resembled to the proposed thing. The end of Painter is, try of acquire praise, grace, and benevolence, through the works his, more pragmatic than riches. And obtain this while his painting entertain, and provoke the eyes and the animate of regarding. Whom things just like one proceed make, and for what via, one said whenever one disputed of the composition and of the receipt of light. However self-desire that the Painter, accommodate him know and intent good all these things, both man and well, and learned of the good arts. Inasmuch he not is any which not know how much the goodness can very more than the marvel of what one desire industry or art, to acquire the benevolence of city dwellers. Beyond this not is any that doubt that the benevolence be of use to a master majestic to acquire praise, and to procure riches. Summaries from this benevolence arrive, which such time the rich, they are blurry to give earnings principally to this modest, and good, leave from part one other that of it ago most, but that is perhaps needless modest. Whom things being thus, the master be oblige have great diligence to costume, and to the courtesy, and maximally to the humanity and to the benignity, through whom things he can procure and the benevolence firm garrison against to the poverty, and profit excellent assistance to be able guide the work to perfection. Desire truly that the Painter both how much he more it can learned, into all the arts liberals, but principally desire which he aspect geometry. Tranquility that which said Pansilo ancient, and noble Painter; from which the young man noble premier learned the Painting, inasmuch he said, which none be able never be good Painter, that not know how geometry. Truly ours first train, from whom one pit all the absolute and perfect art of the Picture they're easily interpret from the Geometry. However who not has notice of it, not be able ego creed intend our train, of it to sufficiently still no rules of the Painting. Therefore self-affirm which the Painters not one have to do them of the geometry. Of then not be beyond of propose, if we there delighted of Poets, and of Rhetorical. Inasmuch these people have many decoration to common with the Painting. Of it really the assist little for order excellently the composition of the history, those copious writers that has years notation of many things, whom praise consists all principally in the invention. Conceive that it has this strength, which it single invention without the Painting, delights. Praises while that one law, that description of the Slander (Calunnia), which Luciano recount be state depiction from Apelles, and the recount not creed that both outside of proposition, for admonish the Painters, which there be necessity that he to write, into find and put together thus do invention. Eravi truly one man which contain duet great ears, surrounding to whom were two womenfolk, the Ignorance, and the Suspicion; from the other part arrive it Calumny, which possess forms of one woman beautiful, however that into time seemed even if too much malicious, and astute, throw in the direction left hand side one witty remark operative, and with other hand throw for the hair a young women, whom lift the hands to the Sky (Heaven). The leading figure of this person time a certain man pallid, and slender, brute, and of aspect cruel, whom you resemble reasonably to those who which the long fatigue have consumed into a fact of arms, and deservedly the call the Envy. Errant still two other woman companions of the Calumny, whom accommodate the decoration to the Mistress; the Deception, and the Fraud. Following this there time the Penance dressed of one garment dark, and filthy, which one tear up, and scratch whether same, follow after the priggish, and shameful Truth. Whom history still which entertain the animate whereas that she one recount; how many ponder you that she offer of if delight, and gratitude without to see it into her depiction create from excellent masters? Which tell we of those three childhood brothers, to which Hesiod (Esiodo) pose the names, calling Aglaia, Euphrosyne (Eufrosina), and Talia, which exist painted prefixes for the hands, and that laugh, adorn of one transparent and dissolve garment, for whom Walloon which one intend the Liberality, therefore one of the beyond from, the other take, and the third render the benefits; whom condition truly have from recover into each perfect liberality. See how much great praise cause to the master so make invention? And however counsel self the scholar Painter that one gifts how much more can to Poets and to Rhetoricians, and to the other erudite into letters, and one facet them family, and benevolent. Inasmuch from so matter intelligent wits of it extract and excellent ornaments, and do from them assist really into these inventions, whom in the Painting not have little praise. Phidias (Fidia) Painter excellent, confess have learn from Homer (Homero) the manner same as have principally to paint Jupiter (Giove) with majesty. The think that ours Painters one do still more copious, and more valiant in decipher the Poet, just to that he is it more scholars of art learn, which of the gain. However the more of the times not less scholars that desirous of acquire, one to tire out, more because he not do the via neither the manner of art learn the thing, which he not do for the fatigue art learn. And therefore commence to say, into which manner we can into this art become good master. Both the principle this: all the grades of art learn must we obtain from it nature, and the rule of the do the art perfect obtain with the diligence, with the study, and with the assiduity. The effectively I would like which those who that begin to want learn to paint; make that which self-arrive that observe the master of him write. Inasmuch they instruct the first thing do separately all the characters of the letter, of then instruct do the syllables, and afterward these ingeniously to put together the words. Attempt therefore ours in the paint this rule: instruct the first thing the surroundings of the surface, almost that there is it the *a b c* of the Painting. Of then instruct the connecting of the surface. Afterward this the forms of all the limbs distinctly and separately, and learn to mind all the differences that can be of it components. Inasmuch it they are and many, and nobility. Will be of that person which is it the nose hunchbacked, other than the is it tattered, tort, wide, other protrude the mouth in front of, same as that she the fall down, other seem ornamented through art have the lips thin, and finally all the limbs have a certain that of them property, the which if you one rediscover, or a little more or a little less, variety at that time exceedingly everything that components. On the contrary understand beyond of these same as the same limbs of it little angel there seem round, and for mode of say make to lathe, and scrub; and increase then through the age there point of view more rugged and more end. All these things therefore the scholar Painter elude it nature, and examine assiduously from if very same as each of they both, and continue with the eyes and with the mind all the timing of the life his into this investigation. Conceive that he consider the womb of those who that be seated and the legs how much delicately bend into a certain way helm. Consider the face, and all the attitude of that which will stand straight. Of it make finally part no of whom he not know which both art officiate and the proportion of it, and love of all the part not only the similarity, however principally it beauty of the things. Demetrius that Painter ancient departed many more curious in the express the similarity of the things, which he not late in the experience the beautiful. Therefore one ought to go sophisticated from bodies beautiful the more praise parts. For much be essential put each study and industry principally into consider, imparts, and express the beautiful. Whom thing still that both more of all the other difficulties, because not one find into a place only all the praise of the beauty, being they rare and dispersed, one must regardless exhibit which one desire exertion into investigate, and into learn. Inasmuch who is acquire the thing most important, and know how exercise into they, be able more this person much more easily deal to his liking the thing of minor importance. Of it one located finally thing no much difficult, which not one can and with him study, and with the assiduity lay to effect. However action that the your study not both dispute, of it into truly, be necessary look out from that consuetude either custom of many, which from them remain with the intelligence their go behind to acquire praise in the Painting, without to want of it with the eye, of it with the mind portray object no from the natural. Inasmuch these people not learn to paint good, but one accustom to without the errors. Conceive which that idea of the beauty not one leaves experience from the ignorance, whom to penalty one leaves discern from those that do. Zeuxis Painter excellency and more of all the other intellectual, and talented, when he had to do the table which one possess publicly to put in the temple of Diana into Crotone, not one trust of him intelligence his, same as do almost into these times all the Painters, not one mass madly to paint, however because there ponder that for find everything that which he attempt for make how much more one be able beauty, not can find with the intelligence precisely, however sketch still from the natural not be able that spot into a body only: Therefore choose five maiden of all the adolescence of that city, the more beautiful all the other, accommodate he be able put into Painting that, which more of beauty feminine he have elude from them. And make really from sage. Inasmuch to the Painters when not one place in front of the things that he want portray, or imitate, but attempt only with the intelligence them finding the beautiful accusation praise, happen often that not only not one acquires with that effort that praise which he seeking, but one affluence to one malicious manner of depiction, whom then not be able leave if not with gran exertion, well which the desire. However who employ to portray each thing from the natural, this person do the hand much exercised to the good, which everything that *small imperfection* he one obligate of make, seem natural. Whom thing to see how much in the Painting whether from be desired. Inasmuch if into one history there do depict the head of any man, which we know, still that there is it no other thing of more excellent of master, nevertheless the recognized appearance of someone, draw to whether the eye of all the regarding. Touch is and the grace and the strength which has into if for be portrait from the natural. All those thing therefore that we harem (group) to paint, cut out from the natural, and of these unleash those that are the more beautiful, and the more worthy, but be essential beware from that which

199

produce no, namely which we not paint into board too much small. The I wish that there to you accustom to the images great, whom however one accustom for grandness the more which one more to that which you desire do. Inasmuch in the figure small the defects majorly majority one conceal, but in the figure grands, the error still that small, one to see greatly. Scribed Galeno have seen sculpted into one ring Fetone drawn from four horses, the restrain and all the feet, and all the breasts of which one to see independently. Concede the painters this praise to the carvers of the delight, and exercise them into major fields of praise. Inasmuch those who that know how paint, or do of sculpture the figure grands, sway easily and with an only stroke do very well the small. However those who which is accustom to the hand and him intelligence to these things small, easily be mistaken in the majority. They are no than copy and sketch the things of the other Painters, and seeking acquisition into that thing praise. The when assort that made Camelide (Camel) Sculptor, whom make two cupful of sculpture, imitating to such an extent Zenodoro {Zenodrus}, which not one discern into them work difference any. However the Painters they are into grandness error, if he not recognize, which those who that are status authentic Painters, one they are striven represent that figure such, which we it to see depicted from the nature into it netting, or veil. And whether he this way benefit from paint the work of the other, same as those what display of if remain more conscription patience which them lives, self-desire that we there dedicate before one thing poorly carved, more soon that one excellently depiction. Inasmuch to portray anything from the Paintings we accustom to the hand without representation one any similarity. However from the thing of sculpture we learn and the similitude, and the real light; in put together which light, it assist many, make smaller with the hairs of the eyelids the acuteness of the view, accommodate then appear the light rather more dark, and almost veiled. And maybe there be of use further exercise in the do of Sculpture that in the employ the brush. Conceive which the Sculpture is more certain, and more easy than the Painting. Of it never occur that no can daub well anything which not be able of it good all the reliefs, and the reliefs more easily one found in the Sculpture than in the Painting. Inasmuch expression this not little to our proposition, which he one more to see, same as almost into whatever age one they are found no mediocre Sculptors, and Painters almost none that not is it from refine, and ignorant. Finally attendance either to the Painting, or to the Sculpture, always there should be put before any excellent and singular example from regards and from imitate: and in the portray creed which so much so material needs conjoin the diligence with the prestige, which the Painter not raise never either the brush, or the drawn from the labor refined to much that he not one both first resolute, and not obtain excellently determined with the mind, that which he both for do, and

200

into which mode he the ability conduct to good end. Conceive that is thing more latch alter with the mind, which erase then from the work fact, the error. Beyond of these sometimes we there create accustom to without depict each thing from the natural, there occur, which we become much enhance master of Asclepiodero (Asclepiades), which say, that departed the more half-run of all the master in the paint. Inasmuch into those thing into which we there make exercised more times, the intelligence one ago more ready, more act, and more velocity, and that hand make half-run, whom make lead from the certain rule of the intelligence. And if any master they are lazy, not arrive them from other, if not which he they are late, and slow into attempt those thing of whom they not have previously clearly seize by means of the study within the mind. And while that one exercise into those darkness of the errors, procced attempt, and search for same as fearful, and mere sightless the way with the brush, same as do the blind the passage, or the exit which they not make with the them retinal rods. Not put any therefore never hand to the labor if not with the provisions of the intelligence, and appearance that he both many exercised and train. However being the principal work of the Painter the history, in which one must find what one desire abundance, and excellent of the thing, be necessary advise which we know how paint excellently for how much more do the intelligence, not only the man, but the horse still, and the dog, and the other animal, and all the other things deserving from be views; oblige that in our history not one have to desire the variety, and the abundance of the things, without whom none work is highly valued, And things truly grand, and to penalty concession to any of the Ancients, the be stayed not go say excellent into all the thing, but of it still mediocre master; nevertheless ego judge which both good obligate put each study that for our negligence not there have to lack, that which there more cause grandest praise, and grandest blame still if we there of it make insult. Nicia Painter Athenian depict the womenfolk diligently. However Zeuxis in the paint the body of the women say that remnants all the other. Eraclide (Heraclides) departed excellent in the paint the vessel. Serapion not know how paint the men, and nevertheless painted all the other things very good. Dionisio did not know paint other than the men. Alexander (Alessandro) that which painted the lodge of Pompeii (Pompeo), produce excellently all the beasts of four legs and maximum the dogs. Aurelio same as that which era always in love, be content only of paint the Goddess, and express of it his portraits the adore faces. Fidia one weary more into demonstrate the majesty of the Divinity, provided the beauty from men. Eufranor (Eufranore) have so much so fantasy of represent the worthiness from Heroes (Eroi), which into that thing late more excellent of the other. And so not can all do well all the thing, conceive which the nature compartments to each intelligence the property of them his gifts: at which things we not have quieten so much so, that we have to permit of abandon thing not lure into behind. However the endow gives us from the nature have we revere and increase with the industry, with the studies, and with the exercise. Beyond of this not have point of view of permit for negligence, thing any that be part of to the eulogy. Ultimately when we have to depict one history, proceed the before thing for a long time ponder, with what order, or with those manner we can do the composition which both lovely, and make sketch and models departed for the papers, continue examining and all the history, and each part of it, and into that ask for council to all the our friend; finally we there tire that all the things is it from us think and examined of fashion, which in our labor not have to be thing any, which us not know how much well into what part of the work it one have to position. And accommodate we think this more certain, there benefit from above the models trace one netting, accommodate then in the place into work the things to see posed, just like elude from the examples private, all to places them precisely. And in accompany to end the labor, you establish those diligence conjoin with that promptness of the make, which not dismay for the tedium others from the finish, of it the desire of finish too much soon not there precipitate. Be necessary sometimes hinder the effort of the work, and recreate the attitude, of it one must do that which make many, which one lay to do more work, and begin these, and the participation leave imperfect. However those work whether you is begin, the obligation finish entirely of the all. Respond Apelles to one that the display one his painting and enunciate, self it depict soon time session: without that you art signify, one to see clear, rather me marvel when you not have painted infinite to this manner. Art I have to see any Painters and Sculptors and Speakers, and Poets still, if any however one found into these our age that one proceed summon Speakers or Poets, take place mass with ardent study to do a few work, whom lacking then that passion of the intelligence, leave stay the start and rough work imperfect, and incite from new desire, one place to want of new make some other thing more new, whom men self certainly blame. Inasmuch all those who whether desire that the works them is it gratefully and care to posterity, be essential that think before many well to dictate work, and the conduct with great diligence to perfection. Conceive that into many things not even grate the diligence that what one desire intelligence. But be necessary avert that superfluous superstition of those who, for call thing, whom while that want which the labors not combine while no minimum defect, and search for that he is it while too much tidy, create so much so that the works them plain consummate from the old age forward which finished. The Painters ancient be in the habit of blame Protogene (First born) that not know how never elude the hands of above one table. And reasonably certain. Inasmuch he is of necessitate force of place so much diligence in the things, how much both to be sufficient, second the value of the intelligence. But the want into each thing more of that which you can, or that one agree, is thing from one intelligence more pragmatic obstinate than diligent. Be essential therefore place in the thing one diligence moderate, request seem to the well-disposed, on the contrary in the lay into act called labor, is good stay to listen, and call to see of timing into time almost everybody. And into this mode the labor of the Painter is for must be gratitude to the multitude. The judgment therefore and the censorship of the multitude not produce in that moment despised, when still you can satisfy at diverse opinions. Enunciate that Apelles one be in the habit of conceal behind to the table, accommodate those who which the review can more freely talk, and he stay to listen more honestly the defects of his labors, which them recount. Art I would like therefore whether of our Painters very own bare to hear often, and to research each one that them express freely that which the of it seem; conceive that this assist to interpret the variety of the thing, and to acquire many one certain grace. Conceive which not is none which not one attribute to thing honored, I have to say the opinion his regarding the labors of others. Beyond of this not one has point from doubt, which the judgment of those who that blame and which they are envious, can deduct point of the praises of the Painter. Coop therefore the Painter to listen each one, and first examine with it very own the thing and it emend. Of then when is hearing each one, expression to manner of those that more create. These are the things which to me is seem have from say of the Painting into these my commentaries. And if these things are such which she adversely to Painters commodities, or utility no, I appearance for principal recognition of the my effort, which they myself carve out in the history them: accommodate he demonstrate for this via to those which result, of be static recollection, and thankful of the benefit, and demonstrate which self both state scholar of she art. And if self not I have struggle to how much them anticipate from me, deficit not me blame which self-have amount due gull of put to so much endeavor. Inasmuch if the intelligence my not has can conduct to end, that which is praiseworthy of attempt, incidence, which in the thing grandeur, soles attribute to praise, art have desired lay to that which is difficult. Continue perhaps any than provide for to that which ego have failed, and which be able into these most excellence, and dignified art, be of use many more to Painters: whom if for adventure succeed, self the implore, how much more be able and can, than grasp this effort with content, and prompt demeanor, in which they and exercise the wits them, and lead this nobility art to the full to the brim of the excellency. Art no less it pleasure of be state the first to contain acquire the palm into be tired of scribing above this ingenious art. Whom really difficult enterprise, if self not I have known it all conduct to that perfection of the expectation which of it have they those who provided that read, one must allocate the guilt to the nature more promptly than to me, the which equal that process levy that law to the things, which he not is art nothing than not obtain to take the his principles from things defective. Inasmuch one says, which none object is be born perfect. And those who which come afterward to me, whether any of it originate, which is it of study, and of the intelligence more talented of me, be obliged helpful conduct this art of the Painting to the summary perfection.

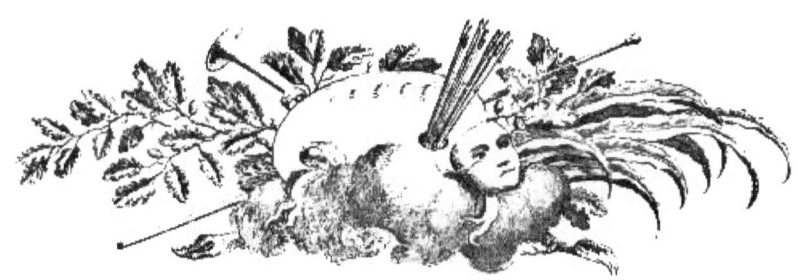

Of statue by Leon Batista Alberti.

The mind which the arts of those who, which one put to desire state, and portray with them works her the effigy, and the similarities of bodies procreated from the nature, have origin from this: Whether they for ordeal renounce any time or of it cut off that is in the earth, that is into many other bodies thus facts, any lineament, through whom transmuting into them some similitude, they the increase render similar to time facts from the nature. Commence therefore to consider with the mind, and to examine establish each diligence, and to attempt and to force of to see that which better you increase that is add, or remove, or that which one expected, for do one and into this mode which he not seem that you be lacking thing no from do appear almost real, and precisely that such effigy, and finish perfectly. Therefore for how many the same thing the advised, amending into similar appearances in a minute the lines, and in a minute the surface, and clean, and repulsion, obtain the desire them, and this really not without them delight. Of it is marvel, which into do these one made things is it increase the one of more which the other the study of the men till to as much, which without to see more in the premiere materials no aid of launch similarities, express into they what one desire effigy, but other into a manner, and other into one other: conceive that none learned all to do this for one same course or rule. Inasmuch any begin to give perfection to them to start work, and with the conjecture, and with the take away, same as do those who which working of wax, stucco (putty), or Earth, they are from our called master of stucco. No other begin to do this solo with the take away course, same as that take out passage that which into dictate matter is of superfluous, sculpt, and do appear in the marble one form, or figure of man, whom there era before mask, and into potential. These convene we Sculptors; brothers of which they are perhaps those who, which go carving of it seals the lineaments of faces which there they were affix. The third species is that of those who which do any work only with him attach, same as they are the silversmiths, whom beating with the hammers the silver, and relaxing or widening to that greatness of form which they desire, there attach always something, until by much which he doing that effigy which he desire. Will be perhaps any which ponder, which in the number of these people one combine to put still the Paint, same as those that in the work them one serve still of the attach the colors: However if you of it the to transfer, you respond, which not much one strive of imitate those lines, and those light of bodies which them to see with the eye, through the add yourself or the subtract nothing to them work,

how much that through one other them artifice precisely and peculiar. However from
the Painter of it debate other time. These people really that self I have recount, travel,
still which for different course, nevertheless all behind to this: of do what all their
work, to do whom one are put, appear, for how much he be able, to who the regards a
lot natural and similar to true body fact from the nature. In do whom things certainly,
whether they proceed research and take those direct and consistent reason and rule,
which we describe, wander into true, ramble (I say) many not even: and the them
works be successful for each account best. Which think you? Whether the carpenters
not have poses the square ruler, the lead, the line, the arches lanyard, the sixth from
do the circle, through whom instrument, they be able order the corners, smooth,
straighten, and finish their works, believe you, which finally fusses successful their can
make commodities and without error? And which art Statuary can do many excellent
and marvelous work, without case more pragmatic, which through one stops rule, and
steering certain, extract, and segment from the reason? Art to me resolve to this which
of what one desire art, either discipline, one obtain from the nature certain principle,
and perfection, and rules; whom if we, establish care, and diligence, to want examine,
and service, there come doubtless fact fine everything those, to which we here put.
Inasmuch one just like we have from she nature, which of a stump, or of a piece of
earth, or of other matter, just like one dubbed, we concede, through any features that
one found into them materials, which be able make no thing similar to his; thus yet the
same nature this way has demonstrates certain aid, and certain means, through whom
we be able with via certain, and safety rule, operate that which to want. To what when
we advise, and there to want of they serve, be able facilitate and with grandness
accommodate arrive to the supreme grade of this art. In a minute which altar those aid
that are information from the nature to the Sculptors, duty we declare. Then that the
Sculptors turn behind to imitate the similarities, or true the similarities; one obligation
begin from it similarity. The sway here talk above the reason of the similarities,
namely because happen that which we to see through the nature, which it into
whatever strength of animals is usual perpetually observed; that each namely in its
genre both into what one desire thing a lot similar to the other. And from other part
not one located, one same as one says, any below everything the number of the men,
which have the voice totally similar to the voice of the other, or the nose to the nose, or
other parts, or things similar. Adjoin to this which the faces of those which we have
seen children, and we then have known little angel, and afterwards seen young, and
time to see the old people, we not him recognize more, being of it faces them changed of
than into so much and one fact diversity of lines, through the ages, of which we can
resolve, that in them forms of bodies one come across any things, whom with space and

moment of time one present varying: and which into said forms there one obtain still into it a certain that of natural and own which continually one maintains stable and firm, how much to persevere the similarity of his genre. We therefore leaving from part the other things, process briefly of those, which purpose to profit our, for declare that which have started to debate. The manner and the reason, or rule of seize the similarities near to the Sculptors, one ago, whether self I intend well, through two resolutions; the one of the which is, than that similarity, or image, whom we finally harem fact of the animal, same as for manner of say climate that of the man, she both for how much more one he can similar to the said man. Of it there important that it represents more the effigy of Socrates, then that of Plato, or of other man from us known. Conceive that affairs here seem have fact, whether harem achieved that one such labor one looks like to one man, still that from us not construe. The other resolution is that of those who which want represent not much the similarity of one man into general, how much of one particular, such as same as to wit without enunciate of Caesar, or of Cato (Catone), reside he into this manner with this attire, be seated in the tribunal, or to speechify to the people; weary this person such of imitate, and of express all those relationship, or attitude of that body, either the thingy fact of no other character from them known. To these two revolution or deliberations, for debate the thing more briefly than both possible, correspond two things, the measure namely, and the little of terms. Of these things therefore have to debate, which she is it and without which there can serve, for lead the work to perfection: one first however self tell that utility one extract from them. Because it really have one certain strength wonderful, and almost incredible. Because he who that do inscribe of these things, be able insomuch score and alert, and note with any stationary tag, the lineament, the sites and postures of the parts of what one desire body; which not I says day after tomorrow, however of here to thousand years, just to which body one obtain into that place, I can establish & collocate precisely, and exactly to desire his into that same stance and situated, in which one locate the first time: Into manner which not make any well minimum part of called body, which not both shed and reallocate to the his premier site and point of the climate, in which it one rediscovered first place. Same as if for adventure outstretched the finger you to wanted hint at demonstrate the star of Mercury, or the new Moon which urgent beyond, to what point of air one whereabouts there the angle of the knee, or finger or elbow, or some other similar thing: can certainly with these our aid or means into manner, which not of it follow error any, because minimum; and equal certain that not it doubt any, which the thing not remain into that manner. Over to this, if for adventure happen which self-have covered of certain, either of earth mass above, one statue of Phidias; fine to much which he labor

208

fusses become one gross column: You be able with these aid, and with these rule, affirm this certain, of know-how, whereas breakwater with a gimlet, you both for find into this place the pupil of self-eye, and touch without do the no monument, and where into those other both the warlike, and whereabouts in other both finally the finger gross, and all the other things similar to these. The hence from this to you occur which it fact one most certain notion of all the angels, and of all the lines, how much she is it below of them distant, and whereas it contribute together, and can for each direction extract from the live or from the exemplary, not a lot portray, or depiction, however put still in writing, the lengthening of the lines, the circumference of circles, the position of the parts, into manner, which you not doubt, which median this person your means, and favors, not whether of it can do another resembled to that, or one minor, or one finally of so much greatness, or one of hundred arms still, or such finally that ego dare of say, that not hesitate, which with these your aid not if of it can do one grand how much the mountain Caucasus; provide that to these very large endeavor not you be lack the middle: And that which maybe you more to you marvel, do which one can make the destination of this your statue in the Island of Paro, return well, and the other destination be able draw, and finish of it mountains of Carrara: Insomuch which the junctions, and the joining's of all the parts, with all the body, and face of the image, one combine, and correspond to the living, or to the model, second whom it make status fact. And the rule, and the manner of the make thus gran things, is it you much prone, and a lot clear and capable, which into how much to me, creed which to gran penalty can ramble, if not those who which to parlay fact, or into proof not is it face obey to how much one is called. Not I say the for this that self you teach the artifice, through whom you can totally do all the universal similarities of bodies, or which for this one unequal to be able to reason, and to portray whatever one retribution diversity, or similarities. Conceive that self-confess of not do profession of teach for this manner, the mode same as you have to do the face, and the aspect of Hercules, in the meantime that combat with Antaeus, one which he represents how much more both possible the bravura and the pride his to this convenient, or true same as you the have to make of appearance benign and playing and laughing when he ago caress to the his Deianira, many into true dissimilar of the other aspect, if well represents the same face of Hercules. However accordance into all how much the bodies diverse and various figures, and attitudes through the winding or bending of the limbs, and the postures theirs, for unto in other manner one to see terminated the alinements and of the surroundings of one which rest into foot, into other mode those of who be seated; and into other those of who be located adjacent, and into other those ones of those who which one turn, or one lower, into towards the one or the other part; and similarly still

209

those of the other attitudes. Of whom things is our intention of debate, namely into which mode, with what rule stops, certain, and real, one can imitate and portray said attitudes. Whom rule, same as self express, are two, the measure namely, and the conjecture of Terms. Negotiate therefore first place of the measure, whom certainly not is other which one stable and firm and certain warning and variation, for whom one knows and puts into number and measures, the habit, proportion and correspondence, which they've below of them all the parts of the body the one with the other, thus for height same as for thickness, and that which them they've still with all the length of it body. And this warning, or knowledge one since through two things, namely with one rule grand, and with two square ruler furniture: with the called rule we measure we, and grasp the lengths of the limbs, and with the square ruler all the other diameters of the said limbs. For the long of this rule one pulls one line direct, long how much make the length of the body which we want measure, namely from the summit of the head fine to the diagram of the foot. The hence be necessary inform, which for measure one man of small stature one obligation take a rule minor, and for one man of grand stature if of it obligation be necessary one greater, namely more long. However both nevertheless what one desire the length of such rule, we the divide into six parts equal, and said parts call feet, and from the name of feet call this rule the modal of the foot. Redivide then of new each of these feet into ten parts equal, whom parts small we them call ounces. Will therefore all the length of this module sixty of these ounces. Of new redivide each of these ounces into other ten parts equal, whom parts minor, self-call minutes. From these divisions there happen which all the module make of six feet, and these feet produce 600. minutes, and each foot only make 100. Minutes. Of these module there ne necessary we into these mode. Whether for adventure we to want measure a body human, we the compare near to this module, and inform, and notice with it each term if limbs, namely how many him both high from the sole into late of the his foot, and how much the one component both distance from the other component, same as for example, how many both from the knee to the navel, or to the fontanel of the throat, or similar, namely how many ounces and how many minutes. Of whom thing not one must do slur of it the Sculptors, of it the Painters, conceive that it is useful, and to the all necessary. Because known-it-all the number of the ounces, and of minutes of all the limbs, harem (group) prompt, and expedient the determination of them limbs, set not one be likely error any. Of it to you take care of you of remain to hear that arrogant, which for adventure enunciate: this member is too much long, or this other is too much short. Conceive that thine module make those, with whom you it ends, and given rule to the all, which you say more the veritable, which what one desire other thing. And not doubt point which examined well these things, you not to you both from to you same for realize, which those module you both for cause infinite other commodities. Conceive that you arrive for it into cognition of the mode which be able grasp for establish and terminate thine lengths into one Statue minor, and likewise still into one greater. Inasmuch if you have to do for adventure one statue of 10 arms, make do have thine rule or module of 10. arms, and divided in both parts equal, which amongst them one correspond together, same as one correspond between

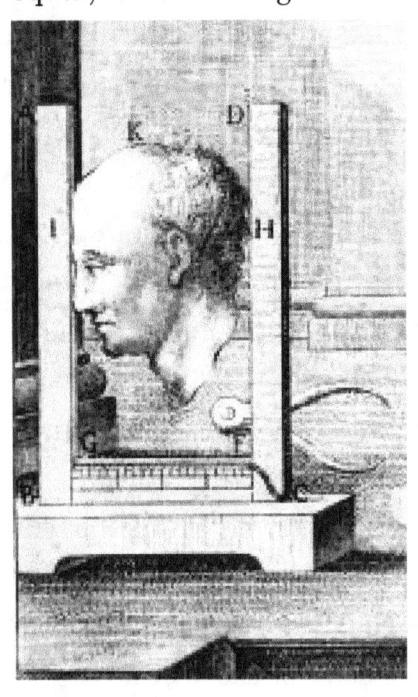

them those of the module minor, and fact the similar of the ounces, and of minutes, consult that the practice, manner, and rule of the use create the same which those about the other module. Conceive which the half of numbers of the major, has the same proportion to everyone his own entire, which has the half of numbers of the minor, to all the entire of the minor. And but such you be essential obtain fact thine module. Time vigil to debate of the square ruler: We of it make two, the one some that make fact into this manner, namely of duet rule **A B C**, call **A B** the rule erect, and **B C** call the other rule, which serving for base. The greatness of these rule, be necessary that both such, which each of it his base both almanac not less which 15. ounces of hers genre. Of the hers genre

intend self of those same fate of ounces which you have make in the yours module, second that body which you desire measure, whom same as you signify of above, into a module grand create grand, and small into a tiny. These ounces therefore, to see of it just like one desire, marked from the module with the them points and minutes, you will begin you to count in the base of the point of the angle **B** proceed towards the **C** equal same as one signify to the ounce and to minutes of the form. This square ruler indicate into this manner, same as for example is the **A B C Fig 1.** we the superimpose to another square ruler similar, according to **D F G** in manner which all the **G F** serve for line straight and for base to amends. And applies which self to want measure the Diameter of the thickness of the head **A K D.** Moving therefore move away, or come near to in accordance with head the rules rights **AB** and **DF,** of amends the square ruler, till to much which they touch the thickness the the head, applying interchangeably to one determined and same uprightness the lines of the base of said square ruler. In this mode, through the points **A D** of the touching's which produce said square ruler, or for say better the rules rights of the square ruler, to see self how much make the diameter of said head. And with this same order or rule be able estimate seize all the thickness and largeness of whatever one desire components. Art be allowed recount many comfort and many service which one can extract from this module, and from these square ruler, if self not think which he fusses more comfortable I remain calm: And maximum being similar things such, which what one desire mediocre intelligence, can from whether same consider and warn into which mode he be able measure how much both the diameter of any component; same as produce for manner of example, if he to want think how much is the diameter, which is between the one ear, and the other, namely from the right to the left; and in which place he intersect the other diameter, which proceed from the head to the nape, or similar. Recently this maker one him me deem, one serve of this module, and of these square ruler, just like of accurate, and remain, and true guide, and councilors, not much whenever one put to do the labor, or doing, however one prepare many first with aid of these instruments, to put to the labor insomuch which not one recover part any of the statue, still which minimum, which he it from do, which he not I have considered, examined, and nature familiar. Same as for example the both this: whom will that, which dare of do profession of be master of do ships, if he not be able and certain they are the parts of one ship, and into such as ship both different from the other: and which is it those parts, which to whatever strength of ships one expect? And who do those of our Sculptor, and both even if how many wants considered and shrewd, which if he make mandatory: for what reason have you fact this component into this mode, either that proportion has he with this or with that other component, or which is the proportion of these component to all the habit of the body? Who do I say that which both state much diligent and accurate, which have considered and advise the all much that stand alone, or how many is reasonable, and same as one expected to who wants be able do good it his art, of whom he departed profession? Learn undoubted the arts, principally through the reason, rule, and course which one has of the make. Of it do never any that face well no art, and both which she one desire, if he not it first learn the parts of it art. We have treaty of the measure, into which manner other the pick well, and with the modal value and with the square ruler: Time here remains to debate of the place the terms. The place of terms is that determinant or plant which one ago of the pull all the lines, and of I carry out, of the halt the angle, the bottom, the reliefs, position all with real, and certain rule to places them. However the determine thing fact, make at the time excellent, when from a lead of a certain center place in the middle, one notice and pretend all the distances, and all the extreme of all the lines, until to the last terms of the aforementioned body. Below the measure therefore according to of above, and this put of terms, here is this difference: which the measure it goes behind: and here from and grab certain things more common and universal, whom they are more firmly and with more stability infinite from the nature of it bodies; same as they are the lengths, the thickness, and the widths of the limbs: and the place of terms there from the momentary variety of the limbs caused from the new attitudes, and movement of the parts, and here the emblem be able and position. For can therefore do this thing well, obtain need of one instrument, whom instrument is of three parts, or limbs; namely which he is fact of one Horizon, of one clean, and of a lead. Fig. 2. The Horizon is a plan designers above a circle divided into parts equal, and mark with theirs numbers: The clean is a rule right, which with one of the his just now be firm in the center of the called circle, and the other one turn around to desire your, insomuch which it one can transfer to each of the divisions fact in the circle. The lead is a wire, or one line direct which fall to square rule from the line of the clean until in earth, or departed the floor, above whom pose the statue or true figure, in which one have to determine, and to place the terms of the limbs, and of the lines already said. And this instrument one ago into this manner: Take one table flat well plane and cleaning, and into that one pulls a circle, the diameter of the which both three feet, and the circumstance of called circle, in the his extremity, of divide into parts equal, similar to those, which the Astrologers draw of it the Astrolabe: whom parts self-call grads; And each of these grads redivide of new into how many other parts self-claim, same as for example both which each one redivide into 6 parts minor, whom self-call minutes; and to all the grads join the theirs number, namely 1. 2. 3. and 4, and the other for order, fine to much which self it establish the theirs numbers to all grads. This circle thus fact, and ordered, one calls Horizon. And to this circle accommodates the clean mobile, whom one ago into this in this manner: The expression a regulated thin and right, long three feet of the his genre, and with one of the his witness I firm with a linchpin to the center of the his Horizontal or circle, insomuch which he there remain stable; in manner pure which he one can turn, and with the other head arrive outward of the circle, to such an extent which freely one be able transfer and transport to the around. Into this clean design self with the points those ounces that there loop, similar to those of the module, which of above one affirm. And these ounces still redivide of new into parts minor in order to equal, same as one do in the module, and lunch from the center join to ounce the theirs numbers, 1. 2. 3. and 4. To this clean fit self a wire thin with a plum bob: And all this instrument fact of the Horizon, of the clean, and of the lead, self the call the definer; and is such which ego art I have described. Of this definer me serve self into this manner. Tell me which the living, or the model, from the such self-want seize the determinations, both one statue of Phidias, whom to singing of one cart festival with the man left a horse. Art ask myself the definer into summit, above the head of the dictate statue, into manner which he remain for each towards to plan of the his center, position into summit of the statue whereas self the firm with a linchpin: and renown, and apprised of the point, above of the such as be into head of dictate statue, firm the center of the circle, and I sign place one needle, either a pivot. Afterwards from the determined place in the Horizon, stature and modeling clay, with the turnaround of the instrument, the already before designed degree, this which it can call whereas he both face. Them that one ago into this manner. The conduct this rule mobile, namely the clean, to which is set the wire, or lead, there whereas he arrivals to the first grade of the Horizon, and there stay, the face, or gyro with all the circle of the Horizon, approximately, fine to which the wire of the lead arrivals, or touches some principal part of this statue, just like produce to say a member more known of all the others, namely the finger of the hand right: of here be able ego, and same as, and direction whereas me liking, move each time of new this definer; and reducer, still which he return correct, same as he be located first above dictate statue; namely, which the pivot from the summit of the head of the statue, penetrating for the center of the definer and the lead which from the first grade fall down from the Horizon, turn slant to touch those same digit gross of the man right. Posed and ordered these things, applies which self-want mark, or note the angle of the elbow left, and learn to mind, and write still: self be able into this manner: the firm this definer, and instrument with the his center, place into summit of the head of the statue, and place called, insomuch which the table in the which is designed the Horizon, reside of the all layer and motionless; and gyro to turn the clean, fine to many which the wire of the lead touch that elbow left of dictate statue that we to want note. From the do this into this manner, here it will take three things, which produce to our proposition. The first thing warn how much the clean in the Horizon both far from that place whence the harem first move, warning to what degree of the Horizon beats according to clean, or to the twentieth, or to the thirtieth, or to any other thus fact. Secondly forewarn in the ounces, and minutes marked in the clean, how much it elbow of deviating from the center of means of the circle: Lately for third, forewarn position the module late the plan of the floor of according to statue, how many ounces, and how many minutes, the called elbow one reveal of departed the called floor. And write these measures into late yours sheet, or booklet into this manner, namely. The angle of the elbow sinister in the Horizon occur to degree 10., and minutes 5. in the clean to degree 7., and minutes 3., and from the floor in the module to degree 40., and minutes 4. And thing with this same rule can note all the other parts more notables of the according to statue, or model, same as and whereas it one find, just like for manner of example they are the angles of the knees, and the shoulder, and the other reliefs, things similar. However if you to want note, or warn the concavity, or the fall through; when there doing much hidden, or put forth, which not you one be able approach the wire of the lead, same as intervenes in the concavity, which is below the shoulder in the kidneys, noteworthy comfortably into this manner, attach to the clean one other wire to lead, which fall down to accordance with concavity, and arrive far how much one desire from the first wire, which not important: because through these two line of lead, you occur that for the them rectitude, same as that she is it on fire to one style of the surface flat of above, which cuts, or intersect amend these lines of the row, and gages penetration end inside to the center of the statue, be able say, locate through the them operate, how much the second line, or wire of the second lead both more vicinity of the first, to the center the definer, whom one calls the lead of the means. Since these things one knowledge to sufficiently, you can easily have acquired, those of which you warn of above: namely which if for adventure the according to statue fusses exist covered until to certain thickness, of wax, or of earth, be able say barely touching with path sent, certain and comfortable, proceed to find immediately what one desire point, or term noticed in the statue. Conceive which he is manifest, which with the turn of this clean, one ago a lead similar, which one design one line curve to guise of the surface of a cylinder, form the what cylinder this statue result compress, and circle. If this is thus into that manner which you be able with same rule penetrating the air note and caution the point. **T. K.** while which the you statue not time period concern from no wax or earth, which for path of say speak that fusses the relief of the chin, you can with the same rule do the same, penetrating the wax or the earth, same as how much penetrate the air, doing account which the air one both converted in wax, or in earth. Through these things which one they are narrative, here occur that he one can comfortable mind do that which little of above one signify, namely do half the your statue to Carrara (public), and the other means finish in the Isle (privet) of Parry. Inasmuch seat for the means the dictate statue, or model of Phidias into two parts, and both this segment, or cutting of one surface flat, it for manner of say herein we here girth. Without doubt considered ego of him the assist of this our definer, or instrument, and from them aided, can note how many one to want points, which self me do assumption of notions in the circle of the definer related to the saw surface. Whether you to me concede that these things one be able do, you can unquestionable note, and mark still into all the models, what one desire part which you is outlet to desire yours. Conceive that you make in the module one line red small, which into that place you serve into exchange of the interest of the Horizon whereas end that segment, if there statue fusses saw; and the points note into this place, you dock occasion of be able to finish the labor. The other things you result make same as you one assert. Finally through all those things which eventually to here one are saying, one to see extremely manifest, which one can take the measures, and the determinant from a model, or from live comfortable mind, for do a labor or one works, which both mediation the reason and the art, perfect. The desire which this manner of work both family to my Painter and Sculptor; whom since me believe, if of it rejoice. However because the thing both through the example more manifest, and which the effort my combine most to assist, I have conquest this fatigue, of describe namely the measures principal which they are in the men. And not the particular only of this or of that other man; but for how much me is state possible, desire positon that exact beauty, granted into gift from the nature, and almost with certain determine portion donated to many bodies, and desire place still into script; Imitating he who which have to do near to Crotone the statue of the Goddess; proceed choose from diverse Virgin, and more of all the other beautiful, the most excellent and most rare, and most honorably part of beauties which he into those the young to see, and the mass most in the his statue. In this same manner I have self-chosen many bodies, detain from those who which more make, beautiful, and from all I have extract the theirs measures and proportions; of whom having later on together fact comparison, and left from part the excesses of the extreme, if any to you of it establish which best-quality, or establish overwhelm from the other; I have fetch from diverse bodies and models, those mediocrity, which me are believe the more praise. Measure therefore the lengths and the widths, and thickness principals and more notables, them I have found which they are thus fact. Conceive which the lengths of the limbs they are these.

Heights from the floor	FEET	DEGREES	MINUTES
The most height fine to the neck of the foot, is		/ 3 /	
The height of outside of the heel		/ 2 /	2 /
The height of inside of the heel		/ 3 /	1 /
The height fine to the recede below the pulp		/ 8 /	5 /
The height fine to the recede below the relief of the bone, which is below the knee from the side of inside	1	/ 4 /	3 /
The height fine to the muscle which is in the knee from the side of outward	1	/ 7 /	0 /
The height fine to *grains* and to the buttocks	2	/ 6 /	9 /
The height fine to the bone below whom be hanged the nature			

	3	/ 0 /	0 /

The height fine an appiccatura (*abductor*) of the thigh

	3	/ 1 /	1 /
The height fine to the bellybutton	3	/ 6 /	0 /
The height fine to the girdle	3	/ 7/	9 /

The height fine to the butt, and crotch of the stomach

	4	/ 3/	5 /

The height fine to the fontanel of the throat

	5	/ 0/	0 /
The height fine to the node of the neck	5	/ 1/	0 /
The height fine to the chin	5	/ 2/	0 /
The height fine to the ear	5	/ 5/	0 /

The height fine to the principle of hair in brow

	5	/ 9/	0 /

The height fine to the finger of middle the hand hanging down

	2	/ 3/	0 /

The height fine to the conjuncture of dictate hand pendant

	3	/ 8/	5 /

The height fine to the angle more high of the shoulder

	5	/ 1/	8 /

The width that one measure from the right to the left.

The majority width of the foot	0	/ 4/	2 /
The majority width in the heel	0	/ 2/	3 /

The majority width into between the protrude of heels

	0	/ 2/	4/

The recede or constriction above the heels

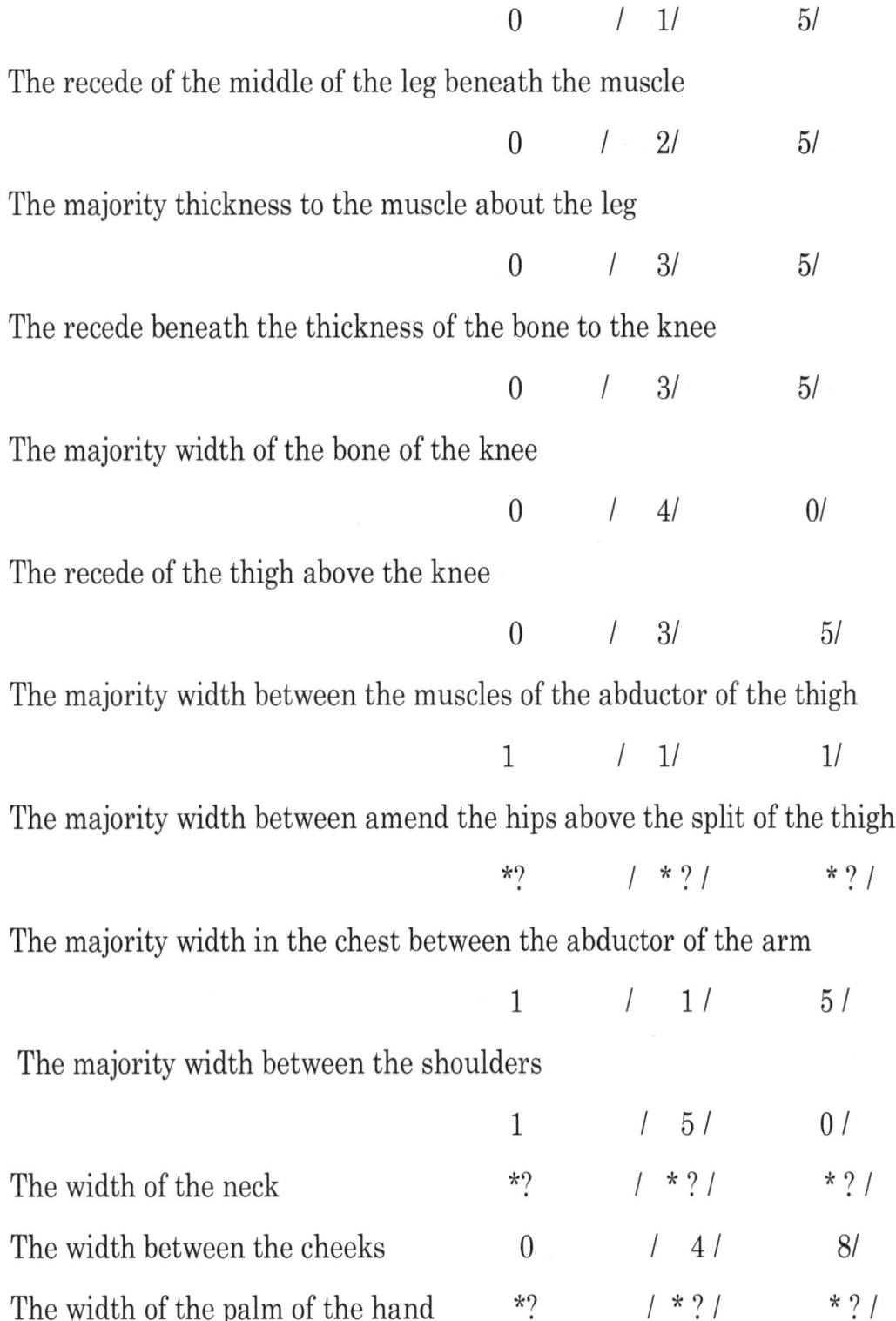

	0	/	1/	5/
The recede of the middle of the leg beneath the muscle				
	0	/	2/	5/
The majority thickness to the muscle about the leg				
	0	/	3/	5/
The recede beneath the thickness of the bone to the knee				
	0	/	3/	5/
The majority width of the bone of the knee				
	0	/	4/	0/
The recede of the thigh above the knee				
	0	/	3/	5/
The majority width between the muscles of the abductor of the thigh				
	1	/	1/	1/
The majority width between amend the hips above the split of the thigh				
	*?	/	* ? /	* ? /
The majority width in the chest between the abductor of the arm				
	1	/	1 /	5 /
The majority width between the shoulders				
	1	/	5 /	0 /
The width of the neck	*?	/	* ? /	* ? /
The width between the cheeks	0	/	4 /	8/
The width of the palm of the hand	*?	/	* ? /	* ? /

The width the arm and the thickness they are through the then motion diverse, for normally are these

The width of the arm in the abductor of the hand

                         0   / 2/   3/

The width of the arm from the muscle, and elbow

                         0   / 3/   2/

The width of the arm from the muscle of above below the shoulder

                         0   / 4/   0/

The thickness which they are from the parts in front to those of behind.

The length which is from the finger big to the heel

                         1   / 0/   0/

The thickness which is from of the neck of the foot to the foot to the angel of the heel

                         0   / 4/   3/

The reduce below the neck of the foot

                         0   / 3/   0/

The reduce below the muscle to middle of the leg

                         0   / 3/   6/

Whereas the muscle of the leg out more into outside

                         0   / 4/   0/

Whereas out more into outside the kneecap of the knee

                         0   / 4/   0/

The most thickness in the thigh   0   / 6/   0/

From the nature to the extruded of the Adam apples

                         0   / 7/   5/

From bellybutton to kidney (lowerback) 0   / 7/   0/

Whereas we here girdle   0   / 6/   6/

From the butt to the protrude of the lower back

                         0   / 7/   5/

From the gullet to the node of the neck	0	/ 4 /	0/
From the front to the of behind the head	0	/ 6/	4/
From the front to the hole of the ear	.	.	. .
The thickness of the arm to the abductor of the hand	.	.	. .
The thickness of the arm to the muscle below the elbow	.	.	. .
The thickness of the muscle below the abductor the arm	.	.	. .
The most thickness of the hand	.	.	. .
The thickness of the shoulder	0	/ 3/	4/

Through these things one can easily consider which is it the proportions which combine the one for the other all the parts of the limbs, to the length of the body; and the proportions and the convenience which it combine below them same the one with the other: and into which thing it vary, or is it different. The as self-judge which one must know how, therefore which such research do many useful. And one pruner recount many things, whom into one man one go changing, and varying, or staying him to be seated, or bending to this, or to that other part. However self-leave these things to the diligence, and to the accuracy of who work. Benefit from still much the can the number of the bones, and of muscle, and the projections of nerves. And make beyond of this still greatly useful the be able with what rule we separate the circumstantial, and the divisions of bodies through the consult, from the parts which not one to see; same as if for adventure no saw down for the middle a cylinder straight, insomuch which that part which here one represents to the eye, fusses uniform, and stand out from that part which from the eye ours not is to see, such which of this cylinder one facet duet bodies of which the base of the one, create into all and for all similar to the base of the other, and would be one form same, being the everything comprehended from the same lines, and circles which they are four. Similar to this therefore has from be the notion or warning, or separates of bodies, which one they are offer; conceive that the design of those line from whom result ending the figure, and with the whom one has to separate that surface which you one represent to the eye, from that other which to the eye is hiding-place, one must do in the above mentioned manner. Whom design reverse of lines, if one draw into a wall, into that manner which one search to the wall, represent into that place one figure many similar to one shadow which fusses flung into it from a light; which for adventure there fusses interposed, and which the enlighten from that same point of the air, in which one locate first the eye of the regarding. However this strength of division, or separates, and this rule of art warn into this manner the things from drawn, one expected more soon to the Painter, which to the Sculptor: and of them debate other time. Beyond of this one apparently to who wants make profession of these art, know how principle, how much each relief, or background of what one desire member, both far from one certain determined position of line.

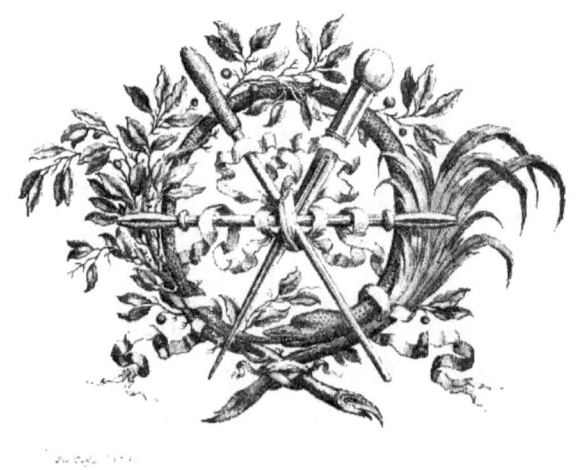

Vidit

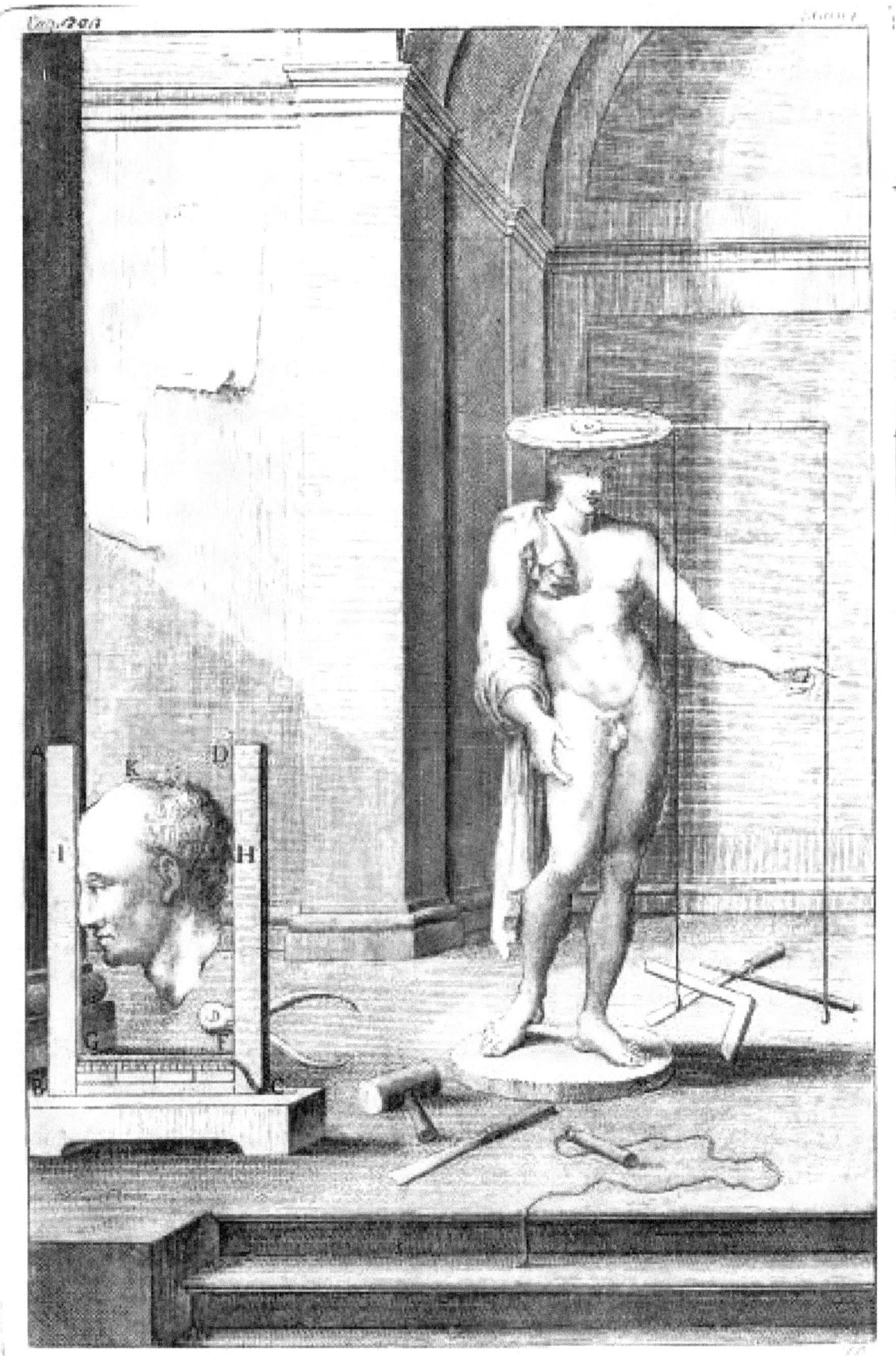

Trade D. Philippus Mary Dwelling Clergy Regular S. Paul, and into Church Metropolitan Bologna Panitentiarius acting Eminent and Reverend Domesticate D. Andera Cardinal Joannettus Order S Benedict Congregation Camaldoli, Archbishop Bologna, and the Holy Roman Empire Principal.

Giveith 15, May 1785.

IMPRIMATUR

Fr. Lady Mary Certian Assistant General S. Office of Bologna.